THE BEST
AMERICAN
RECIPES
2000

The Year's Top Picks

from Books, Magazines,

Newspapers, and the Internet

THE BEST AMERICAN RECIPES 2000

Fran McCullough and Suzanne Hamlin
SERIES EDITORS

With a Foreword by

Paul Theroux

Houghton Mifflin Company
Boston   New York
2000

contents

foreword

IT IS ALMOST INEVITABLE that a novelist will be interested in cooking, for typically the fiction writer works at home for long periods—years on end, not far from the kitchen—in this noble cottage industry. So it was that I came to understand that the profession of writing is more involved with food, cooking, and mealtimes than almost any other sort of employment. No matter where you are in a house, you are never very far from the odors of cooking that give a home its distinctiveness. Growing up, I could identify any of my friends' houses by scent, always food odors.

In the seemingly arbitrary world of writing at home, mealtimes divide the day into coherent parts, giving it a structure. I began to cook seriously only when I began to write full-time, at home, in 1971—and I imagine this to be the case with many writers, for whom the most welcome words are "Your dinner is ready." For various reasons, it has seldom been my privilege to hear such a summons. Out of necessity, I became a cook, at first reluctantly and then enthusiastically. I am not surprised that so many writers are passionate chefs. The sensuous pleasures of food, the satisfying complexity of cooking, and the

formalities of the table are bewitching, but cooking is, ideally, about congeniality—deliberately overcoming solitude. The social element—the pleasantly charged atmosphere of the companionable meal—is an alluring promise to anyone who labors alone. A great deal of religious ritual, which actively depends on sharing common experience, is based on eating or drinking. People who eat together are engaged in an intense peacemaking activity approaching something holy, no matter the circumstances. There are few more compelling images of worship than the Last Supper, and that singular episode in the life of Jesus, that meal, is celebrated in the Catholic Mass.

Traveling, I have always felt that I have been accepted when invited to share a meal. In every culture, offering food is a way of offering friendship. Meals have all sorts of meanings. In Europe, sharing lunch is a token of acceptance, though lunch is casual and improvisational in the tropical world, where cooking fires are stoked in the evening. Dinner is a commitment—in America it is a serious affair, and it is even more formal in Europe. Treating someone to a meal in a restaurant is a characteristic of urban socializing; I prefer a country's hinterland, where being asked to eat in someone's house is more likely. In almost every culture, the invitation to the stranger to share a meal at home is something special, for it is in a home that people are at their most vulnerable, their lives most revealed. Such an invitation is the ultimate compliment.

Every society's food embodies its history, its wisdom, its symbolism. Food is, literally and figuratively, a society's source of health and strength, something of almost mystical importance. Most people on earth eat the same meal every day—the same starch, the same protein, vegetables mainly, and more beans than meat. To see this unvarying diet as monotonous is misleading. The eater would regard any change as confusing and irrelevant, if not subversive.

People can seem amazingly adaptable until they are faced with a different diet. In the Buganda region of Uganda, where in the 1960s I ran a residential education center and had to feed Africans from all over the country, the students from other, rice-growing areas claimed that the banana-based diet of Buganda weakened them. They said that being denied their usual food made them unwell and accounted for their low grades and lassitude. In one respect, there was a snobbish aspect to their attitude. They were deeply superstitious about eating the food of people they regarded as their inferiors. During the Falklands War, the British troops ridiculed the Argentine soldiers as "bean eaters." In a similar spirit, in the seventeenth century, the Yeomen of the Guard, with their tradition of being trenchermen—as well as valued,

strong, effective royal protectors—were nicknamed Beefeaters. There is also an echo of my Ugandan students' lament in the Book of Daniel. In this text, with its numerous references to vegetarian foods, a much-weakened Daniel, in exile, persuades the king's eunuch to bring him lentils and water instead of the meat and wine that Nebuchadnezzar had been serving him. Restored to his simple fodder, Daniel recovers his strength, and he is able to work magic.

Great variety in food has its origin in feasting, an occasion when, to celebrate a holiday or event, people eat special foods for a day or more and gorge themselves. The word "feast" comes from "festival," which in turn derives from a word meaning "joyful." Even the most rigid and unvarying society allows itself to celebrate now and then, and food is always the symbol of that celebration, involving the elaborate preparation of rich dishes and delicacies. In *The Kingdom by the Sea*, about my travels around Great Britain, I described how I happened upon a small town in Scotland that had welcomed the queen the day before. The royal visit was marked with a meal, a banquet at a local hotel, and the most coveted souvenir was the engraved menu.

FEASTING, THE KEYNOTE of many cookbooks, is certainly a theme in *The Best American Recipes 2000*, but it is not the only one. What strikes me about many recipes in this book is their familiarity—they are variations on traditional, and therefore comforting, dishes. I am thinking of Macaroni Gratin, with French flourishes such as cooking the pasta in milk, then dropping ice cubes into the just-done pasta to stop the cooking; mashed potatoes, served as a special creamy dish; and the English Sunday staple Yorkshire Pudding, with a Craig Claiborne emphasis.

Many Mediterranean people would agree that Skillet-Roasted Mussels, especially with the accents here, are superb. (I grew up on the Massachusetts coast, where the general feeling was that only seagulls ate mussels — and weren't they clever the way they cracked them open by dropping them on the road?) In Africa, corn on the cob is usually grilled, as described on page 206, but the next steps in the recipe are a wonderful surprise. I enjoy cooking seafood, and the Basque-style grilled shrimp or scallops (page 176) are pleasing and tasty. My love for bouillabaisse drew me to the Mediterranean Seafood Stew, a grand version of that Marseilles specialty. My mother regularly made codfish cakes, but the Spicy Codfish Cakes with Cilantro Aïoli are better than Mother's. Slow-Roasted Salmon has much to recommend it — the simplicity, the variation with the kelp, the fact that it was inspired by the chef's Irish mother. Another notable feature is that the recipe serves eight, which reminds us that eating is about sharing.

PAUL THEROUX

introduction

PEOPLE ALWAYS ASK US how we choose the recipes that make up the annual *Best American* collections. And although we do have some criteria—taste first and foremost, recipes that solve problems, dishes we get excited about and can't wait to make again—the fact is that we've developed a kind of radar for these distinctive recipes. It's as though a little bell goes off in our heads when we first read them, and then we have to go back and see why.

To a reader, it may seem odd to have a fancy recipe such as chef Thomas Keller's elegant cheese crisps molded in an egg carton in the same book with an unabashedly down-home recipe such as Beer Can Chicken. But to our taste, the barriers between haute and earthy have all but disappeared. You wouldn't necessarily serve these radically different dishes in the same meal, but one can be dressed up and the other dressed down so that they definitely belong in the same kitchen and fall into the category of favorite recipes you make over and over again. They're both unusual, and they both deliver exciting food for a minimum of effort.

Most of all, we love smart recipes that maximize flavor. They may be smart because they're fast (or for that matter, slow, the better to develop flavor), or because they're foolproof, or because they give a classic dish a new life. Or they may just be a best-ever version of a beloved American classic, or an exotic dish we could scarcely imagine ourselves making even five years ago.

We're also mindful of what's really useful to our readers. We know you need a quick potato dish that tastes brand-new and goes with everything (that's Roasted Potato Crisps with Fresh Herbs); we know there are never enough delicious Christmas cookies (and that you'll love Christmas Casserole Cookies); we know you need a big salad that can go to a picnic or sit on a buffet table for hours (Cauliflower, Broccoflower, and Frisée Salad with Olives). All of us need a delectable dinner we can make in nothing flat, like Green Chile Cheese Puff. And we have to admit that we also love to have fun in the kitchen, which is why we couldn't resist the completely outrageous Texas Lemon Bombe, with its meringue topping swirled in the unmistakable style of former Texas governor Ann Richards's coiffure.

It seems almost incredible that we're still discovering new kitchen tricks for dealing with standard ingredients, but fortunately that's the case. This year we hope to entice you to change the way you cook potatoes as well as salmon fillets, not to mention the simplest possible way to cook mussels.

What about magical ingredients? Our vote this year goes to two Asian spice blends: Chinese five-spice powder and Japanese seven-spice powder. These fragrant blends do wonders for grilled food and vegetables. As we become more familiar with Asian dishes casually produced in our own kitchens, Asian spice blends will become as common as chili powder.

And we're also rediscovering old tricks: after roasting several standing rib roasts last year in a fruitless search for the perfect roast beef, we feel our prayers have been answered this year with the republication of a long-lost high-temperature roast beef, which was developed by kitchen wizard Ann Seranne. For us, this is the all-time best roast beef, the one that defies all the fancy high-tech thermometers to produce a sensational rare roast beef so easy you can practically cook it in your sleep. And the oven stays free for last-minute side dishes.

As always, our sources are virtually endless: the perhaps 600 cookbooks published each year, the many food magazines and the recipe sections of general magazines, the food sections of newspapers everywhere, newsletters, handouts, press releases, the back of the box—and most mind-boggling of all, the Internet. In cyberspace, millions of cooks work day and night, contributing a steady stream of hundreds of thousands of recipes—and in the process create a lively community of passionate cooks. Have we looked at every single recipe? Of course not. Have we found some great food on the Internet? Absolutely, and many of the best recipes made our list this year.

In short, we've looked at thousands of recipes, cooked hundreds of them, and come up with this carefully considered collection of what are, for us, the essential recipes of the year. So here they are, with notes to the cook, serving suggestions, wine choices, and variations. The proof of the pudding will be, as always, in your kitchen. Let us know what you think, and let us know (in care of our publisher) when you find a truly superb recipe you think we ought to consider, especially if it's from a source outside the mainstream world of food. If we haven't seen it before and we decide to use it, we'll not only credit you with discovering it, we'll send you a copy of the collection it appears in. So cook up a storm, and may you eat as well this year as we have.

FRAN McCULLOUGH

the year in food

As WE ASSEMBLED the recipes for this collection, we couldn't help noticing certain recurring ingredients, techniques, and general food manias that preoccupied the nation's cooks throughout the year. But it wasn't until we made our final selection that we noticed some surprises: red grapes and sweet little cherry tomatoes, for instance, had sneaked right by us, only clearly announcing themselves in the number of recipes in which they were star players. Here's how the year looked to us.

THE TOP TEN

1. COMEBACK OF THE YEAR
Eggs

There were a number of strong candidates in this category, but we think the winner is good old eggs. We've been feeling sorry for eggs for years now, as they've been lambasted for supposedly raising cholesterol levels to alarming heights and thereby setting people up for an early death. But in fact we now know that eggs do no such thing, thanks to extensive studies on the subject. These dynamic nutritional packages are nearly perfect: high-quality protein that almost everyone loves. We were startled by the number of egg recipes we included—but they're all delicious, and, we have to confess, we dearly love eggs. So welcome back, you good egg, and may ersatz egg products disappear along with ersatz cheese.

2. ADDICTION OF THE YEAR
Fried Everything

Fried food was everywhere this year, from chicken (which appeared in all the food magazines) to french fries to olives. OK, we admit it; we're completely crazy about perfectly fried food ourselves. But we don't cook it at home too often because it's such a production and has to be done at the last minute. We make an exception for West Texas Onion Rings, however. These are just unbelievably good, a treat we'll enjoy at least once a year from now on.

3. SPICE OF THE YEAR
Ginger, Ginger, Ginger!

Ginger is everywhere, and frankly we can't get enough of it. Part of the reason may be that we have high-quality young crystallized ginger in the market now, but home cooks are also starting to realize that a little fresh ginger in everything from coleslaw to icebox cake is a guaranteed hit. Ginger is working hard in both savory and sweet dishes and in all its forms: fresh, dried, and crystallized.

4. NOVELTY OF THE YEAR
Smoked Spanish Paprika (Pimentòn de la Vera)

This intoxicating oak-smoked condiment from the Extremadura region of Spain comes in both hot and sweet forms and transforms everything it touches, from eggs to vegetables to grilled foods. You can use it anywhere you'd use ordinary paprika. Chefs have been playing with smoked paprika for several years now, but it's perfect for home cooks too—we keep a tin of both kinds on the spice shelf and use it several times a week. Check out Creamy Mashed Potatoes for an interesting way to use it. You can order smoked paprika from Formaggio Kitchen: (888) 212-3224.

5. VEGETABLE OF THE YEAR
The Potato

Spuds took over this year, in everything from Mashed Potato Dip (with wasabi and flying fish roe—trust us, it's great) to Roasted Potato Crisps to potatoes in pizza dough. Recipes now call for potatoes by their first names, as in "Get Yukon Golds for this recipe or forget it." The first runner-up is cherry tomatoes, those sweet little orbs that remind us how much we love tomatoes all winter long. Grape tomatoes elbowed out cherry tomatoes in many markets this year, and we use them interchangeably. We're very partial to the roasted cherry tomato sauce in food writer Nancy Harmon Jenkins's excellent Pasta with Baked Tomato Sauce, a great light

supper at the end of winter when you're just dying for a good tomato.

6. TECHNIQUE OF THE YEAR
Slow Roasting

We've had fast, high-heat roasting for years now, so it's time for slow food. And to usher it in, there's an entire Slow Food movement from Italy that's captured the hearts of many American chefs and cooks who like deeply satisfying flavor, the kind that comes only from slow cooking, and are willing to trade their kitchen time in exchange. A good example is Twelve-Hour Roast Pork. A corollary movement is to roast everything in sight, from olives to grapes to cheese. Count us in.

7. DESSERT OF THE YEAR
Anything Chocolate

Maybe everyone fell out of love this year and needed consolation from the brain chemicals chocolate provides—whatever it was, we all tumbled. It may have been partly a response to the new bittersweet chocolates on the market, with much higher cocoa content. We also have a new homegrown high-quality chocolate industry in which we can take great pride (see the Scharffen Berger cake on page 317). Whatever accounts for it, the chocolate passion has been unleashed, and it's raging across the land.

8. FRUIT OF THE YEAR
The Quince

It seems amazing that a hundred years ago there were quince trees all over America and this delectable fruit appeared on many tables with no fanfare at all. But this year the medieval-looking quince was rediscovered, and fragrant bowls of quinces turned up in kitchens and dining rooms across the country. Once you have a taste for quince, you'll look forward to its brief harvest every fall. Not quite a pear, not quite an apple, with its own wild dimension, this excellent fruit deserves more fans. Runner-up fruit of the year is red grapes. Roasted, frozen, baked into bread, teamed with walnuts and olives for a condiment—grapes are coming on strong.

9. DRINK OF THE YEAR
Beer!

This year, Americans have discovered beer as a fascinating drink in its own right. From Sierra Nevada Pale Ale to Brooklyn Beer, microbreweries all across the country have contributed a new sophistication to the beer market. Increasingly, beer is holding its own with wine as the beverage of choice with food, and not only to accompany ethnic food. Beer has another life as an ingredient—in this book alone, you can find Beer-Braised Short Ribs, Beer Can Chicken, and Beer Bread. It doesn't hurt, of course, that the latest science on the subject shows beer has actual health benefits, with its high vitamin B_6 levels that protect against heart disease.

Runner-up for the drink of the year is port, formerly considered a fuddy-duddy confined to the Ye Olde restaurant scene and a few connoisseurs. Sensational on its own, port is also a secret ingredient that transforms a couple of the dishes in this book: the insanely simple Port Wine Grapes and a succulent prizewinning salad with Gorgonzola and walnuts.

10. GADGET OF THE YEAR
The Japanese Mandoline, aka Benriner Slicer

These inexpensive little slicers (from $8 to $60, depending on their complexity) enable the home cook to shave vegetables into gorgeous salads. They make short work of recipes such as Shaved Asparagus and Parmesan Salad, and Roasted Potato Crisps with Fresh Herbs. Even if your knife skills are appalling, you can turn out professional-looking dishes in just a few minutes. And it's a curious fact that how a vegetable is sliced changes its taste, so you can come up with some surprising new flavors as well.

French chefs have been using their expensive mandolines to do the same thing for centuries now, and the newly redesigned Matfer mandoline (available from Williams-Sonoma, 800-541-2233, as are several Japanese mandolines), is the last word on fine slicing, as easy to use as a box grater.

All of these mandolines are extremely sharp, so you need to be very careful when using them. Some vegetables—radishes, turnips, beets—come with their own convenient handles to protect your fingers. But you should also wrap your cutting hand with a kitchen towel to avoid injury.

Best of all, these slicing gizmos are inspirational: once you're familiar with using them, you'll be inspired to mix appealing colors and tastes in new combinations—an exciting way to eat your vegetables!

starters

Roasted Eggplant Dip 2

Radish and Goat Cheese Wreath 3

Mashed Potato Dip 4

Hungarian Jewish Chopped Liver 6

Roasted Black and Green Olives with Whole Garlic 8

Apricot Thrones with Cheese and Pecans 10

Homemade Potato Chips with Crème Fraîche and Caviar 12

Parmigiano-Reggiano Crisps with Goat Cheese Mousse 14

Ceviche Verde 17

Florentine Ravioli *(Nudi)* 20

roasted eggplant dip

It's the generous use of spices and fresh herbs in this eggplant puree that elevates it above similar dips. Steve Johnson of Boston's Blue Room uses it as part of his vegetable antipasto plat-

COOK
Steve Johnson

SOURCE
Foodline.com

ter, but there's no reason it can't be served by itself. The dip is at its very best in late summer, when eggplants hit their peak. Serve with crostini or toasted pita bread wedges.

serves 8 to 10; makes about 3 cups

- 4 medium eggplants
- ½ cup chopped fresh mint
- ½ cup chopped fresh flat-leaf parsley
- 4 garlic cloves
- 1 tablespoon ground cumin

- 1 tablespoon ground coriander
- ¼ cup olive oil
- 1 tablespoon soy sauce
- 1 tablespoon balsamic vinegar
- 1 tablespoon fresh lemon juice
  Salt and freshly ground pepper to taste

Roast the eggplants whole over a gas or charcoal grill for 25 to 35 minutes, or until very soft. Or preheat the oven to 350 degrees, halve the eggplants lengthwise, place them cut side down on a greased, foil-lined cookie sheet, and roast for 30 to 40 minutes, or until the eggplants are very soft and mushy. Let cool cut side up.

Scoop out the eggplant flesh, being careful to avoid bits of charred skin. Place the eggplant flesh and the remaining ingredients in a food processor and puree. Taste and adjust the seasonings. The dip tastes best when it is freshly made, but it can be covered and refrigerated for 1 to 2 days before serving.

radish and goat cheese wreath

COOK

Rozanne Gold

SOURCE

Entertaining 1-2-3

If you're looking for a simple but gorgeous, not-too-filling holiday hors d'oeuvre, here it is. The only trick is to find truly beautiful radishes, fat ones with pretty, perky greens still attached. Guests will ooh and aah at your lovely red-white-and-green wreath, then pick up the radishes by the convenient little handles of their attached stems and rave again over the taste of these exhilarating bites. For all this acclaim, you'll spend about 10 minutes of your precious time. We love this clever idea from the diva of minimalism, Manhattan chef Rozanne Gold.

serves 8; makes 48 cocktail bites

12 fat red radishes with perky
   greens (about 2 large
   bunches)
4 ounces fresh goat cheese
2 teaspoons water

1 tablespoon whole cumin
   seeds, lightly toasted in a
   skillet until fragrant
1/4 teaspoon salt

Remove the leaves from the radishes, leaving 1 inch of stem attached, and wash and dry the leaves well, saving the prettiest for your wreath. Scrub each radish with a brush, cutting off their tails if necessary.

Arrange the leaves in a circle on a platter or just cover the surface of the platter with the leaves. Cut the radishes in half lengthwise.

In a small bowl, combine the remaining ingredients, stirring with a rubber spatula until smooth. Spread the cheese mixture evenly over the cut sides of the radishes. Arrange the radish halves cut side up on the leaves and refrigerate until serving time.

mashed potato dip

COOK

Michel Richard

SOURCE

Cooking with Patrick Clark,
edited by
Charlie Trotter

This is not just any old mashed potato dip, but Michel Richard's wantonly luxurious one that almost qualifies as an entire meal. He gives rich American mashed potatoes a wonderfully Asian twist: a zing of wasabi and a scoop of orange fish roe.

Richard, a French-born, cigar-smoking chef and restaurateur, chose this as his contribution to a cookbook assembled by Charlie Trotter in honor of their fellow chef, the late Patrick Clark. From one ebullient chef to another, it is a very fitting tribute.

If you make this dip once, you'll probably want to double the recipe the second time around. Surrounded by strips of green peppers or other raw vegetables, it is invariably devoured in record time.

serves 6 to 8; makes about 2 cups

- 1 teaspoon wasabi (see note)
- 2 tablespoons olive oil
- 1 tablespoon rice wine vinegar
- 1 tablespoon flying fish roe (see note) or salmon roe
- 1 pound yellow potatoes, such as Yukon Gold, peeled and quartered

- ¼ cup heavy cream
- 8 tablespoons (1 stick) butter, softened
- Salt to taste

tip

Don't think of this as just a dip; it's equally good served warm as a side dish, particularly with fish.

First, prepare a vinaigrette by whisking together the wasabi, olive oil, and vinegar in a small bowl. Gently stir in the roe. Set aside.

Steam the potatoes or boil them gently until thoroughly cooked. Drain and push them through a sieve with a wooden spoon or pass them through a Mouli grater into a large bowl. Stir in the cream and butter and mix thoroughly. Season to taste with salt and stir in the wasabi vinaigrette.

---

cook's notes

🍃 Wasabi, the sinus-clearing Asian horseradish, is sold as a powder and as a paste, both frozen and in a tube, in Asian markets and many supermarkets. Any form of wasabi can be used in the dip; the powder is the most potent.

🍃 Most people will recognize flying fish roe by sight, even if it sounds unfamiliar. Tiny orange grains of roe are often found on sushi rolls. The neon orange color is actually nature's own, and the crunchy texture of the minuscule grains is very appealing. Flying fish roe is available in Asian markets or—often more conveniently—at any sushi restaurant; a tablespoon usually costs about $2.25.

---

starters

hungarian jewish chopped liver

COOK
Valerie Alia

SOURCE
Allrecipes.com

This is for those of you who think you make the world's best chopped liver or who think you don't like chopped liver.

When Valerie Alia submitted this recipe to Allrecipes.com and identified herself as Hungarian, it was not necessary to say more. After all, Hungarians are undoubtedly among the best cooks in the world. It is their particular attention to detail that makes a Hungarian meal special. In the case of Alia's chopped liver recipe, she advises other cooks that "under NO circumstances would you add beef or any other kind of liver or filler; this will spoil the flavor." Note, too, how the livers are mashed (not pulverized). And the way the onions are added is crucial: not once, but three times.

Blessed with a Jewish uncle, one of us grew up knowing that there was always a crock of chopped chicken liver in the refrigerator. That's not such a bad idea today either: chopped liver can provide instant satisfaction for snackers, quick meal seekers, and unexpected guests.

serves 8; makes about 5 cups

2 tablespoons vegetable oil

1–2 tablespoons unsalted butter (optional)

1 large white onion, diced

2 pounds fresh chicken livers

4–6 large eggs, hard-cooked

1 bunch scallions, finely chopped

1 small white onion, grated or finely chopped

Salt and freshly ground pepper to taste

1–2 tablespoons paprika, or to taste (see note)

2 tablespoons chopped fresh flat-leaf parsley

Flat-leaf parsley sprigs, for garnish

In a large skillet, heat the oil and butter, if using, over medium-high heat. Add the diced onion and sauté for 5 minutes, or until soft. Add the chicken livers and sauté over high heat, stirring frequently, for 5 minutes, or until cooked through (no longer pink inside and the juices run clear). Transfer the liver mixture to a large bowl.

Mash the liver mixture with a potato masher or the back of a large wooden spoon. You will need to use your fingers to remove the membranes as you go. The livers will be quite juicy; be sure to retain the juice.

In a medium bowl, mash the eggs and add to the liver mixture. Add the scallions and the grated or finely chopped onion and mix thoroughly. The liver mixture should still be warm and will cook the raw onion slightly. Season the mixture with salt and pepper to taste and add at least 1 tablespoon paprika (more if you're Hungarian!). Stir in the chopped parsley. Cover with plastic wrap and refrigerate for at least 1 to 2 hours or up to 2 days. Bring to room temperature. Garnish with the parsley sprigs and serve with crackers, toasted mini-bagels, or toast, or as a sublime sandwich filling.

---

cook's note

Choose your paprika carefully. Standard supermarket paprika is not worthy of this heavenly mash, and rarefied smoked Spanish paprika—an interesting ingredient in other dishes—overpowers the livers. Aromatic, sweet Hungarian paprika is perfect. Real Hungarian paprika can be found in gourmet stores and some supermarkets.

roasted black and green olives
with whole garlic

In Marlena de Blasi's baroque opera of a cookbook, there are a number of amazing recipes we've never seen before, all gathered from the remote regions of southern Italy. It was hard to choose just one, but in the end the recipe we'd make often is this luscious Sicilian olive dish, redolent of gently cooked garlic and the unusual taste of dry marsala. Totally unexpected is the

COOK

Marlena de Blasi

SOURCE

*Regional Foods
of Southern Italy*

touch of mint tossed in at the end.

De Blasi says it best, in her typically over-the-top prose: "Roasting the olives plumps them, renders them voluptuously fleshy, tender. And when whole, fat garlic— caramelized in a long, slow roasting— confronts the salt-tinged meat of the warm olives, the whole becomes quietly paradisical." Yes, yes …

serves 4 to 6

4 large heads garlic
¼ cup extra-virgin olive oil,
   plus more for oven-toasting
   the bread
1 teaspoon salt
   Freshly ground pepper to taste
1½ pounds Sicilian, Greek, or
   Spanish black, green, or
   purple olives, or a
   combination, unpitted

1 loaf crusty coarse-textured
   bread, torn into chunks
½ cup dry marsala (see note)
½ cup fresh mint leaves

> **tip**
> You may want to choose pit-
> ted olives instead, which will
> be easier for your guests to
> handle.

Preheat the oven to 325 degrees.

Cut through the garlic heads at the root ends and separate the cloves, leaving their skins intact. Place the garlic cloves in a medium ceramic or terra-cotta casserole dish, add ¼ cup olive oil, and toss to coat the garlic well. Sprinkle with the salt and grind pepper generously over the garlic.

Roast the garlic for 20 minutes. Add the olives and stir to combine. Roast for 20 minutes more, or until the garlic cloves are beginning to collapse and the olives have plumped.

Meanwhile, anoint the bread chunks with the remaining olive oil and place on a cookie sheet. Pour the marsala over the olive mixture, increase the oven temperature to 400 degrees, and roast for 5 minutes more, along with the bread.

Remove the olive mixture from the oven, strew with the mint leaves, and serve warm with the bread and iced dry marsala. Give each guest a small plate and knife to spread the roasted garlic cloves (which pop right out of their papery husks) on the toast. Encourage everyone to dip the toast into the delectable juices that collect at the bottom of the serving dish.

---

cook's note

The marsala called for here is not the usual sweet industrial spirit sprinkled over veal marsala, but rather a dry one, such as Marsala Superiore Riserva or Marsala Vergine. For most of us, this is a completely new and exhilarating taste.

apricot thrones with cheese and pecans

These delectable little tidbits have everything going for them: they're simple, quick to make from ingredients you probably have on hand, can be made ahead, and are just as good for dessert as they are with cocktails. California chef Hugh Carpenter serves these up in his

COOK

Hugh Carpenter

SOURCE

Fast Appetizers,
by Hugh Carpenter
and Teri Sandison

aptly titled *Fast Appetizers,* but there are no compromises here: these are elegant, perfectly balanced, sweet-tart morsels.

They're perfect candidates for a potluck dinner or a buffet because they're served at room temperature and need no last-minute attention.

serves 6 to 10

15 pecan halves
2 ounces cream cheese, softened
    (about ¹/₄ cup)

2 ounces blue cheese
    (about ¹/₄ cup), crumbled
15 dried apricots (see note)

Preheat the oven to 325 degrees.

Place the pecans on a cookie sheet and toast in the oven until golden brown, about 15 minutes. Transfer to a plate and set aside to cool .

Combine the cheeses in a small bowl and mix thoroughly. Divide the cheese mixture into 3 pieces, then divide each third into 5 pieces.

Place 1 piece of the cheese mixture on each apricot and top with a toasted pecan half. Transfer the apricots to a serving plate and serve, or cover with plastic wrap and refrigerate for up to 8 hours. Bring to room temperature before serving.

VARIATION

Instead of combining cream cheese and blue cheese, you can use soft Brie alone for a subtler taste.

---

cook's note

Be sure your dried apricots are moist and not desiccated, or your guests will have to gnaw their way through these appetizers. Look for unsulfured apricots for the best flavor.

---

homemade potato chips
with crème fraîche and caviar

COOK

Joachim Splichal

SOURCE

InStyle

For a party for Eric Clapton, Los Angeles chef Joachim Splichal of Patina came up with these terrific chips, which are so good that you might want to serve them without the topping as a side dish or a snack. With the crème fraîche and caviar treatment, however, the humble chips turn completely elegant—just the thing to serve with New Year's Eve champagne.

If you'd rather not get into the caviar business, a little smoked salmon would be just as delicious.

serves 4

2 tablespoons butter, melted
1 baking potato (about 9 ounces)
¼ teaspoon salt
⅛ teaspoon freshly ground pepper

⅓ cup crème fraîche
1 teaspoon fresh lemon juice
2 teaspoons minced fresh chives
½ ounce caviar (see note)

Preheat the oven to 350 degrees. Brush a cookie sheet with 1 tablespoon of the melted butter.

Peel the potato and cut it into ⅛-inch-thick slices. Place the potato slices on the cookie sheet and brush them with the remaining 1 tablespoon butter. Sprinkle with the salt and pepper.

---

to drink

Champagne, of course, but beer, especially India Pale Ale, is also wonderful with caviar.

Bake for 25 minutes, or until golden, turning once.

In a small bowl, combine the crème fraîche and lemon juice. With an electric mixer, beat the mixture until soft peaks form, then add the chives.

To serve, place the warm chips on a serving platter and top with the crème fraîche mixture and caviar.

VARIATION

Gourmet magazine had a similar recipe this year and had the bright idea of cutting the raw potato slices into star shapes with a cookie cutter. That set us thinking about other shapes in our cookie-cutter collection, such as crescent moons. You can have a lot of fun with this recipe.

---

cook's note

Since beluga sturgeon from Russia has been overfished, classic caviar has become astronomically expensive. Look for American caviar, which is quite respectable and reasonably priced—bowfin, paddlefish, whitefish (aka American golden), and Chinook (salmon) are all worth seeking out.

tips

- It's a good idea to reeducate your eye about how thick ⅛ inch actually is, because if your slices are too thick, they won't cook properly, and if they're too thin, they'll burn. So get out a ruler and be sure you know what they're supposed to look like.
- If you use a cookie sheet with sides, your potato chips may be soggy, so you may want to turn it upside down.

parmigiano-reggiano crisps
with goat cheese mousse

COOK

Thomas Keller

SOURCE

The French Laundry Cookbook

We adore every conceivable form of melted Parmesan cheese, but these little morsels stole our hearts because of the ingenious way they're formed: in an egg carton. If anyone knows about delectable morsels, it's chef Thomas Keller. At the French Laundry in the Napa Valley, he creates a staggering parade of sensational small bits, each more enticing than the last. Most of these are well beyond the home cook's repertoire, but these lacy crisps are a cinch.

The goat cheese mousse is fresh and lovely, creamy against the crunch of the crisps—and you don't need us to tell you that you can also fill these tiny tulip-shaped baskets with an almost endless variety of treats, such as smoked salmon.

serves 8

PARMIGIANO-REGGIANO CRISPS

1 cup finely grated Parmigiano-Reggiano cheese, from a moist piece of cheese

GOAT CHEESE MOUSSE

6 ounces fresh goat cheese (about $^3/_4$ cup)

4–6 tablespoons heavy cream

1 tablespoon minced fresh flat-leaf parsley

Salt and freshly ground pepper to taste

FOR THE CRISPS

Have ready a clean egg carton. Preheat the oven to 325 degrees.

Line a cookie sheet with a Silpat sheet (a reusable nonstick cookie-sheet liner) or a piece of parchment paper.

(Here Keller uses a 2½-inch ring mold to form the crisps. If you don't have one, you could use the ring from a tuna can or just make a free-form circle about the same size with your fingers. Since you're probably not cooking at the French Laundry, it doesn't matter if your circles aren't perfect.)

Place a 2½-inch ring mold in the corner of the baking sheet and put 1 tablespoon of the cheese inside it, spreading the cheese into an even layer—or do this free-form. Make 7 more circles of cheese, at least 1 inch apart.

Bake for 8 to 10 minutes, or until the crisps begin to turn golden. Remove the cookie sheet from the oven and let the crisps firm up for about 30 seconds.

One by one, remove the crisps with a spatula and press them gently into the hollows in the egg carton to form tulip shapes. After a few minutes, remove the cooked crisps from the egg carton and repeat the process with the remaining 8 tablespoons cheese, making 8 more crisps.

FOR THE GOAT CHEESE MOUSSE

Place the goat cheese in a food processor and process briefly—depending on the cheese, it may look crumbly or smooth. Pour 4 tablespoons of the cream through the feed tube and process until the mixture is smooth but will hold a shape when piped. If necessary, add a little more cream. Add the parsley and salt and pepper, and process just to combine. Taste and adjust the seasonings. The mousse can be refrigerated for 2 to 3 days; let stand at room temperature for about 30 minutes to soften slightly before piping.

Place the mousse in a pastry bag fitted with a medium star tip or a heavy-duty plastic freezer bag with a corner tip cut out for piping. Pipe 2 to 3 teaspoons of the mousse into each crisp and serve.

VARIATION

Michael Chiarello, another legendary Napa Valley chef, makes a big crisp he calls a *fritelle*, which means "toasted" in Italian. It's a cup of grated Parmesan cheese spread in a thin, even layer on a cookie sheet lined with well-buttered foil, then toasted at 350 degrees for about 5 minutes, or until golden. Slide the cheese on the foil sheet onto the counter and let cool. Pry the cheese off the foil and crumble into bits. It's suitable for sprinkling on salads, soups, pasta, or vegetables or just for eating out of hand. The *fritelle* will keep for several days in an airtight container in the refrigerator. Reheat in a nonstick skillet before serving.

ceviche verde

COOK

Roberto Santibanez after Lila Lomeli

SOURCE

Fondasanmiguel.com

When Roberto Santibanez, the chef at Austin's superb Fonda San Miguel restaurant, tasted his friend Lila's green ceviche in Mexico City, he knew he'd discovered the best. We agree; this exhilarating mild and sweet ceviche is full of herbs (but not cilantro, as you might expect), and the delicate fish is spiked with chile and pungent green olives and brightened with fresh lime juice—a sensational combination.

The crucial thing is to find a very fresh fish that came in whole to the fishmonger. Santibanez uses black drum from the Gulf of Mexico, but most of us can't get that. Other possibilities are Gulf red snapper, halibut, grouper, or mahimahi (be careful to cut out the bloodline). Avoid frozen supermarket fish, which will have a mushy texture and very little flavor. Oilier fish such as sea bass will destroy the delicacy of this dish.

It's essential to taste the herb mixture carefully and adjust it so it sparkles with exactly the right balance of salt, olive oil, and garlic.

The ceviche needs at least 4 hours to "cook" the fish. Santibanez uses small Mexican limes, which aren't as acidic as our larger supermarket Persian limes, and he lets it marinate overnight in the refrigerator, then just whizzes up the herb sauce shortly before serving. If you're using regular limes, cut the fish a little finer and marinate it for only 4 hours.

serves 6

---

to serve

We like to serve the ceviche in an avocado half, with extra lime wedges passed at the table.

---

starters

2 pounds fresh mild white fish
   (see headnote)
½ teaspoon dried oregano,
   preferably Mexican (see
   note), crumbled
½ teaspoon salt
   Fresh lime juice

HERB MIXTURE
1 cup packed fresh flat-leaf
   parsley leaves, including a
   little stem

½ cup fresh mint leaves
½ cup fresh basil leaves,
   including a little stem
10 large pitted green olives
1 habanero or serrano chile,
   or to taste
1 small garlic clove, or to taste
   Salt to taste
1 cup olive oil

Lettuce, for serving

Cut the fish into ¼-inch cubes and place in a large bowl. Add the oregano, salt, and lime juice to cover. Cover and marinate in the refrigerator for at least 4 hours or overnight to "cook" the fish.

About 20 minutes before you plan to serve the ceviche, strain the fish in a sieve, pressing down and squeezing to remove as much moisture as possible. Place the fish in a medium bowl and set aside.

cook's note

Mexican oregano is worth looking for and often turns up at the supermarket. It has a more refined flavor than Greek oregano and can be used interchangeably in most recipes.

The herbs should be as dry as possible. Place all the ingredients except the olive oil in a blender. Blend to a very fine sauce, adding a little water to release the blades as necessary. Pour in the olive oil in a slow, steady stream to emulsify the sauce. Taste and adjust the seasonings until you have a sparkling flavor.

Add enough sauce to the fish to coat each cube completely and serve on a bed of lettuce within 15 minutes. This dish doesn't keep.

VARIATION

You might prefer more lime or more chile. If you have very acidic limes but you'd still like to marinate the fish overnight, use a different Mexican marinade: equal parts lime juice, white vinegar, and water.

florentine ravioli *(nudi)*

COOK
Giuliano Bugialli

SOURCE
Food & Wine

Only in Florence would ravioli be served with not so much as its underwear: no pasta covering at all. That's why these tasty morsels are called *nudi*. When Italian cooking authority Giuliano Bugialli was growing up in Florence, his mother believed that only a true Florentine could make these celestially light spinach-cheese dumplings, so she refused those of her sisters-in-law, who came from Siena. And even though Mama herself couldn't cook, somehow *nudi* became "her" ravioli, the ones she craved. The task falls to Bugialli when he's in Florence to make them for the family, since they've all but disappeared from restaurant menus.

Light as these ravioli are in texture, they are also very rich—a bit overwhelming for more than a first course. But they're sublime; make them with fresh spinach and the best ricotta you can find, and they'll become a trademark recipe.

serves 8

15 ounces ricotta cheese (about 2 cups)
  Salt to taste
3 pounds spinach, large stems discarded
3 cups freshly grated Parmesan cheese (about $3/4$ pound)
$1/2$ teaspoon freshly grated nutmeg

  Freshly ground pepper to taste
5 extra-large egg yolks
1 cup all-purpose flour
8 tablespoons (1 stick) unsalted butter
  Fresh sage leaves, for garnish

---

to drink
A perfect companion is the local Tuscan rosato.

Spoon the ricotta into a large coffee filter set in a strainer and drain for 1 hour.

Bring a large pot of salted water to a boil. Add the spinach and cook for 10 minutes, then drain in a colander and cool under cold running water. Drain the spinach thoroughly. Working with one handful at a time, squeeze the spinach until very dry. Finely chop the spinach.

In a large bowl, combine the drained ricotta, spinach, 2 cups of the Parmesan, and the nutmeg. Season generously with salt and pepper, add the egg yolks, and stir until evenly combined.

Bring a large pot of salted water to a boil. Spread the flour on a plate. Form level tablespoons of the ricotta mixture into balls. Roll the balls lightly in the flour until coated. Arrange the balls on a lightly floured cookie sheet.

Melt the butter and pour it into a large warmed baking dish; keep warm near the stove.

Gently drop one-third of the balls into the boiling water and cook just until they rise to the surface. Using a wire skimmer or a slotted spoon, transfer the ravioli to the baking dish in a single layer. Return the water to a boil and cook the remaining balls in two

---

tips

- For the most ethereal ravioli, dust off any excess flour before cooking them.
- You can make the ravioli up to the point of boiling them the day before you serve them.

batches. Sprinkle the ravioli *nudi* with as much of the remaining 1 cup Parmesan as desired and garnish with the sage leaves before serving.

To reheat, preheat the oven to 400 degrees. Bake the ravioli for 10 to 15 minutes, or until the cheese is melted and the ravioli are lightly browned. Serve.

---

cook's note

Truth to tell, we love the *nudi* best when they're baked in the oven before serving, as in the reheating directions.

soups

Hot Avocado Soup with Poblano 24

Rich Red Pepper Soup 26

Italian Pumpkin Soup 28

Roasted Butternut Squash Soup 30

The Lentil Soup (Shurbat al-'Adas) 32

Red Lentil and Apricot Soup 34

Fabio's *Farinata* (Cornmeal and Kale Soup) 36

Puree of Barley Soup with Chicken Liver Butter 38

Senegalese Peanut Soup 40

Mexican Pistachio Soup 42

Sweet Pea Soup with Crispy Rock Shrimp Salad 44

Cream of Celery Root with Shrimp Butter 46

Heavenly Carrot Soup 48

hot avocado soup with poblano

COOK

Jeff Vaccaro

SOURCE

Avocado.org

We tasted a number of avocado soups this year, both hot and cold, but this Mexican one is special, full of deep but delicate flavor and garnished intriguingly. Jeff Vaccaro was the sous chef at the Silo Restaurant in San Antonio when he created this soup, which the California Avocado Commission recommends to other professional cooks.

We've cut the restaurant proportions in half to serve six. You won't mind having leftovers, since the soup is good the next day as well— just taste it carefully and add seasonings as needed. This dish depends on just the right balance to make the flavors sing. It's perfect for lunch or a light supper.

serves 6

2 Hass avocados, peeled, pitted, and diced
3 tablespoons fresh lime juice
1 teaspoon vegetable oil
1½ cups chopped white onion
1 yellow bell pepper, seeded and chopped
1 poblano chile, seeded and chopped
1½ tablespoons chopped garlic
½ cup dry white wine
4 cups water or chicken broth, plus more if needed

1 teaspoon ground cumin
½ teaspoon chili powder
¼ teaspoon freshly ground white pepper
Salt
6 cilantro sprigs
1 tablespoon finely diced tomato
1 tablespoon thinly sliced scallion
Crumbled queso fresco, for garnish (see note)
Deep-fried corn tortilla strips, for garnish

In a medium bowl, combine the avocados and all but 1 teaspoon of the lime juice. Set aside.

In a large skillet, heat the oil over high heat and sauté the onion, bell pepper, poblano, and garlic until lightly browned, about 5 minutes.

Add the wine and scrape up the browned bits on the bottom of the skillet. Simmer until the liquid is reduced by half.

Add the water or broth, cumin, chili powder, white pepper, and 2¼ teaspoons salt. Simmer, covered, for 1 hour.

Puree the broth mixture in a blender along with the reserved avocado mixture and the cilantro. Thin to the desired consistency with additional water or broth. Taste and adjust the seasonings.

In a small bowl, combine the tomato, scallion, remaining 1 teaspoon lime juice, and a pinch of salt.

Serve the soup hot. Garnish each cupful with a teaspoon of crumbled cheese, a teaspoon of the tomato mixture, and a few crisp fried tortilla strips.

---

cook's note

Queso fresco is a mild, crumbly Mexican cheese. If it's not available, use feta instead. If the feta is very salty, soak it in cold water for 1 hour and drain well to remove some of the salt.

rich red pepper soup

W e'd like to be invited to dinner at the home of Kathy Born, a Boston psychiatrist who gave a stellar dinner party recorded in the pages of *Modern Maturity*. The menu included this fine red pepper soup—the result of one of those add-a-little-of-this and a-little-of-that until-you-get-it-right creations. The

COOK

Kathy Born

SOURCE

Susan Goodman,
Modern Maturity

richness of the soup comes not from cream, but from fruits and vegetables, which include a pear and carrots.

The soup can be served hot or cold, but we like it best at room temperature, when the flavors seem to bloom into more than the sum of their parts.

serves 8

2 tablespoons olive oil

8 large red bell peppers, seeded and coarsely chopped

3 carrots, peeled and cut into ¼-inch-thick slices

3 shallots, chopped

2 garlic cloves, chopped

4 cups chicken broth

1 ripe pear, cored, peeled, and chopped

1 teaspoon salt

⅛–¼ teaspoon cayenne pepper

¼–½ cup orange juice (optional)

Sour cream or plain yogurt, for garnish

Chopped fresh cilantro leaves, for garnish

> **tip**
>
> You can make the soup ahead if you like, but be warned: the cayenne will grow a little hotter as it sits.

In a large skillet, heat the oil over medium heat. Add the bell peppers, carrots, shallots, and garlic. Cover and cook for about 15 minutes, stirring occasionally, until the vegetables are soft but not browned. Add the broth and pear and simmer for 20 to 30 minutes, or until the vegetables are tender. Let cool.

Puree the soup, using a food mill for a smoother texture or a food processor. Season to taste with salt and cayenne pepper. If the soup is too thick, thin it with the orange juice, if desired. Serve hot, cold, or at room temperature with a dollop of sour cream or yogurt and a sprinkle of cilantro.

italian pumpkin soup

COOK
Maria Pia

SOURCE
Palio restaurant press release

At Manhattan's glamorous Palio restaurant, this refined first-course soup is served with a puff-pastry top—but that's a flourish home cooks can safely pass up. The soup is perfect for Christmas dinner or any other celebration for which you want to pull out all the stops.

At some point during the cooking process, you'll suddenly understand what an absolutely brilliant combination of ingredients we have here. The amaretto liqueur and the amaretti cookies are key elements in this divine chemistry: they add a distinct almond flavor and an enriching texture without making the soup sweet. The result is very unusual and very delicious.

serves 6 to 8

1 sugar pumpkin or butternut squash (about 2 pounds)
1/3 cup extra-virgin olive oil
4 tablespoons (1/2 stick) butter
1 large onion, finely chopped
Salt to taste
6–8 cups vegetable broth

1 cup heavy cream
1/3 cup amaretto liqueur, such as Amaretto di Saronno
1/3 cup amaretti cookies (without sugar on top), crushed

---

to serve

This is the perfect beginning to an elegant Thanksgiving dinner or before any roast bird or fish.

Preheat the oven to 450 degrees. Place a rack at the middle level. Line a cookie sheet with foil, grease it, and set aside.

Peel the pumpkin or squash and cut it into small (about 1-inch) pieces. Remove and discard the seeds. Spread the pieces on the cookie sheet in a single layer and roast, stirring once, for 10 to 20 .minutes, or until almost tender.

Meanwhile, in a large pot over medium heat, heat the olive oil and butter, add the onion and a pinch of salt, and cook, stirring frequently, for about 7 minutes, or until totally wilted.

Add the pumpkin or squash and 4 cups of the vegetable broth to the onion mixture and simmer over medium heat until the pumpkin or squash is completely soft, 15 to 20 minutes. Reduce the heat to low and stir in the cream, amaretto, and amaretti. Remove from the heat and let cool for 15 minutes.

Transfer the soup to a food processor and puree. Return to the pot and stir in 2 cups of broth, or more to taste. Taste and add a bit more salt, if desired.

> **tip**
>
> The soup can be made up to 1 day ahead, covered, and refrigerated. Just before serving, reheat it gently, stirring frequently, until hot. It freezes well, so don't worry about making too much.

roasted butternut squash soup

Of the dozens of squash soups we've seen this year, this all-purpose, elegantly seasoned version has become our favorite. It's a great lead-in to a holiday dinner, and it cohabits beautifully with pork and grilled fish, as

COOK

Barbara Hom

SOURCE

Russian River Valley Winegrowers press release

well as big and small birds. Roasting intensifies the flavor of the squash, and the small but judicious amounts of "warm" spices give the soup an added dimension.

serves 8

1 butternut squash
 (about 2 pounds)
 Salt and freshly ground white
 pepper to taste
4 tablespoons olive oil
1 medium onion, chopped
½ teaspoon five-spice powder
½ teaspoon ground cardamom

¼ teaspoon ground allspice
4 cups vegetable broth or
 chicken broth
1 cup heavy cream
 Sour cream flavored to taste
 with freshly ground nutmeg,
 for garnish (optional)

---

to drink

Russian River Valley Pinot Noir is a harmonious match for the squash soup. In general, Pinot Noir is a good fall-moving-into-winter wine because it goes so well with the produce harvested at that time of year.

Preheat the oven to 350 degrees. Place a rack at the middle level. Line a cookie sheet with foil and set aside.

Cut the squash crosswise into 1-inch-thick slices. Sprinkle the slices with salt and white pepper and toss them with 2 tablespoons of the olive oil. Arrange the slices in a single layer on the cookie sheet and roast for 25 to 45 minutes, or until the squash is very tender. Let the squash slices cool, then discard the seeds and pull off and discard the skin.

In a medium skillet, heat the remaining 2 tablespoons olive oil over medium heat, add the onion, and sauté until golden, about 8 minutes.

Place the onion, squash, spices, and 1 cup of the broth in a food processor and puree. Transfer the puree to a large saucepan, add the remaining 3 cups broth, and heat over medium heat, stirring, until combined and heated through.

Right before serving, reduce the heat to low and stir in the cream. Adjust the seasonings and serve, with dollops of flavored sour cream, if desired.

---

cook's note

Start by adding 1/4 to 1/2 cup of cream; it may be enough enrichment for you. We favor the "less-cream" version ourselves.

the lentil soup
(shurbat al-'Adas)

This must be the original earth-brown lentil soup, the biblical Esau's pottage, the essence of sustenance—arguably the most satisfying soup in the world. This version, popular in Lebanon and Egypt, is from Clifford Wright's estimable compendium of Mediterranean dishes, and the recipe is from his former wife, Nawja al-Qattan, a Palestinian.

COOK

Nawja al-Qattan

SOURCE

A Mediterranean Feast,
by Clifford A. Wright

The elegance of this particular recipe comes from the technique applied to the humble ingredients. The cooked soup is passed through a food mill, leaving the thin lentil skins behind; the resulting puree is as smooth as velvet. Don't be tempted to use a blender or a food processor, which would change the texture as well as the taste of this divine soup.

serves 8

2 cups dried brown lentils
8 cups chicken broth
1 large onion, grated
2 teaspoons ground cumin,
    preferably freshly ground
  Salt and freshly ground pepper
    to taste

2 tablespoons fresh lemon juice
2 cups olive oil, for frying
1 large pita bread, cut into
    1/2-inch squares
  Extra-virgin olive oil,
    for drizzling

Rinse the lentils in a colander under cold running water, picking out any stones. In a large saucepan, bring the broth to a boil and add the lentils and onion. When the broth returns to a boil, reduce the heat to low, cover, and simmer for 1 hour. Do not stir.

Pass the lentils and broth through a food mill set over a large bowl. Add the cumin and season with salt and pepper. Return the soup to the saucepan over medium heat. Taste to check the seasonings. Stir in the lemon juice and heat until the soup begins to bubble slightly. The soup will start to thicken very quickly. If it becomes too thick, thin it with some broth or water. Taste again to check the seasonings and add whatever it needs.

Meanwhile, in a medium saucepan or skillet, heat the 2 cups olive oil to 375 degrees, or until a cube of bread turns golden in 30 seconds. Fry the pieces of pita bread until golden, about 1 minute. Serve the soup with the fried pita croutons and extra-virgin olive oil passed at the table.

VARIATION

By substituting vegetable broth for the chicken broth, you could make this into a vegetarian soup.

---

cook's note

This will look like any old bowl of thick brown soup. Don't worry about that; just close your eyes and taste. But if you like, you can garnish each bowl with minced parsley.

red lentil and apricot soup

This absolutely delicious soup has a sweet, tangy flavor all its own. It's terrific with a warm piece of black bread slathered with butter, or just with toasted pita bread.

Red lentils are available in Middle Eastern and Indian stores. Even though they lose their color when they are cooked, their

COOK
Karena

SOURCE
Allrecipes.com

delicate texture and flavor are key to this recipe.

Only the cook will know there are dried apricots in the soup; they just add richness and depth. In fact, if anyone you make this for can guess all the ingredients, write and tell us; we'll think up a prize, which no one we know has ever qualified for.

serves 6 to 8

3 tablespoons olive oil
1 large onion, chopped
1/3 cup dried apricots, chopped
2 garlic cloves, minced
1 1/2 cups dried red lentils, rinsed and picked over
5 cups chicken broth or vegetable broth

3 plum tomatoes, peeled, seeded, and chopped
1/2 teaspoon ground cumin
1/2 teaspoon dried thyme
Salt and freshly ground pepper to taste
2 tablespoons fresh lemon juice

In a large, heavy pot, heat the olive oil over medium heat and sauté the onion, apricots, and garlic; do not let them brown. Add the lentils and broth, bring to a boil, reduce the heat to low, and simmer for 30 minutes, stirring occasionally.

Add the tomatoes, cumin, thyme, and salt and pepper, and simmer for 10 minutes more. Stir in the lemon juice and let the soup stand off the heat for a few minutes. Transfer half of the soup to a blender or food processor and puree. Return the puree to the pot, stir, and reheat. Taste for seasonings and serve.

cook's note

It's simply a matter of taste, but we like to puree three-quarters of the soup, or even all of it. It can be made a day in advance and reheated; add a bit more broth if it is too thick.

soups

fabio's *farinata*
(cornmeal and kale soup)

Faith Willinger, one of television's *Chefs of Cucina Amore*, lives in Florence—which means she can often go to her favorite restaurant, Cibreo, and have this wonderfully rustic soup. Fabio Picchi, the owner-chef, has taken home cooking into the realm of high art, and this soup is a good example. Nothing here is at all complicated, and yet it's an extraordinary dish that's un-

COOK

**Faith Heller Willinger
after Fabio Picchi**

SOURCE

The Chefs of Cucina Amore, **edited by Vincent Schiavelli**

like anything you've ever tasted—but if you can imagine a polenta soup, you'll be close. The garlic is more perfume than pungence, and the final trickle of olive oil and grinding of pepper bring it all together.

Look for *lacinato* or dinosaur kale (an Italian kale), which isn't quite as strong as the American variety—but regular kale is fine, too.

serves 4

½ pound kale or green cabbage
6 cups water
1½ teaspoons salt
¾ cup cornmeal
4 garlic cloves, minced

½ cup freshly grated Parmesan cheese
½ cup extra-virgin olive oil
Freshly ground pepper to taste

> **to serve**
> This hearty soup would be wonderful with roast chicken or pork, but we prefer it shining on its own as a light evening meal. Add a green salad and serve pears with Gorgonzola for dessert.

Wash the kale or cabbage. Remove the tough central ribs of the kale or the core of the cabbage. Chop the leaves finely. In a heavy 3-quart pot, bring the water to a rolling boil. Add the salt and kale or cabbage and simmer for 5 minutes. Gradually sprinkle in the cornmeal, stirring with a whisk to prevent lumps. Reduce the heat to low and cook, stirring occasionally, for 20 to 25 minutes, or until creamy. Alternatively, you could place a pot in a larger pot of boiling water—an improvised double boiler—and cook, stirring occasionally, for 45 minutes.

Add the garlic and cook for 5 minutes more. Whisk in the cheese and ¼ cup of the olive oil. Serve immediately, ladled into bowls and drizzled with the remaining ¼ cup olive oil and freshly ground pepper to taste.

---

tips

- Use stone-ground cornmeal if possible—a medium grind is fine. Finely ground cornmeal will produce a more porridgelike soup.
- It's essential to use a heavy pot such as a Dutch oven for this soup.
- It will help to avoid lumps if you hold a little cornmeal in your fist and slowly release it into the pot as you whisk. To avoid all possible lumps, start the soup with only 5 cups of water and mix the sixth cup with the cornmeal in a small bowl to make a slurry. Pour the slurry very gradually into the soup, whisking constantly.

cook's note

If you have any leftovers, they'll solidify in the refrigerator. Gently reheated the next day (not in the microwave), this soup becomes a delicious side dish.

puree of barley soup
with chicken liver butter

COOK
Michael Roberts

SOURCE
Parisian Home Cooking

When Los Angeles chef Michael Roberts returned to his beloved Paris for a year, he discovered a whole new world of food and cooking. Things had changed since he served his apprenticeship there, and he was captivated by the simple, deeply flavored food he found his friends cooking.

This barley soup is a good example. Though he adores barley soup, Roberts didn't even recognize it without whole barley floating in it. This smooth puree is another thing altogether—and the inspired addition of the chicken liver butter makes it even more appealing.

serves 4 to 6

2 teaspoons vegetable oil
1 small onion, diced
1 celery rib, thinly sliced
1 carrot, peeled and diced
2 garlic cloves
4 cups chicken broth
1 cup white wine
1/2 cup pearl barley
Salt and freshly ground pepper
to taste

1/2 teaspoon dried savory
2 ounces chicken livers
1/4 cup Madeira
3 tablespoons butter, softened
1 cup milk
1 tablespoon finely chopped
fresh flat-leaf parsley, for
garnish

---

cook's note

You may need to add water to thin the soup once it's pureed.

In a 3-quart pot over medium heat, heat the oil. Add the onion, celery, carrot, and garlic and sauté, stirring, until soft but not browned, about 10 minutes. Add the broth, wine, barley, 1½ teaspoons salt, ½ teaspoon pepper, and savory. Cover, reduce the heat to medium-low, and simmer until the barley is completely tender, about 1 hour.

Meanwhile, combine the livers and Madeira in a small saucepan and cook over medium heat for about 3 minutes, until the livers are cooked to medium. Remove from the heat and let cool to room temperature.

Transfer the liver mixture to a food processor or blender, add the butter, and process until smooth. Scrape into a small bowl and set aside.

Process the soup in a food processor or blender until smooth, then pour back into the pot. Add the milk, cover, and reheat over medium heat, stirring to prevent the soup from sticking to the bottom of the pot. Taste and add more salt and pepper, if desired. Pour the soup into bowls, sprinkle with the parsley, and place a spoonful of the liver butter in the center of each bowl. Serve immediately.

serve with

A simple roast chicken
Champ (page 230)
Garlicky spinach
℥

Apple and Armagnac
Croustade (page 295)

senegalese peanut soup

COOKS

Leslie Kaul, Bob Spiegal, and Peter Siegel

SOURCE

The Daily Soup Cookbook,
edited by Leslie Kaul

It was Manhattanites who first became obsessed with soup. At the many outposts of Daily Soup, the staggeringly good take-out shop empire that now stretches well beyond the borders of New York, people do indeed line up every day for their favorite meal-in-a-bowl.

Among their signature soups is this charmer from Senegal. You'd swear it's a complex brew with coconut milk, perhaps a little cilantro, some chiles, possibly some exotic spices—but in fact it contains none of these things, unless you consider curry powder to be exotic. The soup couldn't be simpler; the secret ingredient is peanuts—a whole pound of them—simmered slowly in a fragrant base of onions, celery, and tomatoes. As it cooks, the fragrance becomes almost overwhelming—and the finished soup delivers the full taste its aroma promises.

This soup is at once consoling, intriguing, and invigorating—and now that we've gotten a taste for it, we try to keep some in the freezer for a rainy day.

serves 8

- 1 pound dry-roasted salted peanuts (about 3 cups)
- 2 tablespoons peanut oil
- 1 large Spanish onion, chopped
- 2 celery ribs, chopped
- 2 leeks, well rinsed and chopped
- 2 teaspoons sugar
- 2 teaspoons curry powder
- 2 teaspoons ground cumin
- ½ teaspoon cayenne pepper
- ½ teaspoon salt
- 1 28-ounce can whole tomatoes, drained and diced
- 6 cups water
- ½ cup chopped scallions
- ½ cup heavy cream
- 1 teaspoon minced garlic

Chop ½ cup of the peanuts into small pieces and set aside to use as a garnish. Puree the remaining 2½ cups peanuts in a blender or food processor until a thick paste forms; set aside.

In a large pot over medium heat, heat the oil. Add the onion, celery, and leeks and sweat for 4 minutes, or until tender.

Stir in the sugar, curry powder, cumin, cayenne, and salt. Add the tomatoes, water, and peanut paste. Bring to a boil, reduce the heat to low, and simmer, uncovered, for 1 hour.

Stir in the scallions, cream, and garlic and simmer for 2 minutes more, or until heated through.

To serve, ladle the soup into bowls and sprinkle with the reserved chopped peanuts.

VARIATIONS

❧ For a more sustaining soup, add cubes of tofu (vegetarian version) or cooked chicken (poach 1 pound of boneless skinless chicken breasts in rapidly boiling water for 10 minutes, then cool and dice). Add the chicken or tofu to the soup along with the scallions and cream.

❧ If you like, you can use regular roasted salted peanuts instead of the dry-roasted ones.

---

cook's note

This soup freezes beautifully.

mexican pistachio soup

We've tasted a few delicious nut soups, but most of them fall into the curiosity category. Not so with this extraordinary Mexican soup, a bowl of luscious green so sensual it might have come right from the pages of *Like Water for Chocolate*. It's the creation of Julietta Ballesteros, a native of Monterrey, Mexico,

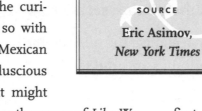

COOK

Julietta Ballesteros

SOURCE

Eric Asimov,
New York Times

who serves it in her charming Manhattan restaurant, Mexicana Mama. She was inspired by a mole sauce made in southern Mexico. Part of the reason it's so delicious is that Ballesteros first roasts the tomatillos, chiles, onion, and garlic in the classic Mexican way to bring out their depth of flavor.

serves 6

½ medium white onion
4 tomatillos, peeled and halved
4 serrano chiles, stems removed
3 garlic cloves, unpeeled
1 teaspoon vegetable oil
1½ cups unsalted shelled pistachios
2 cups chicken broth

1 cup loosely packed fresh cilantro leaves
2 bay leaves
¼ teaspoon sugar
¼ teaspoon dried oregano
3 black peppercorns
Salt and freshly ground pepper
2 cups heavy cream

Preheat the oven to 425 degrees.

Cut the onion half in two and place on a cookie sheet with the tomatillos, chiles, and garlic cloves. Rub the vegetables with the oil and bake until tender and lightly browned, about 20 minutes. Peel the garlic cloves and transfer them to a large saucepan along with the other roasted vegetables; leave the oven on.

Place the pistachios on a cookie sheet and bake until lightly toasted, 5 to 7 minutes. Reserve ¼ cup of the pistachios for a garnish and add the remaining 1¼ cups to the saucepan with the vegetables.

Add the broth and all the remaining ingredients except the cream to the saucepan. Simmer over medium heat for 15 minutes. Let cool for 15 minutes and discard the bay leaves.

Puree the soup in a food processor or blender. With the motor running, slowly add the cream and process until the soup is smooth. Transfer the soup to a clean saucepan and reheat over low heat; do not boil. Serve hot, garnished with the reserved pistachios.

---

cook's notes

℘ This is a very rich soup, so serve small portions.

℘ The complex flavors in the soup develop with time—we like it best several days later.

sweet pea soup
with crispy rock shrimp salad

COOK
Anne Rosenzweig

SOURCE
New York Observer

When fresh peas arrive in the market in late spring, here's a great thing to do with them, courtesy of Manhattan chef Anne Rosenzweig. It's the mint and tarragon that make this soup so special, and in spring the mint is sweet and tender, like the peas. The place to shop for all of these ingredients is the farmers' market, which will be full of beautiful peas, pea shoots, mint, and tarragon.

Not content with creating a superb soup, Rosenzweig gilds the lily with her rock shrimp salad. This takes just minutes to make, and the crisp shrimp are tossed with the sweet little pea shoots. This is a lovely touch, but the soup is also delicious on its own.

serves 6

3 tablespoons unsalted butter
6 cups fresh peas
5 cups vegetable broth or chicken broth
¼ cup chopped fresh mint leaves
3 tablespoons chopped fresh tarragon
Salt and freshly ground pepper to taste

CRISPY ROCK SHRIMP SALAD
3 cups vegetable oil
½ cup cornmeal
¼ cup all-purpose flour
1 cup rock shrimp, shells removed (see note)
½ cup fresh pea shoots, cut into 2-inch pieces

cook's note

Rock shrimp are lobsterish-tasting crustaceans that come already shelled. If you can't find them, use small shrimp to make this tasty salad.

In a medium saucepan over medium-high heat, combine the butter and peas, stirring until the peas are fully coated. In a separate medium saucepan, heat the broth until almost simmering. Pour the broth over the peas and bring to a boil. Remove from the heat and add the herbs and salt and pepper. Chill the soup in an ice-water bath to preserve its color. Puree the soup in a blender or food processor and refrigerate in a covered container while you make the salad.

FOR THE SALAD

In a medium saucepan, heat the oil over medium heat until it reaches 375 degrees, or until a cube of bread turns golden in 30 seconds. In a medium bowl, combine the cornmeal and flour. Toss the rock shrimp in the cornmeal mixture until fully coated. Place the shrimp in a strainer and shake off the excess flour. Fry the shrimp in two batches until they are golden brown, about 3 minutes. Remove and drain on paper towels. Toss the rock shrimp with the pea shoots in a medium bowl.

TO ASSEMBLE

Pour the soup into individual bowls and top with the salad.

cream of celery root with shrimp butter

COOK
Marcia Kiesel

SOURCE

Food & Wine

When the kitchen staff of *Food & Wine* set itself the mission of concocting a supremely luxurious soup, this sensational but subtle bisque floated to the top. The shrimp butter is a complete — and delightful — surprise, as is the refreshing tart apple garnish. For a major holiday meal, you couldn't ask for a more appropriate starter.

serves 10

8 tablespoons (1 stick) plus
      1 tablespoon unsalted butter
3 large leeks (white and tender
      green parts only), halved
      lengthwise, well rinsed, and
      thinly sliced crosswise
2 thyme sprigs
½ cup dry white wine
6 cups chicken broth
2½ pounds celery root, peeled,
      trimmed, quartered, and
      cut into 2-inch chunks
½ pound Yukon Gold potatoes,
      peeled and cut into 2-inch
      chunks

Salt to taste
½ cup heavy cream
1 tablespoon minced shallot
½ pound medium shrimp,
      peeled, deveined, and halved
      lengthwise, shells reserved
Freshly ground pepper to taste
¼ cup finely diced tart green
      apple, such as Granny
      Smith, for garnish
1 teaspoon minced fresh thyme,
      for garnish

In a large Dutch oven, melt 3 tablespoons of the butter over low heat. Add the leeks and thyme sprigs and cook until softened, about 8 minutes. Add the wine and simmer over medium-high heat for 2 minutes. Add the broth, celery root, potatoes, and a large pinch of salt and bring to a boil. Cover and simmer over low heat until the vegetables are tender, about 45 minutes.

Working in batches, puree the soup in a blender or food processor until very smooth. Return the soup to the Dutch oven and stir in 1/4 cup of the cream.

In a medium skillet, melt the remaining 6 tablespoons butter over low heat. Add the shallot and the shrimp shells and cook, stirring, for 8 minutes. Strain through a coarse strainer, pressing on the shells to extract as much butter as possible; you should have about 2 tablespoons. Set aside and keep warm.

In a small saucepan, bring the remaining 1/4 cup cream to a simmer over low heat. Add the shrimp and a pinch of salt and cook, stirring, until just cooked through, about 1 minute. Remove from the heat.

Reheat the soup and season with salt and pepper. Ladle the soup into warm shallow bowls. Spoon the shrimp mixture into the bowls. Drizzle each serving lightly with the shrimp butter, garnish with the diced apple and minced thyme, and serve immediately.

heavenly carrot soup

Carrot soup is by definition both sweet and gorgeous. Here a very simple soup is taken to another level by the addition of coriander and a little white wine. It's a versatile soup —you can serve it hot, cold, or at room temperature—and it's made of staples you usually have on hand.

COOK

Susan Riherd

SOURCE

Smith & Hawken
The Gardeners'
Community Cookbook,
edited by Victoria Wise

Susan Riherd, who created this soup, lives in Santa Fe, and she suggests garnishing the soup with cilantro sprigs. We love that idea, not only for its look and taste, but also because coriander is the seed of the cilantro plant, so it seems fitting to bring them together again.

serves 4

- 4 tablespoons (½ stick) butter
- 1 small onion, finely chopped
- 1 pound carrots, peeled and finely chopped
- ½ cup white wine
- 1½ teaspoons ground coriander

- 4 cups chicken broth
- ½ teaspoon salt
- ¼ teaspoon freshly ground pepper
- Cilantro sprigs, for garnish (optional)

In a large soup pot, melt the butter. Add the onion and sauté for 5 minutes, or until slightly wilted. Add the carrots, wine, and coriander. Cover and cook over low heat for 30 minutes, stirring occasionally, until the carrots are soft enough to mash. Remove from the heat and let sit until cool enough to handle.

Puree the carrot mixture and 1 cup of the broth in a food processor or food mill. Return the puree to the pot and stir in the salt, pepper, and remaining 3 cups broth. Reheat and serve immediately if serving warm, or chill if serving cold. Garnish with the cilantro, if using, just before serving.

salads

Savannah Salad with Avocado Dressing 50

Tomato Salad 52

Avocado, Jicama, and Watercress Salad 53

Purslane Salad with Baby Greens and Cabbage 54

Cauliflower, Broccoflower, and Frisée Salad with Olives 56

Spicy Coleslaw 58

Watercress Slaw with Toasted Coconut 60

Hijiki Salad 62

Fresh Fig, Gorgonzola, and Walnut Salad with Warm Port Vinaigrette 64

Shaved Asparagus and Parmesan Salad 66

Vitello Tonnato Salad 68

Prosciutto with Apple Salad 70

savannah salad with avocado dressing

COOK

Elizabeth Terry

SOURCE

*A Celebration
of Women Chefs,*
edited by Julie Stillman

This wonderfully delicate salad of refreshing orange, sweet pecans, and creamy avocado speaks with a definite southern accent. We especially love this salad with ham—or any variety of pork, for that matter.

Elizabeth Terry, the chef-owner of Elizabeth's on 37th in Savannah, Georgia, is a self-taught home cook who takes historical southern cooking to a new level.

You need to make the dressing the day you serve the salad, or the avocado will turn brown—but you can make it a few hours before serving. The other elements can be prepared well ahead of time and combined at the last minute.

serves 4

DRESSING

- 1 Hass avocado, peeled, pitted, and diced
- ½ cup water
- 1 tablespoon apple cider vinegar
- 1 tablespoon fresh lemon juice
- 1 teaspoon minced garlic
- ½ teaspoon freshly ground pepper
- ½ teaspoon salt

SALAD

- 6 cups mixed salad greens, washed, dried, and torn
- 2 oranges, peeled and diced
- ¼ cup chopped toasted pecans (see note)
- 2 tablespoons minced dried cranberries or raisins (optional)

---

to serve

This winter-spring salad is delicious with holiday fare, especially ham.

In a food processor, combine all the ingredients and process until they have the consistency of heavy cream.

FOR THE SALAD

Just before serving, divide the greens among four salad plates. Spoon the dressing over and sprinkle each salad with the oranges, pecans, and cranberries or raisins, if using.

---

cook's notes

℘ We find a huge difference between regular cider vinegar and organic apple cider vinegar, which is much more delicate and has more character. Even when you're using just a tablespoon, we think it makes a difference to use the organic version.

℘ To toast pecans, spread them in a single layer on a cookie sheet and oven-toast at 300 degrees, stirring frequently, for about 30 minutes, or until they smell good.

s a l a d s

tomato salad

In her charming and moving memoir of an exotic childhood in Cairo, the French-born Colette Rossant tells of learning to cook both in Egypt and in France. It was essential to master the perfect crepe, the perfect vinaigrette, and mayonnaise from scratch. The young Colette had no idea she'd actually succeeded until her grandmother, who never complimented her, announced that Colette's tomato salad

COOK

Colette Rossant

SOURCE

Memories of a Lost Egypt

was the best she'd ever tasted.

Her grandmother was right: This fresh salad with its perfectly balanced lemon and herbs works with both casual and more formal meals. Ordinarily, this sort of salad would be relegated to the few weeks of local tomato season, but made with tasty cherry tomatoes cut in half and sprinkled lightly with salt, it's delicious in winter too.

serves 4

4 ripe tomatoes, peeled and sliced
1 shallot, minced
1 tablespoon chopped fresh tarragon

1 tablespoon chopped fresh chives
2½ tablespoons olive oil
1 tablespoon fresh lemon juice
Salt and freshly ground pepper to taste

Place the tomatoes in a salad bowl. In a small bowl, whisk the remaining ingredients until emulsified, and pour over the tomatoes. Toss and serve.

avocado, jicama, and watercress salad

COOK

Stephan Pyles

SOURCE

**Recipe handout,
Regional Flavors
of Mexico conference**

As much as we love Mexican food, Mexican salads have been a predictable romaine with tomatoes, avocados, onion, and maybe a little radish. This gorgeous salad is light-years away from all that: it's crisp and a little sweet with jicama, rich with avocado, sharp with watercress, and zingy with a serrano chile and fresh lime vinaigrette.

We love this salad with Mexican dishes, barbecued meat or fish in the summer, and roasts in the winter.

You can make the vinaigrette ahead and refrigerate it; just bring it to room temperature before serving.

serves 4

SERRANO-LIME VINAIGRETTE
Juice of 2 limes

3 serrano chiles, or to taste, thinly sliced

1/4 teaspoon salt

Freshly ground pepper to taste

1/2 cup extra-virgin olive oil

SALAD
2 cups watercress, heavy stems removed

1 jicama, peeled and cut into fine julienne

2 avocados, peeled, pitted, and sliced

FOR THE VINAIGRETTE

Combine the lime juice, serranos, salt, and pepper in a small bowl. Drizzle in the olive oil in a steady stream, whisking constantly to emulsify.

FOR THE SALAD

In a medium bowl, combine the watercress and jicama. Add the vinaigrette and toss. Carefully fold in the avocado and serve.

purslane salad
with baby greens and cabbage

COOK

Paula Wolfert

SOURCE

Food & Wine

What's purslane? It's a weed that's probably growing in your garden if you have one, or possibly pushing up the gravel in the driveway. But purslane is no ordinary weed; it's a trendy green that Mediterranean cook Paula Wolfert has introduced to restaurant kitchens all across the country.

In an article about purslane for *Food & Wine*, Wolfert points out that it's a nutritional powerhouse—a great plant source of omega-3 fatty acids, otherwise found in sardines and cod-liver oil. Purslane is also succulent and delicious, great in salads and soups and stews. Look for it at the farmers' market—and in your own backyard.

This exhilarating salad mixes greens with refreshing cucumber and brings out their flavors with mint and lemon.

serves 6

½ small green cabbage
(¾ pound), cored and
finely shredded
¾ pound young purslane
2 cups baby greens or mesclun
4 medium scallions (white part
only), thinly sliced and
separated into rings
1 large cucumber, peeled,
seeded, and cut into
½-inch dice

2 tablespoons extra-virgin
olive oil
1½ tablespoons fresh lemon juice
Salt and freshly ground pepper
to taste
¼ cup small fresh mint leaves,
for garnish

Soak the cabbage in salted cold water for 30 minutes. Drain and spin dry in a salad spinner. Trim the purslane, leaving only the small sprigs and leaves; you should have about 2 cups. Wash well and spin dry. In a large bowl, toss the cabbage and purslane with the baby greens or mesclun, scallions, and cucumber.

In a salad bowl, whisk the olive oil with the lemon juice and season with salt and pepper. Add the salad and toss to coat. Garnish with the mint leaves and serve.

VARIATION

For a minimalist purslane salad, which will give you the pure flavor of the greens, just toss it with a little minced garlic, olive oil, and salt.

to serve

This densely green salad is particularly good with lamb or roast chicken.

cauliflower, broccoflower, and frisée salad with olives

This superb Spanish-accented salad from Deborah Madison, the vegetarian cook sine qua non, is full of flavor and crunch, but that's just the beginning of its virtues. You can cut up the vegetables well ahead, take it to a covered-dish party,

COOK

Deborah Madison

SOURCE

Food & Wine

keep it on the buffet table for hours with no problem, and add or leave out vegetables. *Food & Wine* included this recipe in its December issue—good thinking: it's perfect holiday fare.

serves 8

2 garlic cloves, coarsely chopped
Salt to taste

2 large eggs, hard-cooked, yolks separated from whites

2 tablespoons sherry vinegar

2 teaspoons Dijon mustard

½ cup extra-virgin olive oil
Freshly ground pepper to taste

1 pound broccoflower or broccoli, cut into florets and very thinly sliced lengthwise

1 pound cauliflower, cut into florets and very thinly sliced lengthwise

4 cups frisée or yellow escarole

1 European cucumber, halved, seeded, and coarsely chopped

2 cups thinly sliced celery hearts and leaves

1 cup fresh flat-leaf parsley leaves

½ green bell pepper, seeded and thinly sliced

½ cup Spanish green olives, pitted, or pimiento-stuffed green olives, halved crosswise

4 scallions (white and tender green parts), thinly sliced

2 tablespoons salt-packed capers, rinsed and drained (see note)

In a mortar or mini–food processor, puree the garlic with ¼ teaspoon salt. Add the egg yolks and pound or process until smooth. Stir in the vinegar and mustard and transfer to a small bowl. Slowly whisk in the oil and season with salt and pepper.

In a large bowl, combine the broccoflower or broccoli, cauliflower, frisée or escarole, cucumber, celery, parsley, bell pepper, olives, scallions, and capers. Add the dressing and toss well. Finely dice the egg whites, scatter them over the salad, and serve.

salads

spicy coleslaw

COOK

Patrick Clark

SOURCE

Cooking with Patrick Clark,
edited by Charlie Trotter

Patrick Clark was a Halley's comet of a chef, bursting onto the scene and burning bright for a mercilessly short but amazingly rich life. At one point, he was the chef for not just one but two major Manhattan restaurants, turning out his signature brightly flavored food, which always had an element of soul.

This recipe for the most subtle of slaws was contributed to *Cooking with Patrick Clark* by his son, Cameron, now a student at the Culinary Institute of America.

This is a slaw that crunches, but not aggressively; the briefly cooked, tangy dressing mellows out the vegetables. It's the perfect accompaniment to ribs and fried chicken, of course, but also to fish. The slaw needs at least half an hour for the flavors to marry—beyond about 4 hours, though, it begins to lose its crunch.

serves 6

3 cups shredded green cabbage
1 1/2 cups julienned carrots
1 cup julienned jicama
1 sweet onion, cut into julienne
Salt and freshly ground pepper to taste
1 cup apple cider vinegar

3 shallots, chopped
1 jalapeño pepper, sliced
3 1/4-inch-thick slices peeled fresh gingerroot
2 garlic cloves, sliced
10 black peppercorns
1 cup olive oil

In a large bowl, combine the cabbage, carrots, jicama, and onion and season lightly with salt and pepper.

In a small saucepan, combine the vinegar, shallots, jalapeño, ginger, garlic, and peppercorns and simmer over low heat for 5 minutes. Remove from the heat and let cool. Strain through a fine-mesh sieve into a medium bowl and whisk in the olive oil.

Pour the dressing over the cabbage mixture and toss well. Season to taste with salt and pepper. Refrigerate for at least 30 minutes or up to 3 hours before serving.

tip

If you have a food processor with a julienne blade, this is the time to use it. If not, you can just shred the vegetables in a food processor using the large-hole shredding blade.

watercress slaw with toasted coconut

This unorthodox slaw with its giddy flavors is simply amazing—for starters, there's no cabbage here, and there's coconut, lime, basil, and mint, flavors we tend to associate with Southeast Asian cooking.

COOK
Molly O'Neill

SOURCE
New York Times Magazine

We were quickly converted—this is a delicious slaw, great with fried chicken and grilled foods. It needs to stand in the refrigerator for a while, but don't let it go beyond a couple of hours, or it will get soggy.

serves 4

3 tablespoons mayonnaise
3 tablespoons olive oil
1 tablespoon fresh lime juice
½ teaspoon hot chili oil
1 teaspoon salt
    Freshly ground pepper to taste
2 bunches watercress (leaves and tender sprigs only)

½ red onion, thinly sliced
1 red bell pepper, seeded and thinly sliced
½ cup unsweetened dried coconut (see note)
½ cup chopped fresh basil
½ cup chopped fresh mint

In a small bowl, whisk together the mayonnaise, olive oil, lime juice, chili oil, salt, and pepper to taste. Set aside.

In a large bowl, combine the watercress, onion, and bell pepper. Pour the mayonnaise mixture over the watercress mixture, toss to coat, and refrigerate for at least 30 minutes.

Meanwhile, heat a small, heavy skillet over medium heat. Add the coconut and toast, shaking the pan, until it is lightly browned, 2 to 3 minutes. Transfer to a small bowl and set aside to cool.

When ready to serve, toss the slaw with the basil and mint. Transfer to a serving bowl, garnish with the toasted coconut, and serve.

cook's note

You need unsweetened coconut here, most reliably found at natural food stores.

salads

hijiki salad

COOK
Ming Tsai

SOURCE
Blue Ginger, by Ming Tsai
and Arthur Boehm

Y ou may have eaten seaweed salads at Asian restaurants and marveled over their crunchy-sweet flavor and texture. But most American cooks don't think of making seaweed salad at home, which is a pity, because it's so easy and good for you and such a surprise at the table.

Ming Tsai, the famous television chef, makes this salad with either hijiki (a tea-flavored Japanese seaweed) or wakame (which grows off the coast of Maine), both readily available at natural food stores as well as Asian markets. The seaweed needs a half-hour soak in boiling water to reconstitute itself (it will swell three to five times in volume), becoming a little chewy, almost al dente, and offering some of the pleasure of eating a very unusual pasta.

serves 4

- 4 cups water
- 1 cup dried hijiki seaweed
- 1 cup peeled, seeded, and finely diced cucumber
- 2 tablespoons ¼-inch-thick scallion slices (green parts only)

- 2 tablespoons rice wine vinegar
- 2 teaspoons toasted sesame oil
- 1 teaspoon sugar
  Salt and freshly ground white pepper to taste

to serve

Hijiki salad is a great partner for grilled or roasted seafood as well as for Asian-style chicken. It's also an excellent item for the buffet table.

In a small saucepan, bring the water to a boil. Place the hijiki in a medium bowl and add boiling water to cover. Let stand for 30 minutes; drain well.

In a medium bowl, combine the hijiki, cucumber, scallions, vinegar, sesame oil, and sugar. Season with salt and white pepper and toss well. Serve within 30 minutes.

---

tips

- If you're using wakame, which has a different flavor from hijiki, remove any large veins.
- To keep the salad longer, use a European seedless cucumber. Salt the diced cucumber well and drain in a colander for 30 minutes; rinse well and drain thoroughly. The salted cucumber will remain crisp.
- If you're using seasoned rice wine vinegar, it already contains both sugar and salt, so you may not need to add those to the salad—taste first.
- If you'd like a slightly less chewy texture, soak the seaweed in cold water for 10 minutes before covering it with boiling water.

fresh fig, gorgonzola, and walnut salad with warm port vinaigrette

This lovely sweet-and-savory salad is a winner—specifically, it's the winner of a contest sponsored by the Walnut Marketing Board and Colavita, the olive oil folks. It's the creation of a San Francisco culinary student, not (yet) a famous chef.

Although it's intended as an appetizer, we'd also be happy to see this elegant salad served at the end of a meal, with a glass of

COOK
Theresa Landis

SOURCE
Create with the Best cooking contest

vintage port. In fact, the dish combines a salad course and a cheese course, and it's just sweet enough to be a satisfying ending to a meal. All the elements can be prepared ahead of time and the salads composed—but it's crucial to serve the vinaigrette warm, so make that at the last minute and dress the salads right before serving.

serves 8

1³/₄ cups walnuts
1 pound arugula (about 4 bunches), stemmed, or mesclun mix
12 fresh Mission figs, halved lengthwise
2 cups crumbled Gorgonzola cheese

1 cup ruby port (see note)
1 tablespoon sugar
¹/₄ cup balsamic vinegar
³/₄ cup extra-virgin olive oil
Freshly cracked pepper (optional)

Preheat the oven to 350 degrees. Spread the walnuts on a cookie sheet and toast until they are lightly browned, about 8 minutes. Coarsely chop the walnuts and transfer to a small bowl. Set aside.

Divide the arugula or mesclun among eight salad plates. Arrange 3 fig halves on each plate and divide the cheese and walnuts evenly among the plates. Set aside.

In a small saucepan, simmer the port over medium-high heat until reduced by half, being careful to keep the heat low enough not to ignite the port. Add the sugar and stir to dissolve. Remove from the heat. Add the balsamic vinegar and slowly whisk in the olive oil.

While the vinaigrette is still warm, drizzle it over the salads. If desired, lightly season with freshly cracked pepper.

---

cook's note

You don't need a great port for this salad—a good California port is fine. For drinking, there are some delicious ports—Ficklin and Warre are both good possibilities— that aren't expensive. And if you have a truly vintage port, you're a lucky duck.

shaved asparagus and parmesan salad

At Chez Panisse, the legendary Berkeley restaurant, the café serves asparagus every which way all spring. One of the most beguiling preparations is this raw asparagus salad—a revelation if you've never eaten the delicate vegetable au naturel. The key to success is using very fresh, sweet asparagus; in just a couple of days, it will turn grassy. Look for your asparagus at the farmers' market and check the cut ends, which should be white and moist. Once you have the right asparagus, this crisp, perfectly balanced salad is simplicity itself.

COOK

Alice Waters

SOURCE

*Chez Panisse
Café Cookbook*

serves 4

2 shallots, finely diced
2 tablespoons champagne
   vinegar
2 tablespoons fresh lemon juice
   Salt to taste

⅓ cup extra-virgin olive oil
12 large asparagus spears
   Freshly ground pepper to taste
   Wedge of Parmigiano-Reggiano
   cheese, for shaving

In a small bowl, macerate the shallots in the vinegar and lemon juice, adding a little salt to taste, for 15 minutes. Whisk in the olive oil.

Snap off the tough bottom ends of the asparagus spears. Using a Japanese mandoline set on the thinnest setting, very carefully shave each asparagus spear into long, wide, paper-thin ribbons.

Place the shaved asparagus in a salad bowl, season with salt and pepper, and dress lightly with the vinaigrette.

Divide the salad among four salad plates. With a vegetable peeler, shave large curls of cheese over each serving.

---

cook's note

Japanese mandolines, called Benriner slicers, are available in Asian markets and some gourmet stores. You can also use a French mandoline, if you have one. And if you have no such fancy tools, you can just cut the asparagus in half lengthwise and sliver it.

vitello tonnato salad

COOKS

**Louise Fiszer
and Jeannette Ferrary**

SOURCE

A Good Day for Salad

Who doesn't love Vitello Tonnato, the classic Italian summer dish of veal in tuna sauce? We do, but it may seem a little too fifties for contemporary tastes—we haven't seen the dish on a menu for a long time.

Enter California cooks Louise Fiszer and Jeannette Ferrary, who lighten up this classic by turning it into a salad with punchy greens and making it with chicken, not veal. The result is a lighter, zesty, fresh look at a great dish, with its authentic flavors still very much intact.

serves 8

3 whole skinless chicken breasts
2 heads radicchio, cut into strips
1 bunch watercress, stemmed

DRESSING
½ cup reserved chicken-poaching liquid (see below)
1 6½-ounce can tuna packed in olive oil, drained (see note)

2 tablespoons capers, rinsed and drained
6 anchovy fillets, rinsed and patted dry
1 cup mayonnaise
Salt and freshly ground pepper to taste

1 tablespoon capers, rinsed and drained, for garnish

Place the chicken breasts in a saucepan just large enough to hold them. Add cold water to cover. Bring to a boil, cover, and simmer for 1 minute. Remove from the heat and let cool with the lid slightly ajar. Remove the chicken and reserve ½ cup of the poaching liquid for the dressing. Remove and discard the chicken bones and tear or cut the meat into strips. In a large bowl, combine the chicken, radicchio, and watercress.

FOR THE DRESSING

In a blender or food processor, process the chicken-poaching liquid, tuna, capers, and anchovies. Transfer to a small bowl, stir in the mayonnaise, and season with salt and pepper. Toss the dressing with the chicken mixture, garnish with the capers, and serve.

---

cook's note

It's important to use tuna packed in olive oil, which is infinitely more tasty than the bland, characterless tuna packed in water.

---

salads

prosciutto with apple salad

COOK
Mario Batali

SOURCE
Wine & Spirits

When Mario Batali, the irrepressible no-nonsense Italian chef (and host of *Molto Mario*), was asked by *Wine & Spirits* to come up with a Super Bowl menu, there wasn't a chip in sight. For the first quarter, Batali suggests this unusually refreshing composed salad with no greens.

It's just artfully arranged prosciutto, little batons of apple, and—surprise—poppy seeds, bound together in a vinaigrette and served with grilled bread.

This winter salad can be lunch, a snack, a first course, or a midnight treat. Waldorf Salad, *arrivederci*.

serves 5

- 3/4 pound thinly sliced prosciutto, preferably San Daniele (see note)
- 2 Granny Smith apples, peeled and cored
- 2 Golden Delicious apples, peeled and cored

- 1 McIntosh apple, peeled and cored
- 1/4 cup extra-virgin olive oil
- 1 1/2 tablespoons red wine vinegar
- 1 1/2 tablespoons poppy seeds
- Salt and freshly ground pepper to taste
- Grilled rustic bread slices

Fan the prosciutto slices around the edges of a large platter. Julienne the apples and place them in a medium bowl. Add the olive oil, vinegar, poppy seeds, and salt and pepper, and toss to coat. Arrange the salad in the center of the platter and surround with the grilled bread. Serve immediately.

---

cook's note

Mario prefers San Daniele prosciutto, which comes from the Friuli region, to the more intense Parma prosciutto for this dish because it's a little sweeter and therefore a better complement to the apples.

breakfast and brunch

Cinnamon Buns from Heaven 72

Stuffed French Toast with Lemon-Cheese Filling and Blueberries 75

Puffy Maine Pancakes 78

Sour Cream Coffee Cake 80

Airy Scones 82

Crystallized Ginger Scones 84

Kona Inn Banana Muffins 86

Mini-Frittatas with Wild Mushrooms 88

Green Chile Cheese Puff 90

Goat Cheese and Herb Skillet Soufflé 92

Caramelized Onion Waffles with Smoked Salmon and Radish Salad 94

cinnamon buns from heaven

COOK

Nicki Cross

SOURCE

Oregonian,
Portland, Oregon

Somewhere in the back of most Americans' minds, there's a vivid memory of an archetypal cinnamon bun, against which all others must be measured and found wanting. Nicki Cross had such a memory from her eastern Oregon childhood, and she knew the source: a school lunchroom worker in Prairie City. Although she never found the exact recipe for those buns, she worked out this version, which gathers so many raves it's been reprinted four times in the *Oregonian.*

We were determined to find a great cinnamon bun this year and baked our way through a number of disappointments before we found Cross's. This is the real thing: rich, sweet, and huge. We preferred making slightly smaller rolls (18 instead of 12) and skipping the glaze (see note, page 74).

serves 12 to 18

DOUGH

- 1 cup warm water (105–115 degrees)
- 2 envelopes active dry yeast
- 1 teaspoon plus ⅔ cup sugar
- 1 cup milk, heated to lukewarm
- ⅔ cup (1⅓ sticks) butter, softened
- 2 large eggs, lightly beaten
- 2 teaspoons salt
- 7–8 cups all-purpose flour, or more as needed

FILLING

- 1 cup (2 sticks) butter, melted
- 1¾ cups sugar
- 3 tablespoons ground cinnamon
- 1½ cups chopped walnuts (optional)
- 1½ cups raisins (optional)

CREAMY GLAZE

- ⅔ cup (1⅓ sticks) butter, melted
- 4 cups confectioners' sugar
- 2 teaspoons pure vanilla extract
- ¼–½ cup hot water

Combine the warm water, yeast, and 1 teaspoon sugar in a cup and stir; set aside. In a large bowl, combine the milk, remaining ⅔ cup sugar, butter, eggs, and salt. Stir well and add the yeast mixture. Add 3½ cups flour and beat until smooth. Stir in enough of the remaining flour until the dough is slightly stiff—it will be sticky.

Turn out the dough onto a well-floured surface and knead for 5 to 10 minutes, adding just enough flour to keep the dough from sticking. Place in a well-buttered glass or plastic bowl. Cover and let rise in a warm place, free from drafts, until doubled in volume, 1 to 1½ hours. Punch down the dough and let it rest for 5 minutes. Roll out on a lightly floured surface into a 15-by-20-inch rectangle.

FOR THE FILLING

Spread ½ cup of the melted butter on the dough. In a small bowl, combine 1½ cups of the sugar and the cinnamon. Sprinkle over the dough, then sprinkle with the walnuts and raisins, if desired. Roll up like a jellyroll and pinch the edges together to seal. Cut the roll into 12 or 18 slices.

If making 12 buns, use the remaining ½ cup melted butter to coat

---

tip

To save time in the morning, make the rolls a day ahead up to the final rise, then let them rise slowly overnight in the refrigerator. Bring to room temperature before baking.

---

the bottoms of a 13-by-9-inch baking pan and an 8-inch square baking pan; if making 18 buns, use two 13-by-9-inch pans. Sprinkle the pans with the remaining ¼ cup sugar. Place the cinnamon bun slices close together in the pans. Cover and let rise in a warm place until the dough is doubled in volume, about 45 minutes.

Preheat the oven to 350 degrees. Bake for 25 to 30 minutes, or until the buns are nicely browned. Let cool slightly before glazing.

FOR THE GLAZE

In a medium bowl, combine the melted butter, confectioners' sugar, and vanilla. Add the hot water, 1 tablespoon at a time, until you have a spreadable glaze. Spread the glaze over the buns and serve.

---

cook's notes

❧ A simple dusting of confectioners' sugar is a great topping for the buns, which are already so over the top that the glaze is almost too much.

❧ You can play with the filling ingredients: try golden raisins or currants, use pecans instead of walnuts, add some nutmeg or mace and a little grated lemon zest.

stuffed french toast with lemon-cheese filling and blueberries

COOK

Donna Leahy

SOURCE

Fine Cooking

We've seen several inventive versions of French toast this year, one of which featured an entire quart of melted ice cream, but none of them stole our hearts the way this one did. Donna Leahy is the chef-owner of the Inn at Twin Linden in Narvon, Pennsylvania, and her guests are always begging her for the recipe for her amazing stuffed French toast —a bit of theater on a plate. The stuffing varies from day to day and season to season, but the basic idea is to cut a pocket into a thick slice of firm bread and stuff it with a cheesy filling and perhaps some preserves. Once the toast is stuffed, it's soaked in a creamy egg mixture and left overnight in the refrigerator for its flavor to develop (see tip, page 77).

In the morning, you just sauté the toasts and bake them in the oven briefly to heat through—so simple you could just about do it in your sleep.

serves 6

6 thick (1½-inch) slices bakery cinnamon bread or challah

FILLING

4 ounces cream cheese, softened
2 tablespoons sugar
1 teaspoon lemon extract
1 teaspoon finely chopped lemon zest
¾ cup part-skim ricotta cheese

EGG MIXTURE

6 large eggs
½ cup heavy cream

1½ tablespoons unsalted butter, melted
1½ tablespoons canola oil

BLUEBERRY SYRUP

2 cups fresh or frozen blueberries
½ cup sugar
2 teaspoons fresh lemon juice

Create a pocket in each slice of bread by inserting a sharp knife into the center of the top crust and working the knife in both directions, cutting to within ³/₄ inch of the sides and bottom. Be careful not to puncture the sides.

FOR THE FILLING

In a medium bowl, combine the cream cheese, sugar, lemon extract, and lemon zest and beat with an electric mixer on high speed until smooth, scraping the sides of the bowl as necessary, about 1 minute. Gently stir in the ricotta until just combined.

To fill the bread slices, squeeze the bread gently from both sides to part the opening. Spoon in a few tablespoons of the filling, being careful not to overstuff or tear the bread. Wipe any extra filling from the opening with a clean paper towel.

FOR THE EGG MIXTURE

In a large, shallow bowl, whisk together the eggs and cream. Dunk the stuffed bread into the egg mixture to coat both sides. Place the bread in a baking dish, cover with plastic wrap, and refrigerate overnight.

When you are ready to serve, preheat the oven to 375 degrees. Lightly grease a cookie sheet. Heat the butter and oil in a large skillet over medium-high until the butter is melted and foamy. Sauté as many of the stuffed-bread slices as will fit comfortably at one time, turning once, until golden brown on both sides, about 2 minutes per side. Continue with the remaining pieces. Place the sautéed pieces on the greased cookie sheet and bake until the filling is heated through, 6 to 8 minutes.

While the French toast is baking, combine the blueberries, sugar, and lemon juice in a medium saucepan. Heat over low heat, stirring constantly until the sugar dissolves, 2 to 3 minutes. Increase the heat to medium and simmer for 2 minutes more, stirring constantly. Remove from the heat. Serve warm over the stuffed French toast.

VARIATIONS

❧ You can experiment with this basic recipe, mixing fresh cheeses and preserves, such as apricot or apple butter, or almost anything you can dream of—it's that flexible. The bread is equally variable, as long as it's relatively firm.

❧ If there's any mascarpone cheese around, substitute ¼ cup mascarpone for the cream cheese and increase the ricotta to 1 cup. If you have no lemon extract—or don't like it—use lemon oil (such as the excellent product made by Boyajian, available through Williams-Sonoma or Dean & DeLuca) instead, or just double the amount of lemon zest.

---

tip

You don't have to soak the bread overnight, but it will save a little time in the morning.

---

breakfast and brunch

puffy maine pancakes

During an interminable doctor's office wait, one of us happened to pick up a special millennium magazine put out by Martha Stewart, transfixed by a photo of a beaming Martha, bearing a huge platter of what appeared to be crusty flying saucers called Puffy Maine Pancakes. Someone else had been intrigued earlier; the page was ripped out.

When we finally tracked down the recipe, it turned out to be those classic American oven pancakes, Dutch Babies. Martha had simply poured the batter into several crepe pans—doesn't everyone have several small crepe pans?—and made individual pancakes, what appeared to be dozens of them. Telling this story to friends, we discovered that most of them didn't know about this terrific recipe. In case you don't, we're reprinting it here— and if you don't have the crepe pans, just use a single 12-inch skillet.

COOK

Martha Stewart

SOURCE

*Martha Stewart's
Millennium 2000*

serves 3

2 large eggs, lightly beaten
½ cup all-purpose flour
½ cup milk
  Pinch of salt

  Pinch of freshly grated nutmeg
3 tablespoons unsalted butter
  Confectioners' sugar, for
    dusting

Preheat the oven to 425 degrees.

In a medium bowl, whisk the eggs, flour, milk, salt, and nutmeg until well combined; the batter may be slightly lumpy. The batter may be made a day ahead and chilled overnight.

For each pancake, melt 1 tablespoon of the butter in a 4-inch crepe pan or ovenproof skillet over medium-high heat. Using a ladle, pour one-third of the batter into the very hot pan. Transfer the pan immediately to the oven.

For a single large pancake, melt all the butter in the skillet and pour in all the batter when the pan is hot. Transfer the pan immediately to the oven.

Bake until golden brown and very puffy, about 10 minutes. Dust with confectioners' sugar and serve immediately.

tip

Bonus: The pancake will be most delicious and convenient if the batter is made the night before—so your morning kitchen time will be minimal.

sour cream coffee cake

COOK

Gladys Martin

SOURCE

The Family Baker,
by Susan G. Purdy

Sour cream coffee cakes with walnuts and cinnamon have been around since at least the fifties—and they've had a little renaissance this year, turning up all over the country as "new." Of all the versions we've seen, this one is the champ: moister, richer, tastier. It also has a tale to tell.

Gladys Martin was a summertime neighbor of baking authority Susan Purdy's in Vermont, and when Gladys died, Purdy went to the auction of her household goods, hoping to find a cache of cookbooks and recipes. She waited all day long in the hot July sun, as the antiques and eventually the crowd itself dispersed. Finally, two bedraggled boxes came out, jammed with recipes, and they went to Purdy. This particular treasure was handwritten in blue ink on a pink file card, an heirloom that might just as easily have ended up in the landfill.

serves 12 to 16

FILLING/TOPPING
1 cup chopped walnuts
1/2 cup sugar
1 teaspoon ground cinnamon

CAKE
3 cups sifted all-purpose flour
1 1/2 teaspoons baking powder
1 teaspoon baking soda

1 teaspoon salt
3/4 cup (1 1/2 sticks) unsalted
   butter, softened
1 1/2 cups sugar
1 1/2 cups sour cream
4 large eggs, at room
   temperature
2 teaspoons pure vanilla extract

Preheat the oven to 350 degrees and place a rack at the middle level. Coat a 9- or 9 1/2-inch Bundt pan with shortening, taking special care to generously coat the tube and any indentations. Dust flour all over the inside of the pan, especially the tube. Tap out any excess flour.

FOR THE FILLING

In a small bowl, toss the ingredients together and set aside.

FOR THE CAKE

In a medium bowl, whisk together the flour, baking powder, baking soda, and salt.

In a large bowl, with an electric mixer or a wooden spoon, beat together the butter and sugar until smooth and well blended. Beat in the sour cream, eggs, and vanilla. Slowly mix in the dry ingredients, stirring just until thoroughly incorporated and no flour is visible.

Spoon about half the batter into the Bundt pan, sprinkle half the nut filling over the batter, cover with the remaining batter, and top with the remaining filling. Lightly press the filling into the batter.

Bake for 50 to 55 minutes, or until the top is golden brown and springy to the touch and a cake tester inserted in the center comes out dry or with just a few moist crumbs attached. Cool the cake in the pan on a wire rack for 15 minutes, then top with a plate and invert. Lift off the Bundt pan. Serve.

The cake will keep for 1 week at room temperature, securely wrapped. You can also double-wrap it in plastic wrap and foil and keep it in the freezer for up to 2 months.

VARIATION

For a different flavor, replace the 2 teaspoons vanilla extract with 1/2 teaspoon each vanilla, lemon, and almond extract.

airy scones

COOK

Gary Clauson

SOURCE

Los Angeles Times

These are the lightest, richest scones imaginable, served for tea at the Hotel Bel-Air in Los Angeles. The secret is using cake flour, which gives them their ethereal quality. But they're also down-to-earth: they're made in just a few minutes with an electric mixer.

Because the scones are so delicate, it wouldn't be a great idea to jam them with dried cherries or cranberries or other chunks of fruit—the currants are perfect, but you can leave them out, if you like. You can also cut the recipe in half; since they don't keep well, it's not worth making more than you need.

serves 12 to 14

3 cups cake flour
2 tablespoons baking powder
2 tablespoons sugar
³/4 teaspoon salt
8 tablespoons (1 stick) unsalted butter, chilled and cut into small pieces

2 cups whipping cream
1 cup dried currants (see tip)
1 large egg yolk, lightly beaten
Butter and/or preserves (optional), for serving

Preheat the oven to 375 degrees. Line a cookie sheet with parchment paper.

In a large bowl, sift together the flour, baking powder, sugar, and salt. With an electric mixer, work the butter into the flour mixture until mealy. Add the cream and currants and mix on low speed until the dough is smooth, about 1 minute.

Turn the dough out onto a floured surface and roll or pat to about ³/₄ inch thick. Cut into 2¹/₄-inch rounds with a biscuit cutter.

Place the dough rounds 2 inches apart on the cookie sheet. Brush with the beaten egg yolk and bake until golden brown, 18 to 20 minutes. Serve with butter and preserves, if desired.

VARIATIONS

❧ Add 1 teaspoon of grated orange zest.

❧ The egg yolk brushed on top gives the scones a lovely golden glow, but you can skip the egg and just brush them with cream before baking.

> **tip**
>
> For particularly delicious scones, soak the currants in the cream for 20 minutes before making the scones.

crystallized ginger scones

COOK

**Chuck Williams
after Judy Rodgers**

SOURCE

Williams-Sonoma catalog

The basic scone recipe here—which may be the best we've ever tried—comes from Judy Rodgers of Zuni Cafe in San Francisco. Rodgers gave her recipe to Chuck Williams of Williams-Sonoma years ago, and this year he came up with the brilliant idea of adding crystallized ginger. Williams uses the wonderful, full-flavored, tender ginger from Australia for these scones (see note).

These are sophisticated scones: not too sweet, very buttery, and with a terrific texture—you won't be able to stop eating them.

serves 12

3 cups all-purpose flour
1/3 cup sugar
5 teaspoons baking powder
1 teaspoon salt
1 cup (2 sticks) unsalted butter, chilled and cut into small pieces

1/2 cup chopped crystallized ginger (see note)
1/2 cup milk
1 large egg

Preheat the oven to 350 degrees and line two cookie sheets with parchment paper.

---

tip

True confessions: It's easiest to cut the butter into the flour in a food processor, just briefly until it comes together. However, don't try to chop the ginger in a food processor; you'll end up with gummy, pasty ginger bits that clump together.

In a large bowl, combine the flour, sugar, baking powder, and salt. Add the butter and, with a pastry blender or two knives, cut the butter into the flour until the mixture resembles pea-size crumbs. Toss the ginger with the flour mixture.

In a small bowl, whisk together the milk and egg until blended and add to the flour mixture. With a fork, stir to form large, moist clumps of dough. Turn out onto a lightly floured surface and press with your hands until the dough comes together. Adding flour as needed, roll the dough into a 10-inch round, about 3/4 inch thick. Cut the dough into 12 equal wedges, transfer to the cookie sheets, and bake until golden, 30 to 35 minutes. Serve.

cook's note

The best crystallized ginger is baby Australian ginger, available at Williams-Sonoma, Trader Joe's, and many gourmet shops. It's exceptionally tender, but any crystallized ginger that's not dried out and hard is fine.

kona inn banana muffins

When you look at the recipe for these banana muffins, you might pass it by since nothing seems particularly special—no cinnamon, no flavorings at all, in fact; just pure banana. In *Learning to Cook with Marion Cunningham*, Cunningham explains that the secret of

COOK

Marion Cunningham

SOURCE

Learning to Cook with Marion Cunningham

these divine muffins is using lots of bananas, five of them in fact, and beating them into submission for an especially tender, moist muffin. The extra banana also means these muffins are great keepers, and they freeze well too. Thanks, Kona Inn!

serves 12

½ cup vegetable shortening, plus
   more for greasing the pan
1¼ cups all-purpose flour, plus
   more for sprinkling the pan
5 very ripe medium bananas

1 teaspoon baking soda
½ teaspoon salt
1 cup sugar
2 large eggs, lightly beaten
½ cup chopped walnuts

Preheat the oven to 350 degrees. Smear the cups of a muffin pan with a little shortening, sprinkle with a little flour, and shake the pan to distribute the flour. Turn the pan upside down over the wastebasket and shake out any excess flour.

Peel the bananas, place them in a large bowl, and beat them well with an electric mixer. The riper the bananas and the more you mash them, the more tender your muffins will be. Don't expect absolute smoothness; there will always be a few lumps. Set aside.

In a small bowl, combine the flour, baking soda, and salt.

Add the sugar, shortening, eggs, and walnuts to the bananas and mix well. Add the dry ingredients to the banana mixture and stir just until the batter is thoroughly blended.

Pour the batter into a large measuring cup with a spout and fill the muffin cups about two-thirds full.

Place the muffin pan in the lower third of the oven. After 15 minutes, check the muffins for doneness. A toothpick inserted in the center of a muffin should come out clean. If not, cook for 5 minutes more and check again. When the toothpick comes out clean, remove the muffins from the oven and let cool in the pan for 5 minutes.

Run a knife around the edges of the muffins and transfer them to a platter. Serve warm.

VARIATION

You can turn these muffins into a cake using the same recipe. Butter two 9-inch round cake pans and divide the batter between them. Bake for 25 minutes, or until a toothpick comes out clean. Cool the cakes in their pans for 10 minutes. Loosen the edges with a knife and turn out onto a platter. To give the cakes a nice finish, place $1/3$ cup confectioners' sugar in a strainer and sift it over the cakes. Serve with whipped cream.

mini-frittatas with wild mushrooms

COOK

**Eileen Weinberg,
Good & Plenty to Go**

SOURCE

**Macy's De Gustibus
recipe handout**

Manhattan caterer-to-the-stars Eileen Weinberg is famous for elegant food that tastes entirely home-made, and in fact she "ghost-chefs" for some of the biggest names in the food world. This divine recipe is one of her trademarks: Guests always beg for the recipe.

It's the mix of several mushrooms and several cheeses—including cream cheese—that makes these little frittatas stand out.

But it's a very simple recipe, and it can be made up to 1 day ahead and re-heated at the last minute. This amount is calculated to feed a small crowd for cocktails, but you can easily cut the recipe in half.

You can also make one large skillet frittata for lunch, dinner, or brunch—just bake it for 1 hour and run it under the broiler to brown just before serving.

serves 12; makes 3 dozen

¼ cup olive oil, plus more for greasing pans
2 cups minced cleaned wild mushrooms or a combination of shiitakes and portobellos
8 large eggs
Pinch of salt
Pinch of freshly ground pepper
½ cup cream cheese, cut into small pieces

¾ cup grated Muenster cheese
¾ cup grated mozzarella cheese
¾ cup grated Swiss cheese
¾ cup freshly grated Parmesan cheese
¾ cup grated white cheddar cheese
½ cup heavy cream

to drink
Champagne

Preheat the oven to 350 degrees. Spray two mini-muffin pans with nonstick cooking spray or rub them with olive oil.

In a small skillet over medium-high heat, heat the ¼ cup olive oil and sauté the mushrooms until they begin to turn brown and reabsorb some of the cooking juices. Set aside.

In a large bowl, beat the eggs well and add the salt and pepper. Stir in the cheeses, cream, and mushrooms. Pour the egg mixture into the muffin pans and bake for 30 to 40 minutes, or until the tops are light golden brown and firm. Serve warm or at room temperature.

---

cook's note

You can also use a regular muffin tin and increase the cooking time slightly.

serve with

Caramelized Onion Waffles with Smoked Salmon
and Radish Salad (page 94)
Shaved Asparagus and Parmesan Salad (page 66)

℘

Peach Sorbet (page 263)
Tuscan Rosemary and Pine Nut Bars (page 306)

---

breakfast and brunch

green chile cheese puff

COOK
Elizabeth
Knowlton-Turney

SOURCE
Gourmet

Imagine a crustless quiche that's divinely light and given an extra dimension by glorious green poblano chiles. You can make this unorthodox quiche in just a few minutes, as long as you roast and peel the poblanos ahead of time, up to one day ahead (see note). Then you will have the perfect breakfast, brunch, or late supper— or, as *Gourmet* suggests, the perfect Mother's Day feast. Add your favorite salsa, and you're done.

serves 6

¹/₄ cup all-purpose flour
³/₄ teaspoon salt, or to taste
¹/₂ teaspoon baking powder
6 large eggs
2 tablespoons unsalted butter, melted
1 cup cottage cheese
¹/₂ pound grated Monterey Jack cheese (about 2 cups)

4 poblano chiles (about ³/₄ pound), roasted and peeled (see note), cut into ¹/₂-inch dice

Fresh store-bought or homemade tomato salsa

---

cook's note

To roast and peel the poblanos, arrange them on a foil-covered cookie sheet and broil until they are blistered and blackened, turning frequently. Wrap them in the foil and set aside so they steam for 10 minutes. Let cool until they can be handled, then peel; the skin should come off easily. Cover and refrigerate until ready to use.

Preheat the oven to 350 degrees. Place a rack at the middle level. Oil a 9-inch glass pie plate.

In a small bowl, sift together the flour, salt, and baking powder.

In a large bowl, with an electric mixer, beat the eggs until doubled in volume, about 3 minutes. Add the butter, flour mixture, and cheeses and beat well. Stir in the chiles and pour the mixture into the pie plate.

Bake until the top is puffed and golden brown and a tester comes out clean, 30 to 35 minutes.

Serve the cheese puff immediately—it will fall slightly—with the salsa on the side.

---

serve with

Avocado, Jicama, and Watercress Salad (page 53)
Hot tortillas

℃

Store-bought dulce de leche ice cream

to drink

Tequila sunrises or Mexican beer

goat cheese and herb skillet soufflé

The very idea of a skillet soufflé is intriguing, and this one really delivers. It's incredibly light but packed with the flavors of basil and chives, as well as savory goat cheese. Although it's a bit like a puffed omelette, it's really not like anything we've ever tasted.

COOK

Tamara Holt

SOURCE

Redbook

But it is a soufflé, so you should dig into this gorgeous golden puff as soon as it emerges from the oven. It's one of those anytime dishes that works as well for breakfast or lunch as it does for a simple supper.

serves 4

8 large eggs, separated
1/2 teaspoon cream of tartar
1/4 teaspoon salt
4 ounces fresh goat cheese or feta, crumbled (about 1/2 cup)

2 tablespoons chopped fresh basil
2 tablespoons chopped fresh chives
1/4 teaspoon freshly ground pepper
2 tablespoons (1/4 stick) butter

Preheat the oven to 375 degrees.

In a large bowl, with an electric mixer, beat the egg whites, cream of tartar, and salt until stiff but not dry. In a separate large bowl, beat the egg yolks for 2 minutes, or until thick. Stir in the cheese, herbs, and pepper. Fold in the egg whites in two batches, stirring until just blended.

In a 10-inch ovenproof skillet, melt the butter over medium heat. Add the egg mixture and cook for 3 minutes. Transfer the skillet to the oven and bake for 18 minutes, or until the soufflé is puffed and golden. Serve immediately.

serve with

Avocado, Jicama, and
Watercress Salad
(page 53)
Sliced tomatoes

Velvet Chocolate Cake
(page 317)

caramelized onion waffles
with smoked salmon and radish salad

COOK

Richard Crocker

SOURCE

Michael Bauer,
San Francisco Chronicle

The *Chronicle*'s food critic, Michael Bauer, doesn't actually like brunch at all, so he wasn't looking forward to his early-bird meal at Kelly's Mission Rock in San Francisco. But this unusual savory waffle knocked his socks off, and we agree entirely; these are nothing like your mom's waffles. What a great idea: tucking caramelized onions into the crisp waffles, paving them with silky smoked salmon, drizzling lemony cream over them, and topping them with a tangle of zesty radish salad.

Don't be daunted if you don't own a waffle iron (see note). And don't be scared off by the long ingredient list: it's very easy to put this dish together, and you can caramelize the onions the night before and let them come to room temperature before stirring them into the waffle batter. Frankly, we'd be just as happy to see these on our dinner plates.

serves 6

LEMON CREAM

1 cup sour cream
¼ cup whole milk
  Zest of 1 lemon
3 tablespoons fresh lemon juice

RADISH SALAD

1–2 bunches radishes, trimmed
2 heads Belgian endive, halved, cored, and separated into leaves
1 head frisée, trimmed of outer green leaves, cored, and chopped
1 3½-ounce package radish sprouts
5 tablespoons fresh lemon juice
2 tablespoons extra-virgin olive oil
  Salt and freshly ground pepper to taste

3 tablespoons butter, plus 5
tablespoons, melted

2 medium onions, finely diced

2 cups all-purpose flour

½ cup chopped mixed fresh
herbs, such as parsley,
thyme, chives, tarragon,
and/or chervil

1½ tablespoons baking powder

1 tablespoon freshly ground
pepper

1 teaspoon salt

1½ cups milk

2 large eggs, at room
temperature

¼ pound thinly sliced smoked
salmon or gravlax

FOR THE LEMON CREAM

In a small bowl, whisk the sour cream, milk, lemon zest, and lemon juice. Refrigerate until ready to use.

FOR THE SALAD

Thinly slice the radishes with a mandoline or Japanese vegetable slicer, or just slice them as thinly as possible with a knife. In a large bowl, combine the radishes, endive, frisée, and radish sprouts. Set aside.

In a small bowl, whisk the lemon juice and olive oil. Season with salt and pepper. Set aside.

---

cook's note

If you have no waffle iron, you can make pancakes with this batter, top them with the salmon and lemon cream, and serve the salad on the side. Not quite as elegant, but still very tasty.

In a large skillet, melt the 3 tablespoons butter over medium heat. Add the onions and sauté, stirring, until golden and caramelized, 7 to 10 minutes. Let cool.

In a large bowl, combine the flour, herbs, baking powder, pepper, and salt. In a medium bowl, combine the milk, eggs, and 5 tablespoons melted butter. Fold the wet ingredients into the dry ingredients, being careful not to overmix. Fold in the onions. The batter should be slightly lumpy.

Preheat a waffle iron according to the manufacturer's directions. Brush the grids lightly with vegetable oil. Pour 1/2 cup batter onto the hot iron. Cook the waffles until golden brown, 3 to 5 minutes. Keep the waffles hot while you cook the remaining batter, brushing the griddle with oil after cooking each waffle.

Place a waffle in the center of each of six plates. Drape the salmon over the waffles around the edges. Drizzle with the lemon cream. Toss the radish salad with the dressing. Top each waffle with some salad and serve.

---

serve with

Fresh fruit in season for dessert, such as strawberries, melon, figs, and grapes, with Zante Currant Cookies (page 300)

to drink

Champagne is the perfect partner for these waffles.

---

main dishes

PASTA, PIZZA, RICE, AND BEANS

CHICKEN, DUCK, AND TURKEY

SEAFOOD

pasta with baked tomato sauce

COOK

Nancy Harmon Jenkins

SOURCE

Cucinaamore.com

It's difficult to imagine a more mundane-sounding dish than Pasta with Baked Tomato Sauce—and yet this extremely simple pasta is a breakthrough, not like any other you're likely to have eaten. And it's so good you'll make it again and again.

The sauce is made from roasted cherry tomatoes, very ripe ones. These diminutive tomatoes with the big taste are then covered with a cheesy–garlicky–bread crumb mixture and set in the oven. Just before serving, you tear some basil leaves into the roasted tomato mixture, and that's your sauce, right in the oven dish. Add some corkscrew or butterfly pasta, and you have dinner.

Italian cookbook author Nancy Harmon Jenkins points out that the only trick to this dish is using really ripe cherry tomatoes—which are easy to find all year long. If they're not available, use any ripe red tomatoes and quarter them.

serves 4

- ⅓ cup extra-virgin olive oil
- 1 pound very ripe cherry tomatoes, halved
- ⅓ cup plain dry bread crumbs
- ¼ cup freshly grated Parmigiano-Reggiano cheese
- 2 tablespoons freshly grated pecorino cheese (see note)

- 2 garlic cloves, finely chopped
  Salt and freshly ground pepper to taste
- 1 pound dried fusilli (corkscrew) or farfalline (butterfly) pasta
- ¼ cup loosely packed fresh basil leaves, torn

---

cook's note

If there's no good pecorino available, just use all Parmesan.

Preheat the oven to 400 degrees. Grease a 13-by-9-inch baking dish with one-third of the oil.

Place the tomatoes cut side up in the dish.

In a small bowl, combine the bread crumbs, cheeses, and garlic and toss with a fork to mix well. Sprinkle the bread crumb mixture over the tomatoes, making sure that each cut side is well covered. Sprinkle with salt and pepper. Bake until the tomatoes are cooked through and starting to brown on top, about 20 minutes.

Meanwhile, bring a large pot of salted water to a boil. Add the pasta and cook for 8 to 10 minutes, or until al dente. Time the pasta so it finishes cooking about the time the tomatoes are ready to come out of the oven.

When the tomatoes are done, add the basil and stir vigorously to mix everything into a sauce. Drain the pasta and immediately transfer it to the baking dish. Add the remaining olive oil and mix well. Alternatively, transfer the pasta to a large heated bowl, then immediately add the hot tomato sauce and the oil. Serve at once.

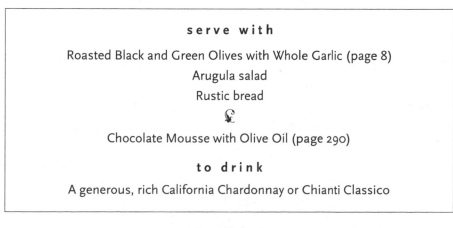

serve with

Roasted Black and Green Olives with Whole Garlic (page 8)

Arugula salad

Rustic bread

℀

Chocolate Mousse with Olive Oil (page 290)

to drink

A generous, rich California Chardonnay or Chianti Classico

main dishes

spaghetti with anna's pesto

Anna Tasca Lanza is the quintessential Sicilian cook. At her cooking school at Regaleali, the wine estate, students come from all over the world to learn the secrets of the deeply flavorful Sicilian way with food. Tasca Lanza herself is always exploring that cuisine. Her latest infatuation is with herbs, and she's written an especially charming little book on the subject, *Herbs and Wild Greens from the Sicilian Countryside*.

One of the recipes is for this amazing

COOK
Anna Tasca Lanza

SOURCE
*Herbs and Wild Greens
from the
Sicilian Countryside*

pesto, a spirited mix of herbs that includes sage, rosemary, and thyme, as well as almonds and pecorino cheese. For any herb gardener, this will become an essential dish. For the rest of us, it's worth buying the herbs to make this truly unusual and intense pesto, which seems to distill the essence of the Sicilian sun. Purists would pound the herbs in a mortar, but Tasca Lanza has no time for that and finds a food processor does a fine —and instant— job.

serves 6

1 cup fresh flat-leaf parsley
   leaves and tender stems
1 cup fresh basil leaves and
   tender stems
1 cup fresh mint leaves and
   tender stems
1 sage sprig, leaves only
1 thyme sprig, leaves only
1 small rosemary sprig,
   leaves only
1 fresh hot pepper, seeded

2 garlic cloves
1 cup olive oil
1 teaspoon sugar
   Salt to taste
½ cup ground almonds
2 tablespoons freshly grated
   pecorino cheese
1 pound dried spaghetti
   or linguine
4 medium ripe tomatoes,
   peeled and diced

In a food processor, puree the herbs, hot pepper, garlic, and oil. Add the sugar and salt. Transfer to a medium bowl and stir in the almonds and pecorino.

Bring a large pot of salted water to a boil. Add the pasta and cook for 8 to 10 minutes, or until al dente. Meanwhile, add a ladleful of the pasta water to the pesto to thin it. Drain the pasta, return it to the pot, and mix in half of the pesto. Transfer the pasta to a serving bowl, scatter the tomatoes on top, and add the remaining pesto. Serve immediately.

serve with

A big green salad

℘

Plum and Raspberry
Sorbet (page 264)

Tuscan Rosemary and
Pine Nut Bars (page 306)

to drink

Regaleali's Rosso or
another easy-drinking
Sicilian red

main dishes

ziti with spicy sausages, goat cheese, tomato, and parsley

Erica De Mane's cookbook sets out to explain the art of improvisation as it relates to pasta. This quick skillet pasta—a cross between a traditional Italian pasta and a North African one—presents an excellent opportunity to play. We couldn't find merguez, North African lamb sausages, in any of our local markets, so we settled for Italian-spiced lamb sausages and added a little cumin, cinnamon, and

COOK

Erica De Mane

SOURCE

Pasta Improvvisata

cayenne to the sauce as it cooked. It's almost startling to have lamb with pasta, but it's delicious—and the goat cheese is a perfect complement.

This dish is ready so quickly that it's imperative to start the pasta water boiling before you do anything else. Once all the ingredients are assembled, it's not more than 10 minutes from start to finish.

serves 4

Salt to taste
3 tablespoons olive oil
1 pound merguez sausages
   (North African lamb
   sausages; see note)
1 pound dried ziti or penne
2 or 3 garlic cloves, thinly sliced

4 ripe tomatoes (about
   2 pounds), seeded and
   chopped, or one 35-ounce
   can Italian plum tomatoes,
   drained and chopped
1 small log (about 6 ounces)
   fresh goat cheese, such as
   Montrachet, cut into pieces
½ cup fresh flat-leaf parsley
   leaves (about 1 small bunch)

---

to drink

Chianti or
a full-bodied rosé

Put a large pot of salted water on to boil.

Heat a large skillet over high heat until very hot. Add 1 tablespoon olive oil and the sausages and brown them on all sides, leaving them slightly undercooked in the center. Remove the sausages from the skillet and cut them into thin slices.

Add the ziti or penne to the pot of boiling water.

In the large skillet, heat 2 tablespoons olive oil over medium heat. Return the sausages to the skillet and sauté, stirring, until cooked through, about 1 minute. Add the garlic and sauté for 1 minute; do not let it color. Add the tomatoes, season with salt, and sauté until they release their juices but still retain their bright red color, 3 to 4 minutes.

When the pasta is al dente, drain and add to the skillet. Toss well, taste for seasoning, and transfer to a large serving bowl. Add the cheese and parsley and toss until the cheese is slightly melted and the pasta is well coated. Serve.

---

cook's note

We love the North African touch here, but you can improvise almost endlessly, by substituting Italian sausage or southwestern sausage, or by substituting cilantro for half the parsley.

serve with

Roasted Eggplant Dip (page 2)
Green salad with cilantro and dill

℘

Peach Sorbet (page 263)
Apricot-Pistachio Bars (page 310)

deep-dish pizza

The world divides into those who are willing to make their own pizza and those who wouldn't dream of it. We think it's definitely worth it to make pizza from scratch—especially if it's an unusual one like this. Even thin-crust pizza lovers will adore it—and yes, there's a secret ingredient: a baking potato. The potato gives the crust a softer, sweeter, more tender character—and the extra sugar in the potato

COOK
Anne Yamanaka

SOURCE
Cook's Illustrated

speeds up the fermentation process (which is already hastened by quick-rise yeast), giving the crust a more complex flavor in a shorter time.

This is a great party dish, and it's vegetarian too. Chances are you don't have a 14-inch deep-dish pizza pan, in which case you can use two 10- or 9-inch cake pans (nonstick is fine).

serves 4 to 6

1 quart water
1 medium baking potato (about 9 ounces), peeled and quartered
3½ cups unbleached all-purpose flour
1½ teaspoons quick-rise yeast
1 cup warm water (105–115 degrees)

6 tablespoons extra-virgin olive oil
1¾ teaspoons salt
Fresh Tomato Topping with Mozzarella and Basil or Four-Cheese Topping with Pesto (recipes on page 109)

---

cook's note

We like to offer both toppings with the pizza, using two cake pans. Just cut the topping recipes in half.

to drink

A Tuscan Sangiovese

Place the water and potato in a medium saucepan and bring to a boil over medium-high heat. Cook until tender, 10 to 15 minutes. Drain and let cool until the potato can be handled. Press the potato through the fine disk of a potato ricer or grate on the large holes of a box grater. Measure 1½ cups tightly packed potato and discard the rest.

Place one oven rack at the highest level and another rack at the lowest level. Preheat the oven to 200 degrees. Once the temperature reaches 200 degrees, maintain the heat for 10 minutes, then turn off the oven.

With a mixer or food processor, mix ½ cup of the flour, the yeast, and ½ cup of the warm water until combined. Cover with plastic wrap and set aside until bubbly, about 20 minutes. Add the remaining ½ cup warm water, 2 tablespoons of the olive oil, the remaining 3 cups flour, the potato, and the salt.

If using a mixer, fit it with the paddle attachment and mix on low speed until the dough comes together. Switch to the dough hook and increase the speed to medium. Continue kneading until the dough comes together and is slightly tacky, about 5 minutes.

If using a food processor, process until the dough comes together in a ball, about 40 seconds. The dough should be slightly sticky.

Transfer the dough to a lightly oiled medium bowl, turn to coat with oil, and cover tightly with plastic wrap. Place in the warm oven until the dough is soft and spongy and doubled in volume, 30 to 35 minutes.

Meanwhile, make the pizza topping.

Oil the bottom of a 14-inch deep-dish pizza pan with the remaining 4 tablespoons olive oil. Remove the dough from the oven and pat it into a 12-inch round. Place the dough in the pan and cover with plastic wrap. Let the dough rest until it no longer resists shaping, about 10 minutes.

Line the lower oven rack with unglazed baking tiles, a pizza stone, or a rimless cookie sheet (not an insulated one) — or if you have none of these, just turn a regular cookie sheet upside down.

Uncover the dough and pull the edges up the sides of the pan to form a 1-inch lip. Cover it with plastic wrap and set aside in a warm place to rise for 30 minutes. Halfway through the rising time, preheat the oven to 425 degrees.

Uncover the dough and prick it generously with a fork. Bake on the lower rack until dry and lightly browned, about 15 minutes. Sprinkle the topping over the hot crust and return to the oven until the cheese melts, 10 to 15 minutes for a large pizza, 5 to 10 minutes for smaller ones.

Transfer the pizza to the top rack and bake until the cheese is golden brown in spots, about 5 minutes. Let cool for 5 minutes. Holding the pan at an angle with one hand, use a wide spatula to slide the pizza onto a cutting board. Cut into wedges and serve hot.

serve with

Antipasto

Big green salad

℘

Plum and Raspberry Sorbet (page 264)

Tuscan Rosemary and Pine Nut Bars (page 306)

Fresh Tomato Topping with Mozzarella and Basil

4 medium ripe tomatoes (about
1½ pounds), cored, seeded,
and cut into 1-inch pieces

2 medium garlic cloves, minced
Salt and freshly ground pepper
to taste

6 ounces mozzarella cheese,
shredded (about 1½ cups)

1¼ ounces Parmesan cheese,
grated (about ½ cup)

3 tablespoons shredded fresh
basil leaves

In a medium bowl, combine the tomatoes and garlic. Season with salt and pepper and set aside.

Top the partially baked crust with the tomato mixture. Scatter the mozzarella, then the Parmesan, over the crust. Bake as directed, then sprinkle with the basil before serving.

Four-Cheese Topping with Pesto

½ cup pesto sauce

6 ounces mozzarella cheese,
shredded (about 1½ cups)

4 ounces provolone cheese,
shredded (about 1 cup)

1¼ ounces Parmesan cheese,
grated (about ½ cup)

1¼ ounces blue cheese, crumbled
(about ¼ cup)

Spread the partially baked crust evenly with the pesto sauce. Sprinkle with the mozzarella, the provolone, the Parmesan, and finally the blue cheese. Bake as directed.

apple and country ham risotto

Just when we thought everything had been said about apples, along came *An Apple Harvest,* in which apples are deconstructed, eulogized, and moved, with great respect, into dishes where they belong. Some of

COOKS

Frank Browning and Sharon Silva

SOURCE

An Apple Harvest

these unusual apple creations are so delicious that we wonder: What kind of eaters are we, that we didn't think of this before? That's exactly the case with this risotto.

serves 4

5 cups chicken broth
4 tablespoons (¹/₂ stick)
   unsalted butter
³/₄ cup diced (¹/₈ inch) unpeeled
   Stayman, Winesap,
   McIntosh, or other firm,
   sweet-tart apple
1¹/₂ cups Arborio rice
6 tablespoons finely diced
   (scant ¹/₄ inch) country ham
   (see note)

³/₄ cup semidry hard cider
   (see note)
Wedge of Asiago cheese
A few paper-thin apple slices
   sautéed in unsalted butter,
   for garnish
A few fresh sage leaves, for
   garnish
Freshly ground pepper to taste

In a medium saucepan, bring the broth to a simmer over medium heat. Reduce the heat to low and keep hot.

---

cook's notes

℘ Pancetta or prosciutto can be substituted for the country ham.
℘ Hard cider is slightly alcoholic and can be found at liquor stores and some supermarkets.

In a small skillet, melt 2 tablespoons of the butter over medium-high heat. Add the diced apple and sauté, stirring, until lightly browned, about 10 minutes. Do not let the apple soften, as it will cook further in the risotto. Remove from the heat and keep warm.

In a large saucepan, melt the remaining 2 tablespoons butter over medium-low heat. Add the rice and ham and cook, stirring, for 2 to 3 minutes, or until the rice is well coated with the butter. Add the cider and cook, stirring, for about 2 minutes, or until the cider is absorbed. Begin adding the hot broth, ¹/₂ cup at a time, and cook, stirring, allowing it to be fully absorbed before adding more, until the rice is almost cooked. Add the cooked apple cubes with the final addition of stock. The risotto is ready when it is firm but tender and creamy and the center of each grain is no longer chalky, about 25 minutes total. You may not need all the broth, or you may need more liquid, in which case hot water can be used. Remove from the heat, cover, and let stand for 5 minutes.

Spoon the risotto onto a warmed serving platter. Using a vegetable peeler, shave curls of Asiago over the top. Follow with the apple slices, a scattering of sage leaves, and a grinding of pepper. Serve immediately.

serve with

Watercress salad with
toasted pecans

❧

Souffléed Lemon Custard
(page 288)

to drink

A light young Riesling or
Pinot Blanc

main dishes

egg and potato skillet supper

COOK
Sarah Fritschner

SOURCE
Louisville Courier-Journal

If you're always on the prowl for an emergency meal that's not pasta, one you can make entirely from staples, here's one for your collection. Food editor Sarah Fritschner was thinking about being snowed in when she devised this dish, which is a cross between a frittata and a quiche with hash browns. You can even make it with evaporated milk on true snow days.

But that's hardly the point; this is a very tasty breakfast, brunch, or supper, and it lends itself to leftovers, vegetarian or not, from broccoli and spinach to ham and sausage, as well as any combination of cheeses. Fritschner notes you can also leave out the cheese altogether, but if you do, add a little more salt.

serves 4

2 tablespoons olive oil
1 medium potato, grated (peeled, if desired)
6 large eggs, at room temperature
1½ cups grated cheddar cheese
½ teaspoon salt

1 12-ounce can evaporated milk or 1½ cups whole milk
½ teaspoon hot red pepper sauce, or to taste
Cooked sausage, crumbled bacon, or thawed frozen chopped spinach (optional)

serve with

Sliced tomatoes and a big green salad

Ice cream sundaes

Preheat the oven to 350 degrees.

In a large, shallow ovenproof skillet, heat the oil over medium-high heat. Tilt the skillet to coat the sides with oil, then add the potato. Cook over medium heat, stirring once or twice, until the potato is golden, about 5 minutes.

In a medium bowl, beat the eggs. Add l cup of the cheese, the salt, milk, and hot pepper sauce and combine.

Remove the skillet from the heat and scrape up any potato that is stuck on the bottom. Pat the potato out to roughly cover the bottom of the skillet. Add the sausage or other tidbits, if using. Pour the egg mixture on top and sprinkle with the remaining $1/2$ cup cheese. Bake for 30 minutes, or until set and golden brown. Serve hot.

tunisian chickpea stew
(lablabi)

COOK

Clifford A. Wright

SOURCE

A Mediterranean Feast

As stews go, this one is almost instant—about 45 minutes start to finish—because it's based on canned chickpeas brightened with spicy harissa, garlic, and cumin. Once the stew is cooked, the fun really begins, because you can garnish it, as the Tunisians do, with a number of intriguing items. Set your choices out in little bowls to pass at the table along with a little vial of olive oil. Add some hot flatbread and a salad, and you have a great vegetarian dinner.

serves 4

4 cups drained canned chickpeas
2 tablespoons harissa (see note)
4 garlic cloves, mashed
1 tablespoon ground cumin, preferably freshly ground
Salt to taste
Juice of 1 lemon
¼ cup extra-virgin olive oil

Garnishes, to taste (optional)
Fresh lemon juice
Coarse sea salt
Coddled eggs

Seeded and finely chopped green bell peppers
Chopped very ripe tomatoes
Dollops of harissa
Capers, rinsed and drained
Pickled turnips (see note)
Preserved lemons (see note)
Croutons
Finely chopped fresh flat-leaf parsley leaves
Finely chopped fresh cilantro leaves
Leftover bread
Extra-virgin olive oil

---

cook's note

Harissa is available in tubes and cans in many supermarkets and most gourmet stores. Pink pickled turnips are sold in jars in Middle Eastern markets and some supermarkets. Preserved lemons are harder to find, but they're not crucial.

Place the chickpeas in a large saucepan and cover with water. Bring to a boil over high heat and cook until soft, about 30 minutes. Stir in the harissa, garlic, cumin, and salt. Reduce the heat to medium and cook for 10 minutes more. Stir in the lemon juice and olive oil. Serve hot with any combination of the optional garnishes, including more harissa and olive oil.

serve with

Arab flatbread

Purslane Salad with Baby Greens and Cabbage (page 54)

℘

Apricot-Pistachio Bars (page 310)

to drink

A bold, dry rosé

main dishes

beer can chicken

This year's most provocative chicken recipe appeared on the barbecue circuit about five years ago, and although nobody knows who actually invented it, we have a pretty good idea it was someone living along the Texas-Louisiana axis, where they've been cooking birds on beer cans for years. The unsung genius sitting next to a barbecue grill with a chicken and a can of beer who put them together is right up there in Nobel territory: This is one brilliant way of cooking chicken.

What happens to a chicken when it's stuck on a half-full can of beer and grilled or smoked is this: the de facto vertical roaster drains off the fat, the skin of the bird becomes incredibly crackling crisp, and the

COOK

Steven Raichlen

SOURCE

Abcnews.go.com/ goodmorningamerica

meat is amazingly tender and juicy because it's moistened by the rising steam of the beer, which carries with it whatever flavorings are used in the beer can.

We've seen this recipe called Barbecue Butt Chicken, Bud Chicken (that was Matthew McConaughey on Rosie O'Donnell's show), and plain old Beer Can Chicken. Some recipes use a spice rub, some don't; some cooks insist the bird has to be smoked (in which case the skin won't really be crisp), others just grill it. And we like Beer Can Chicken so much that we also cook it in the oven (see note).

This recipe, by cookbook author Steven Raichlen, is especially good because he soaks the wood chips in beer first to get a smoky beer flavor going.

serves 4

2 cups hickory or oak chips
2 12-ounce cans beer
1/2 cup of your favorite barbecue rub or Memphis Rub (page 119)

2 3 1/2-to-4-pound chickens (fat removed), washed and patted dry with paper towels

---

to drink
More beer, of course

Place the wood chips in a medium bowl. Pop the tab of each beer can and make two additional holes in each top, using a church-key opener. Pour half the beer from each can over the wood chips. Add additional beer or water to cover the chips and let soak for 1 hour.

Meanwhile, start a charcoal fire in a kettle grill. When the coals are red hot, dump them in two piles at opposite ends of the grill. Place a drip pan in the center and set the grate on the grill. Drain the wood chips.

Sprinkle 1 teaspoon barbecue rub in the neck cavity and 2 teaspoons in the main cavity of each chicken. Add 1 tablespoon rub to each open half-full beer can — don't worry if it foams up. Season the outside of each bird with 2 tablespoons rub.

When you're ready to cook and the coals are red, scatter the wood chips over the charcoal. Stand the beer cans on a work surface and lower each chicken over a can so that the can goes into the main cavity. Pull the chicken legs modestly forward to form a sort of tripod, so the chicken can sit upright on the can. Carefully transfer the chickens to the grill in this position, placing them in the center over the drip pan, away from the heat.

---

cook's notes

❦ To make Beer Can Chicken in the oven, prepare the chicken as described and roast it as you usually do, but perched on the beer can inside a shallow roasting pan. Or make the chicken with just a salt and pepper rub. If you trim off the wing tips and add them to the can along with some garlic and herbs, you'll have a tasty sauce base to add to any drippings in the pan.

❦ We know sooner or later someone's going to ask: Can you use light beer to cook this chicken? Of course you can, but you know what the good old boys on the barbecue circuit would say about that.

---

main dishes

Barbecue the chickens until nicely browned and cooked through, about 1½ hours, or until the thickest part of a thigh registers 165 degrees.

Carefully transfer the birds to a platter in the same position. Carefully lift the chickens off the cans—it helps to squeeze the can slightly. Discard the cans and carve the chickens. Serve.

VARIATION

Flavor options to toss into the beer include garlic, onions, herbs, spices, chiles, crab boil seasoning, and Asian seasonings.

serve with

Guacamole and chips

Roasted Potato Crisps
with Fresh Herbs
(page 224)

Charcoal-Grilled Corn on
the Cob with Mayonnaise,
Cheese, and Chile
(page 206)

Big green salad

Sliced tomatoes

Beer Bread (page 248)

Sour Cream Pound Cake
with Strawberries
(page 312)

Memphis Rub

To rub over the chicken—and add to the beer can too, if you like—try Steven Raichlen's rub, which is also good on pork.

makes ½ cup

¼ cup paprika
1 tablespoon packed dark brown sugar
1 tablespoon sugar
1 teaspoon celery salt
1 teaspoon freshly ground pepper

1–3 teaspoons cayenne pepper, or to taste
1 teaspoon dry mustard
1 teaspoon garlic powder
1 teaspoon onion powder
2 teaspoons salt

In a jar, combine all the ingredients and shake well. Cover the jar tightly; the rub will keep for about 6 months.

garlicky baked chicken

We've always wondered how Sara Moulton manages to appear on *Good Morning America,* cook lunch at the executive dining room of *Gourmet* magazine, race to the TVFN studio to film a cooking show, and have a relaxed dinner with her family. This favorite family chicken recipe may be one reason: Moulton and her family enjoy simple but delicious food every day.

Sara found the idea for this recipe in Jean

COOK

Sara Moulton
after Jean Anderson

SOURCE

Thefoodmaven.com

Anderson's 1982 book, *Jean Anderson Cooks.* She simplified it, dropping some ingredients—herbs, pecans—and adding lots more garlic and cheese. This is a crisp-coated, incredibly fragrant baked chicken that's made in minutes. Of course, you can re-complicate it by adding some sage, parsley, and thyme, not to mention some chopped pecans. But try it once the simple way, and we think you'll be hooked.

serves 4

8 chicken thighs or 4 chicken
    breasts
Salt and freshly ground pepper
    to taste
8 tablespoons (1 stick) butter

4 garlic cloves, chopped
2 cups fresh bread crumbs
1 cup freshly grated Parmesan
    cheese

---

tip

For the crispest chicken, bake the chicken on a rack in a roasting pan. The quality of chicken you use will make a difference, too; regular supermarket chicken will give off a fair amount of water, which may make the bottom of the pieces soggy, so it's best to look for an organic, free-range chicken from a reliable supplier.

Preheat the oven to 350 degrees.

Season the chicken pieces with salt and pepper.

In a small saucepan, melt the butter with the garlic and pour into a shallow bowl.

In a pie plate or shallow bowl, mix the bread crumbs with the cheese.

Dip the chicken pieces, one at a time, into the garlic butter, coating well on all sides. Then dip into the bread crumb mixture, patting them on so the coating is thick.

Place the chicken pieces in a shallow roasting pan, skin side up, and pat on any remaining bread crumb mixture. Drizzle any remaining garlic butter over the chicken pieces.

Bake the chicken for 1 hour, or until crisp and golden brown, basting several times with the pan juices. Serve hot.

---

serve with

Parmigiano-Reggiano Crisps with Goat Cheese Mousse (page 14)
Champ (page 230)
Tomato Salad (page 52)

℘

Souffléed Lemon Custard (page 288) or
Lemon-Yogurt Cheesecake for Jerry (page 279)

to drink

Sauvignon Blanc

---

main dishes

indonesian ginger chicken

At the Barefoot Contessa, a take-out shop in the Hamptons, Ina Garten has been selling this scrumptious chicken for many years to the likes of Lauren Bacall, who gets cranky if it's sold out. Garten's recipe is a variation of one from an earlier Hamptons shop, Loaves and Fishes,

COOK

**Ina Garten
after Devon Fredericks
and Susan Costner**

SOURCE

*The Barefoot Contessa
Cookbook,* by Ina Garten

created by Devon Fredericks and Susan Costner.

The recipe (from *The Barefoot Contessa Cookbook*) is not only amazingly simple, it's also versatile, delicious hot or cold, and as wonderful with pork as it is with chicken. Start the recipe a day ahead.

serves 6

1 cup honey
³/₄ cup soy sauce
¹/₂ cup grated peeled fresh
    gingerroot

¹/₄ cup minced garlic
    (8–12 cloves)
2 3¹/₂-pound chickens, quartered,
    backs removed

In a small saucepan, cook the honey, soy sauce, ginger, and garlic over low heat until the honey is melted. Place the chicken in a large, shallow roasting pan, skin side down, and pour on the sauce. Cover the pan tightly with foil and marinate overnight in the refrigerator. Bring to room temperature before baking.

Preheat the oven to 350 degrees.

Bake the chicken, covered, for 30 minutes. Uncover the pan, turn the chicken skin side up, and increase the oven temperature to 375 degrees. Bake for 30 minutes more, or until the juices run clear when you cut between the leg and the thigh and the sauce is a rich dark brown. Serve hot or cold.

VARIATIONS

❧ You can make this dish with just chicken thighs, which are great for a picnic or other portable feast. And you can easily halve the recipe.

❧ To use the marinade with pork, cover 2 pork tenderloins with the marinade and refrigerate overnight. Bring to room temperature before roasting at 350 degrees for 30 minutes, or until the pork reaches 130 degrees on an instant-read thermometer.

serve with

Sugar Snap Peas with
Sesame (page 199)

Rice cooked in unsweet-
ened coconut milk

❧

Star Anise Ice Cream
(page 266)

to drink

A smooth white Rhône,
such as Viognier

main dishes

dad's chinese chicken wings

The father of Chinese cook par excellence Nina Simonds loved the chicken wings he used to order in Asian restaurants, but he couldn't duplicate them at home. Simonds devised these succulent wings for him, and we find them even better than the standard deep-fried Chinese wings. These are lacquered, like the ducks you see in the windows of Chinese markets, and they have a sweet and slightly spicy taste. They also give off a wonderful fragrance

COOK
Nina Simonds

SOURCE
A Spoonful of Ginger

while they're cooking.

They're great snacks for Super Bowl parties and other traditional chicken-wing occasions. We also like them for dinner, and leftovers are delicious. The wings are very portable, since you can serve them at room temperature as well as hot. You can marinate them a day ahead—in fact they'll be even tastier that way—and bake them right before you serve them.

serves 6

CHINESE MARINADE
1¼ cups soy sauce
1¼ cups rice wine or sake
1 cup water
12 scallions, ends trimmed, smashed with the flat side of a cleaver
10 garlic cloves, smashed with the flat side of a cleaver

1 2½-inch chunk fresh gingerroot, peeled, cut into 10 quarter-size slices, and smashed with the flat side of a cleaver

CHICKEN WINGS
3½–4 pounds chicken wings (about 20), rinsed and patted dry with paper towels

> **tip**
> If the wings are sticking to the foil, loosen them with a spatula during the cooking.

FOR THE MARINADE

In a medium saucepan, combine all the ingredients and bring to a boil. Reduce the heat to low and simmer for 10 minutes. Let cool slightly.

FOR THE CHICKEN WINGS

With a sharp knife, separate the drumettes from the wing tips at the joint. Place the wings in a large bowl and add the marinade. Stir to coat, cover with plastic wrap, and let the wings marinate for at least several hours or overnight in the refrigerator.

Preheat the oven to 500 degrees. Line a cookie sheet with foil.

Place the wings on the cookie sheet and brush liberally with the marinade. Roast for about 40 minutes, turning once, until the wings are cooked through and crispy brown at the edges (see tip). Serve hot, at room temperature, or cold.

serve with

Mashed Potato Dip (page 4), as a side dish

Sugar Snap Peas with Sesame (page 199)

℮

Honey-Poached Quinces (page 270)

Zante Currant Cookies with lemon zest (page 300)

to drink

A light-flavored beer

main dishes

chinese lemon chicken

The traditional version of this recipe calls for the chicken to be marinated with lemon and seasonings and then browned. In the hands of a less-than-expert cook, however, the wet chicken and lemon can make the oil spatter alarmingly, and the honey can easily burn if it's overheated. Grace Young worked out a new way of cooking this sweet-tart dish, and it's so good and

COOK

Grace Young
after Anna Loke

SOURCE

*The Wisdom
of the Chinese Kitchen*

so simple—and so different from all other versions of lemon chicken—that it should become part of our kitchen repertoire.

The chicken is chopped into pieces that include the bone, but for Western tastes the little bits of bone present a problem. For that reason, we like this dish best made with chicken thighs, but you'll need to increase the cooking time by about 10 minutes.

serves 6

2 pounds mixed bone-in chicken
   parts or chicken thighs
1 tablespoon Shao Hsing rice
   wine
1 tablespoon soy sauce

1 tablespoon honey
1 lemon
1 tablespoon vegetable oil
3 slices peeled fresh gingerroot
½ teaspoon salt

If using mixed chicken parts, chop the chicken through the bone into 2-inch pieces with a meat cleaver, or disjoint into serving pieces.

to drink
A dry, full
Sauvignon Blanc

best american recipes 2000

In a medium bowl, combine the rice wine, soy sauce, and honey.

Slice ⅛ inch off both ends of the lemon. Halve the lemon crosswise and cut each half into 4 wedges. Remove any visible seeds.

Heat one large skillet or two smaller ones over high heat until hot but not smoking. Add the oil, lemon wedges, and ginger and stir-fry for 1 to 2 minutes, or until the lemon and ginger are lightly browned. Be careful; the wet lemon wedges will cause the oil to spatter. Transfer the lemon and ginger to a small plate.

Carefully add the chicken to the skillet, skin side down, in a single layer. Fry for 3 to 4 minutes, adjusting the heat between medium and medium-high as the chicken browns. Using a metal spatula, turn the chicken over and fry for 3 to 4 minutes more, or until the chicken is browned on the other side but not cooked through. Pour off any excess fat. Sprinkle on the salt, the wine mixture, and the lemon and ginger. Cover and simmer over medium heat for 3 to 4 minutes (8 to 10 minutes for chicken thighs). Turn the chicken, reduce the heat to low, and simmer for 3 to 4 minutes more (8 to 10 minutes for thighs), or until the chicken is cooked through. Serve immediately.

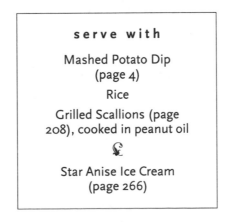

serve with

Mashed Potato Dip
(page 4)

Rice

Grilled Scallions (page
208), cooked in peanut oil

℘

Star Anise Ice Cream
(page 266)

main dishes

balsamico roast chicken and potatoes

COOK
Lynne Rossetto Kasper

SOURCE
The Italian Country Table

The craze for drizzling every imaginable foodstuff with balsamic vinegar seems to have subsided for the moment, but if you want to remind yourself of why it's such a magical ingredient, try this terrific homey chicken dish. The whole chicken is flattened out in the pan, with its backbone removed—a great way to roast it —and then it's stuffed under the skin with a heady mix of fresh and dried herbs (using dried basil is important here), onion, garlic, pancetta, and good-quality balsamic vinegar.

The chicken roasts right along with the potatoes; the skin comes out crisp, the flesh moist and deeply flavored with the stuffing. And because this recipe comes from the Modena and Reggio regions of Italy—balsamic country—it's served with a baptism of more balsamic vinegar. Naturally, the better your vinegar, the more sensational the dish will be. But even a good commercial brand will produce a great result.

If time allows, season the chicken and refrigerate it for several hours or overnight. Bring the chicken to room temperature before cooking.

serves 4

¼ medium onion

3 large garlic cloves

¼ cup packed fresh basil leaves

½ teaspoon dried basil

¼ teaspoon dried marjoram

¼ teaspoon dried oregano

4 slices pancetta (1½–2 ounces), chopped

5 tablespoons good-quality balsamic vinegar (see note)

1 tablespoon extra-virgin olive oil

Salt and freshly ground pepper to taste

1 3½-to-4-pound chicken, preferably organic

6 medium Yellow Finn, Yukon Gold, or red potatoes, cut into 2-inch chunks

½–1 cup dry white wine
Fresh parsley or fresh thyme, for garnish

the cooking time for even browning. If, after 1 hour, the chicken isn't browning, increase the oven temperature to 500 degrees to finish cooking. Or wait until it is done and broil for 5 minutes to crisp the skin.

Let the chicken rest for 5 to 10 minutes at room temperature, then present it on a warmed platter along with the potatoes, sprinkling everything with the remaining balsamic vinegar. Garnish with bouquets of parsley or thyme.

serve with

A salad of sharp
winter greens

Plenty of rustic bread to
sop up the pan juices

℘

Original Plum Torte
(page 280)

to drink

Dolcetto d'Alba

Preheat the oven to 400 degrees.

Mince together by hand or in a food processor the onion, garlic, herbs, and pancetta. Blend in 2 teaspoons of the balsamic vinegar, the oil, salt, and pepper.

Cut out the chicken's backbone and open the chicken out flat, skin side up. With your palm, firmly press down on the breast area to flatten. Wiggle your fingers under the skin to loosen it, then stuff most of the herb mixture under the skin of the thigh, leg, and breast areas. Rub the rest all over the chicken. Place the bird skin side up in a large shallow pan (such as a jellyroll or half-sheet pan). Scatter the potatoes around it and sprinkle everything with salt and pepper.

Roast the chicken for 20 minutes, then pour in 1/2 cup wine. Roast for 70 minutes more, or until the inner thigh reaches about 175 degrees on an instant-read thermometer. Baste the potatoes and chicken frequently with the pan juices, turning the potatoes often to brown evenly and prevent them from sticking. Add more wine if the pan is dry. Turn over the chicken two-thirds of the way through

---

cook's notes

❧ Balsamic vinegar is one of the few food products you can judge by the price. A really cheap one is industrial quality. A really expensive one is actually a condiment, not a cooking ingredient. For cooking, the Fini brand in the frosted bottle is good; anything cheaper will be disappointing.

❧ We don't find it necessary to turn the chicken, and if you do, you'll need to turn it right side up again for a final browning. Just use the broiler at the end if it isn't sufficiently browned.

chicken roasted
with orange, rosemary, and bay leaves

COOK

Amanda Hesser

SOURCE

The Cook and the Gardener

Before she became a *New York Times* food writer, Amanda Hesser spent an apprentice year studying and cooking in France at Anne Willan's legendary cooking school, La Varenne, housed in a seventeenth-century chateau in Burgundy. There she learned French food from the ground up, at the hands of the chateau's master gardener, M. Milbert. As with all gardens, the main lesson for the cook is seasonality. There are, of course, no oranges growing in Burgundy, but they come into the market in February, and Hesser was inspired to combine them with the few remaining winter herbs in this memorable roast chicken dish.

The combination is brilliant: The orange peels caramelize in the pan juices to create a mouthwatering sauce, and the chicken is infused with the perfume of the oranges and herbs. The marinating time is important; even overnight wouldn't be too long.

serves 4

1 4-to-4½-pound roasting chicken, rinsed and patted dry with paper towels
4 juicy oranges, halved and juiced, orange halves reserved (see note)
2 garlic cloves
4 rosemary sprigs
3 bay leaves
Coarse salt or kosher salt and freshly ground pepper to taste
3 tablespoons butter
1 cup water or chicken broth

Place the chicken and orange halves in a large nonreactive bowl. Add the orange juice, garlic, rosemary, and bay leaves, immersing them in the juice. Cover and marinate in the refrigerator, turning the chicken occasionally, for 6 to 8 hours.

Preheat the oven to 400 degrees.

Remove the chicken from the marinade. Place 2 orange halves, 2 rosemary sprigs, and 2 bay leaves in the cavity of the bird, reserving the marinade with the remaining herbs and garlic. Season the bird with salt and pepper, truss it, and place it in a heavy roasting pan along with 2 tablespoons of the butter. Place 2 orange halves from the marinade in the bottom of the roasting pan alongside the chicken.

Roast, turning the bird to cover all sides and basting often with the pan juices, for 1 to 1¼ hours. During the last half hour, the skin may begin to burn, depending on the dimensions of your oven. If this is the case, simply lay a sheet of foil over the top. The chicken is done when it is lifted carefully with large-pronged forks from the roasting pan and the juices from its cavity run clear—or when an instant-read thermometer inserted into the thickest part of the leg for 1 minute registers 160 degrees. Transfer the chicken to a cutting board and let rest for a few minutes before carving. It will continue to cook to its done temperature of 165 degrees while it rests.

---

cook's note

Pretty as they are, navel oranges aren't the best choice here. Look for Valencias, which have lots of delicious juice.

tip

If you have extra rosemary and fresh bay leaves, make a bed of them on the platter and lay the cooked chicken on top. The warm chicken will release the perfume in the herbs.

Meanwhile, make the sauce. Pour off the fat from the roasting pan. Add the water or broth and marinade (discard the orange halves) to the roasting pan and bring to a boil on top of the stove. Stir with a wooden spoon to loosen any pan drippings. Reduce to about ½ cup and whisk in the remaining 1 tablespoon butter. Taste and adjust the seasonings. Strain into a small bowl.

Carve the chicken and arrange the slices on a serving platter. Serve the sauce on the side.

serve with

Hungarian Jewish
Chopped Liver (page 6)

Al Forno's Mashed
Potatoes (page 157)

Garlicky spinach

Souffléed Lemon Custard
(page 288)

to drink

An Austrian
or Alsatian Riesling

main dishes

chicken with yams, fennel, and ginger

COOKS

**Len Allison and
Karen Hubert Allison**

SOURCE

*D'Artagnan's Glorious
Game Cookbook,* by Ariane
Daguin, George Faison,
and Joanna Pruess

We're willing to bet you've never tasted these flavors together before. This one-pot meal starts off in a very French way, with chicken browned in butter and oil (the skillet deglazed with Armagnac, white wine, and chicken broth), lots of shallots and garlic, rosemary, and thyme. Then it goes a little wild: fennel jumps in from Italy, sweet potatoes (the yams of the recipe title) from the New World, and ginger from Asia. Add some dried apricots, and you have quite an amazing dish.

Bonus: It's all made ahead, it smells divine while it's cooking, and it's dinner all by itself. The chicken is falling-off-the-bone tender, and the vegetables melt down into a delicious heap.

serves 4

2 tablespoons clarified butter (see note)

1 tablespoon fruity olive oil

4–6 chicken pieces (white or dark), skinned, washed, and patted dry

1/2 cup Armagnac or cognac

1 cup chicken broth

1/2 cup dry white wine

2 cups very thinly sliced fennel

3 tablespoons sliced shallots

2 tablespoons sliced garlic

1 1/2 pounds sweet potatoes, peeled and cut into 1/2-inch-thick slices (about 3 cups)

1 cup loosely packed dried apricots (preferably whole pitted apricots rather than halves), cut into 1/4-inch dice

1 tablespoon finely julienned peeled fresh gingerroot

5 4-inch rosemary sprigs

2 4-inch thyme sprigs

Salt and freshly ground pepper to taste

1/3 cup toasted sunflower seeds, for garnish (optional)

Preheat the oven to 325 degrees.

In a large skillet, heat the butter and oil over medium-high heat until hot but not smoking. Add the chicken pieces and brown on both sides, 5 to 7 minutes per side. Transfer to a large Dutch oven.

Pour off the butter mixture into a small bowl and set aside. Deglaze the pan with the Armagnac or cognac, stirring up any browned bits from the bottom. Add the broth and wine, increase the heat to high, and boil until the liquid is reduced by one-fourth. Pour the broth mixture over the chicken in the casserole.

Wipe out the skillet and heat 2 tablespoons of the reserved butter mixture over medium heat. Add the fennel, shallots, and garlic. Cover and sweat until softened, 5 to 6 minutes; add to the casserole.

Add the remaining ingredients except the seeds to the chicken and mix. Cover and bake for 1³/₄ to 2 hours, or until the meat falls off the bones. Sprinkle with the seeds, if desired, and serve.

---

cook's notes

 To clarify butter, melt unsalted butter slowly in a heavy pan over medium-low heat. Skim off the foam at the top and carefully pour the clear yellow liquid into a clean jar. Seal tightly and store in the refrigerator for up to 2 months.

 This dish has a frankly sweet aspect; you might want to cut the amount of apricots in half.

serve with

Watercress salad with Belgian endive

Fresh Ginger Cake (page 282)

to drink

California Chardonnay

chicken poached in new beaujolais

T he great chef Paul Bocuse loves Beaujolais, and he devised this recipe, which appeared in *French Chefs Cooking*, to give it a star turn. This is one of those incredibly simple grandmother's dishes that most French chefs love more than their fancy restaurant creations—and we love it too. Because it's so simple, the

COOK

Paul Bocuse

SOURCE

French Chefs Cooking,
by Michael Buller

quality of the ingredients counts: be sure to get a really good chicken—fleshy and tender, as the recipe specifies.

And don't stint on the parsley: delectable as it is, the chicken looks dreadful, and needs a little green to bring it to life.

serves 4

3 tablespoons olive oil
1 3½-pound fleshy, tender chicken
    Salt and freshly ground pepper to taste

1 garlic clove, crushed
½ cup crushed shallots (see note)
½ bottle Beaujolais Nouveau
1½ tablespoons butter
1 flat-leaf parsley sprig, chopped

---

serve with

Warm Leeks with
Vinaigrette (page 202)

Creamy Mashed Potatoes
(page 228)

Winter greens salad

℘

Velvet Chocolate Cake
(page 317)

to drink

More Beaujolais Nouveau

In a large, deep skillet, heat the olive oil over medium heat and sauté the chicken lightly on all sides. Add salt and pepper to taste. Add the garlic and shallots. Pour the wine over the chicken. Bring to a boil, reduce the heat to low, and poach, covered, for at least 1 hour, or until tender: the slower the cooking, the better the taste. Transfer the bird to an ovenproof serving platter and keep warm.

Boil the juices in the skillet over medium-high heat to make a reduction (you should have enough to fill a coffee cup). Blend in the butter, ideally with an electric hand blender. Pour the sauce over the chicken, sprinkle with some chopped parsley and salt and pepper, and serve.

VARIATION

You can substitute chicken thighs—about 10 of them—for the whole chicken.

---

cook's notes

❧ If you don't have a skillet with a lid large enough to hold the chicken, use a Dutch oven.

❧ The chicken looks best with $1/3$ cup chopped parsley scattered over it before serving.

❧ You may find yourself stopping at the line "$1/2$ cup crushed shallots." You crush shallots just as you do garlic: Smack them hard with a meat mallet or the flat side of a chef's knife and peel them.

grilled duck in a jar

Passionate gardener Arayah Jenanyan was marinating some duck pieces to grill later when she had an idea: the duck with its herb seasonings was actually beautiful, and it ought to be on display somewhere as a still life. Then she remembered a large glass jar she'd put away, and *voilà*, a highly decorative way of preparing dinner for her backyard barbecue guests. The duck doesn't actually cook in the jar—it's just on display, ready to be admired by those who will soon enjoy it.

That idea quickly led to vegetables in a jar—two side-by-side jars are even more dramatic. The jars can be anything glass that's large enough to hold the duck, about 2 quarts—old Planters peanut jars, large glass flowerpots, whatever works. A plain glass bowl also is fine.

If we had a party trick file, this recipe would definitely be there.

COOK
Arayah Jenanyan

SOURCE
Smith & Hawken:
The Gardeners'
Community Cookbook,
edited by Victoria Wise

serves 6 to 8

2 4-pound ducks, each cut into
   6–8 pieces
12 thyme sprigs
12 fresh sage leaves
8 bay leaves
12 juniper berries, crushed

1 tablespoon black peppercorns
1 tablespoon coarse sea salt

Grilled Veggies in a Jar (recipe
   page 140; optional)

> **to drink**
> Gigondas

Layer the duck pieces in a large glass jar or bowl, sprinkling each layer with the seasonings as you go. Cover and refrigerate for 12 to 24 hours.

When you're ready to cook, prepare a charcoal fire in a grill with a lid and let burn until white-hot, with no flames.

Remove the duck from the refrigerator, lift out the pieces, and brush off as much salt as you can, leaving as much of the other seasonings as possible. Return the duck pieces to the jar and set it by the grill until the fire is ready.

Place the duck pieces on the grill rack directly over the coals and close the lid. Grill for 20 to 25 minutes, turning once or twice, until golden all over and cooked through. Serve hot or at room temperature.

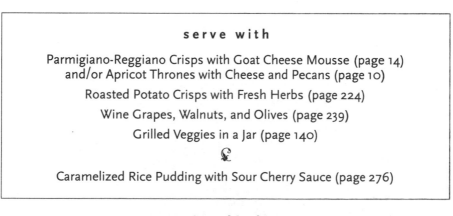

serve with

Parmigiano-Reggiano Crisps with Goat Cheese Mousse (page 14)
and/or Apricot Thrones with Cheese and Pecans (page 10)

Roasted Potato Crisps with Fresh Herbs (page 224)

Wine Grapes, Walnuts, and Olives (page 239)

Grilled Veggies in a Jar (page 140)

℮

Caramelized Rice Pudding with Sour Cherry Sauce (page 276)

Grilled Veggies in a Jar

Fill a large jar with an assortment of garden vegetables in season, such as summer squash, onions, bell peppers, whole heads of garlic, eggplants, and/or leeks. Leave the vegetables whole if small, or cut in half if large.

12 thyme sprigs
12 flat-leaf parsley sprigs
10 garlic cloves, halved
 1 teaspoon freshly ground
    pepper

2 tablespoons balsamic
    or red wine vinegar
    or juice of 1 lemon
¼ cup olive oil

In a small bowl, combine the seasonings and toss with the vegetables. Let marinate for at least 30 minutes or up to 3 hours.

Grill the vegetables around the edges of the rack while the duck cooks. Serve hot or at room temperature.

sam choy's award-winning roast duck

The larger-than-life Hawaiian chef Sam Choy is a legendary cook whose speedy version of the traditional Chinese roast duck is always winning awards. Choy isn't particularly impressed; what matters most to him is that his restaurant customers rave about the roast duck and order

COOK

Sam Choy

SOURCE

Sam Choy's Island Flavors

it over and over again.

What we love about it is not only its addictive taste but its absolute simplicity —you don't even have to baste it. In terms of bang for the buck, this method of making the classic Asian duck is the best in its class, no question.

serves 4

1 5-pound Pekin (Long Island)
   duck
¾ cup soy sauce

3 tablespoons Dry Duck
   Marinade (page 143)

Rinse the duck and remove its wings, neck flap, tail end, excess fat, and drumstick knuckles. Place it in a large bowl and pour the soy sauce over it. Roll the duck in the soy sauce to coat and let stand for about 10 minutes, rolling it several more times.

serve with

Mashed Potato Dip, as a
side dish (page 4)

Sugar Snap Peas with
Sesame (page 199)

Savannah Salad with Avo-
cado Dressing (page 50)

to drink

A young, cold
Gewürztraminer

main dishes

Preheat the oven to 550 degrees.

Place the duck, breast side up, on a rack in a large, shallow roasting pan and sprinkle thoroughly with the dry marinade. Put a little marinade inside the cavity.

Roast the duck for 30 minutes. Reduce the oven temperature to 325 degrees. Cook for l hour, or until a meat thermometer registers 170 degrees on the inner thigh.

Let the duck rest for 15 minutes before carving and serving.

---

cook's notes

❧ If there's one thing—actually, two things—we've learned about roasting a duck, it's (a) to drain the fat, before you begin, by pricking it all over with a kitchen fork or poking it all over with a knifepoint held on the diagonal so you cut only the skin and the fat, not the flesh; and (b) to roast the duck in the shallowest possible pan, such as a sheet pan, so the bottom won't steam and the duck skin will be crisp.

❧ If your oven isn't clean, you may get a lot of smoke during the initial roasting. If so, open all the doors and windows and disconnect the smoke alarms.

Dry Duck Marinade

makes about ¼ cup

1 tablespoon salt
1 tablespoon garlic salt
1 teaspoon garlic powder
1 teaspoon paprika

½ teaspoon freshly ground white
    pepper
1 tablespoon whole coriander
    seeds

Mix all the ingredients together in a small bowl and rub on the duck.

VARIATION

Try this marinade on chicken and pork as well—with the pork, you might add a big pinch of ancho chile powder.

awesome tangerine-glazed turkey

As wonderful as the traditional Thanksgiving roast turkey always is, we and virtually everyone else we know are eager to serve a holiday turkey that's just a little different, a little more interesting, a little unusual. The roasting fragrance alone makes this turkey a standout—it is indeed awesome.

The turkey is stuffed with a hearty sausage stuffing perked up with apple and dried cranberries, but you could use virtually any stuffing that sounds pleasing

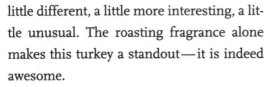

COOK
Stacy M. Polcyn

SOURCE
Allrecipes.com

and has a citrus flavor.

The bird is kept moist with basting and a cheesecloth drape that's soaked in the tangerine mixture.

Note that this is a small turkey, which some experts feel is the tastiest kind. If you're cooking a giant bird, you'll need to increase the ingredient amounts and cooking time accordingly.

Both the Turkey Giblet Broth and the stuffing can be made a day ahead, and the turkey can be stuffed at the last minute before roasting.

serves 6

3 cups Turkey Giblet Broth
    (page 147)
2 quarts Sausage, Apple, and
    Dried Cranberry Stuffing
    (page 148)
1 10-pound turkey, at room
    temperature, neck and
    giblets reserved for the broth
Salt and freshly ground pepper
    to taste

³/₄ cup (1¹/₂ sticks) unsalted
    butter, softened
³/₄ cup canola oil
1¹/₂ cups fresh tangerine juice
    (see note)
3 tablespoons all-purpose flour
    Thyme and rosemary sprigs
    and bay leaves for garnish
    (optional)

---

cook's note

Frozen tangerine juice concentrate is an excellent product—if you can find it. Just reconstitute it and save yourself from having to squeeze the tangerines.

Prepare the broth and the stuffing; both can be made a day ahead and refrigerated.

Preheat the oven to 425 degrees. Place a very low rack in a shallow roasting pan.

Rinse the turkey and pat it dry inside and out. Season inside with salt and pepper. Pack the neck cavity loosely with stuffing. Fold the neck skin under the body and fasten it with a skewer. Pack the body cavity loosely with the remaining stuffing. Truss the drumsticks together with kitchen twine. Spread half of the butter over the turkey and season it with salt and pepper. Place the stuffed turkey on the rack in the pan and roast for 25 minutes.

Meanwhile, in a small saucepan, melt the remaining butter with the oil and tangerine juice. Let cool in the pan.

Reduce the oven temperature to 325 degrees. Baste the turkey with the pan juices and drape it with a piece of cheesecloth soaked in the tangerine mixture. Roast the turkey for 1 hour, then baste the turkey (still draped with the cheesecloth) with the tangerine mixture and the pan juices every 20 minutes for 2½ hours more, or until the juices run clear when the fleshy part of a thigh is pricked with a skewer and a meat thermometer inserted there registers 180 to 185 degrees. Remove and discard the cheesecloth and the twine.

Transfer the turkey to a heated platter, reserving the juices in the roasting pan. Let the turkey stand for 25 minutes before carving and spooning out the stuffing into a serving dish. Skim the fat from

to drink

A fruity, young, dry California rosé or Pinot Noir

the pan juices and reserve ¼ cup of the fat. Add 1 cup of the broth to the pan juices and deglaze the pan over high heat, scraping up the brown bits.

In a medium saucepan, whisk together the ¼ cup reserved fat and the flour. Cook over low heat, whisking, for 3 minutes. Add the remaining 2 cups broth and the deglazing liquid and simmer, whisking constantly, for 10 minutes. Strain the gravy through a sieve into a medium bowl. Add the giblets reserved from the broth and transfer to a gravy boat. If you like, garnish the turkey platter with the fresh herbs.

Thanksgiving Menu

We're of the more-is-more school when it comes to Thanksgiving dinner. We think it's not redundant to have both potatoes and stuffing with the turkey, and we'll take as many side dishes as we can comfortably accommodate on the table—any vegetarians will be delighted to see them.

℮

Apricot Thrones with Cheese and Pecans (page 10)

Italian Pumpkin Soup (page 28)
or Roasted Butternut Squash Soup (page 30)

Awesome Tangerine-Glazed Turkey (page 144)

Sausage, Apple, and Dried Cranberry Stuffing (page 148)

Creamy Mashed Potatoes (page 228)

Creamy Anchos and Onions (page 220)

Northeast Kingdom Maple-Glazed Braised Turnips (page 219)

Green Beans with Parsley-Pecan Pesto (page 204)

Garlicky Cranberry Chutney (page 240)
or Cranberry Horseradish Relish (page 242)

℮

Apple and Armagnac Croustade (page 295)

Chocolate-Dipped Pink Grapefruit Rind (page 319)

Turkey Giblet Broth

makes about 3³/₄ cups

Neck, giblets, and liver from a
10-pound turkey
7 cups water
1 celery rib, sliced
1 carrot, peeled and sliced

1 onion, quartered
Zest of 2 tangerines, white pith
removed
1 teaspoon black peppercorns
1 bay leaf

In a large saucepan, combine the neck and giblets (reserve the liver), water, celery, carrot, onion, tangerine zest, peppercorns, and bay leaf. Bring to a boil, reduce the heat to low, and simmer, skimming the froth occasionally, for 1 hour. Add the liver and simmer for 30 minutes more.

Strain the stock through a fine sieve into a medium bowl. Reserve the liver for the stuffing. Reserve the neck and remaining giblets for the gravy. You should have about 3³/₄ cups broth. If there is more, simmer the broth until it is reduced to about 3³/₄ cups; if there is less, add enough water to make 3³/₄ cups. The broth can be made up to 2 days in advance. Let cool completely, uncovered, then refrigerate in an airtight container until ready to use. The broth also can be frozen for up to 3 months.

Sausage, Apple, and Dried Cranberry Stuffing

serves 8; makes 2 quarts

1½ cups ½-inch cubes whole wheat bread

3¾ cups ½-inch cubes potato bread, sourdough bread, or European white bread

1 pound seasoned turkey or pork bulk sausage, crumbled

1 cup diced onion

Olive oil (optional)

¾ cup chopped celery

2½ teaspoons dried sage

1½ teaspoons dried rosemary

½ teaspoon dried thyme

1 medium Golden Delicious apple, cored and chopped

¾ cup chopped dried cranberries or dried apricots

⅓ cup chopped fresh flat-leaf parsley

Reserved cooked turkey liver, diced

¾ cup Turkey Giblet Broth

4 tablespoons (½ stick) unsalted butter, melted

Preheat the oven to 350 degrees.

Arrange the bread cubes on a cookie sheet and bake until evenly golden brown, about 10 minutes. Transfer the toasted bread cubes to a large bowl and let cool.

---

tip

You can make the stuffing a day ahead and store it, covered, in the refrigerator. Bring to room temperature before stuffing the turkey. Don't stuff the turkey ahead of time, however; that could be dangerous. Cook any extra stuffing in a foil-covered casserole dish alongside the turkey.

In a large skillet, cook the sausage and onion (use a little olive oil if the sausage is very lean) over medium heat, stirring and breaking up the lumps, until cooked through. Add the celery, sage, rosemary, and thyme. Cook for 2 minutes, stirring constantly.

Add the sausage mixture to the bread cubes, along with the apples, cranberries or apricots, parsley, and liver and toss well. Drizzle the broth and the butter over the stuffing and toss well. Let cool completely before stuffing the bird.

barbecued turkey hash

COOK

Susan Wyler

SOURCE

Thefoodmaven.com

Once the post-Thanksgiving turkey sandwiches are eaten and the turkey-bits-with-layered-stuffing-and-gravy casserole has been consumed, before the carcass goes into the turkey soup—what do you do with the rest of the leftover turkey? We vote for this terrific barbecued turkey hash—a flexible dish that makes the perfect supper or farewell breakfast when everyone's leaving to go home. The recipe was originally published in a Pennsylvania country cookbook, *Cooking from a Country Farmhouse*.

If you have leftover potatoes, use them here; if not, steam some little red potatoes—don't even bother peeling them. Spice up the barbecue sauce if you like it hot, as we do.

serves 4

4 medium potatoes (about 1¼ pounds)

2 tablespoons olive oil, or more as needed

2 medium onions, coarsely chopped

Salt and freshly ground pepper to taste

2 cups diced cooked turkey

1 cup tangy barbecue sauce

4 large eggs (optional)

In a large saucepan, cover the potatoes with water and bring to a boil. Continue boiling over medium-high heat for 15 to 20 minutes, or until the potatoes are tender and will drop from a knife inserted in the center. Drain in a colander and let sit until cool enough to handle. Peel and cut into ½-inch dice.

In a large ovenproof skillet, preferably cast-iron, heat the olive oil over medium-high heat. Add the onions and cook, stirring often, until softened, about 3 minutes. Add the potatoes, reduce the heat to medium, and cook, turning occasionally with a spatula, until the onions and potatoes are lightly browned, 5 to 7 minutes, adding more olive oil if necessary. Season generously with salt and pepper.

Add the turkey to the skillet and cook, turning with the spatula, until heated through and crispy around the edges, about 5 minutes. Add the barbecue sauce and cook, turning, until mixed well and heated through.

Serve the hash either as is or as follows: Preheat the oven to 400 degrees. Make 4 equidistant indentations on top of the hash with a large spoon, crack an egg into each indentation, and bake for 5 to 7 minutes, or until the eggs are set and the hash is lightly browned on top. Serve immediately.

---

cook's notes

❧ Instead of dicing the turkey, you can simply pull it off the bones.

❧ Instead of oven-poaching the eggs, you can fry them in a skillet and carefully perch one on top of each serving of hash.

twelve-hour roast pork

COOK

Suzanne Somers

SOURCE

Suzanne Somers' Get Skinny on Fabulous Food

A Hollywood diet book isn't the obvious place to look for great recipes, but this one jumped out at us from the pages of *Suzanne Somers' Get Skinny on Fabulous Food*. It's a re-creation of an Italian dish Somers enjoyed at the River Café in London, and it's meltingly delicious.

The recipe requires a little forethought:

You'll need to order the whole pork shoulder in advance from your butcher. And you may end up cooking it day and night—it's done in 12 hours.

Make the most of the pan drippings by making the sauce—unless you're feeding a crowd, you'll have leftovers, and the sauce will come into its own when you reheat them.

serves 12

1 7-to-9-pound pork shoulder
    with skin (see note,
    page 154)
12 garlic cloves, finely chopped
3 tablespoons fennel seeds
8 small dried red chiles,
    crumbled
    Salt and freshly ground pepper
    to taste

Juice of 6 lemons
1/4 cup olive oil

PAN DRIPPINGS
1 14-ounce can chicken broth
    Juice of 2 lemons (optional)

Preheat the oven to 450 degrees.

to drink
Chianti

best american recipes 2000

Score the pork shoulder all over by slicing deeply into the skin, making cuts ¼ inch apart.

In a food processor or by hand, chop the garlic, fennel seeds, chiles, and salt and pepper until coarsely ground. Rub this mixture all over the pork and into the cuts.

Place the pork on a rack in a roasting pan and roast for 30 minutes, or until the skin begins to crackle and brown. Loosen the shoulder from the bottom of the pan and pour half the lemon juice and 2 tablespoons of the olive oil over the pork.

Reduce the oven temperature to 250 degrees and roast the pork for 12 hours more, basting occasionally with the remaining lemon juice and the remaining 2 tablespoons olive oil, until it's completely soft under the skin. Push it with your finger; it should give and may even fall off the bone.

FOR THE PAN DRIPPINGS

Remove the roast from the pan and spoon off all but 3 tablespoons of the fat from the drippings. Place the pan on the stovetop over medium heat and scrape up all the browned bits stuck to the bot-

serve with

Apricot Thrones with Cheese and Pecans (page 10)

Creamy Mashed Potatoes (page 228), made with the optional garlic and smoked Spanish paprika

Kale sautéed in olive oil with garlic

Watermelon Salsa (page 238)

℔

Texas Lemon Bombe (page 260)

main dishes

tom. When the juices are hot, add the broth and lemon juice (but taste the drippings first; you may not need more lemon), continuing to scrape the pan and reduce the juices for about 5 minutes, or until you have a sauce consistency.

Serve each person a little of the crisp skin along with the meat and pass the pan drippings separately.

---

cook's notes

❧ You'll most likely need to order the pork shoulder (butt) ahead. Unless you have an Italian, Chinese, or Mexican butcher, the idea of a pork shoulder with skin on may draw a complete blank. If you're offered a picnic ham with skin—that is, the forearm—just say no; that meat is sinewy and won't have the same lusciousness as the shoulder. There are two other options: the butcher can take the skin off a fresh ham and wrap it around the butt, or you can just forget about the skin and simply wrap the meat in oiled foil once the initial browning takes place. Don't worry about the basting in that case; just skip it. The meat will brown under the foil, and it will be moist and delicious.

❧ Almost surely you'll have leftovers, which are great for sandwiches, to fold into hot tortillas with some salsa, or to cook with hash browns.

roasted sausages and grapes

COOK

Johanne Killeen

SOURCE

A Celebration of Women Chefs,
edited by Julie Stillman

With her husband, George Germon, Johanne Killeen has been cooking superlative rustic but sophisticated Italian dishes for over twenty years at their Providence restaurant, Al Forno. This traditional Tuscan harvest dish is a good example of their sublimely satisfying food: rich spicy sausages, sweet tannic grapes (we like the red ones best here) roasted to bring out their character, and balsamic vinegar to pull it all together. It's also great no-fuss home food, ready in a matter of minutes.

Germon and Killeen serve this dish with coarsely mashed new potatoes, enriched with a little butter and cream, and we wouldn't dream of serving it without them.

serves 6 to 8

1½ pounds hot Italian sausages
1½ pounds sweet Italian sausages
3 tablespoons unsalted butter
6–7 cups (2½ pounds) seedless red or green grapes, stemmed

¼ cup balsamic vinegar

Al Forno's Mashed Potatoes (page 157)

Preheat the oven to 500 degrees.

In a large saucepan, cover the sausages with water and parboil for 8 minutes to rid them of excess fat.

Melt the butter in a large, flameproof roasting pan. Add the grapes and toss to coat.

to drink
Regaleali's
Rosso del Conte

main dishes

Using tongs, transfer the sausages to the roasting pan and push them down into the grapes so that they don't brown too quickly. Roast, turning the sausages once, for 20 to 25 minutes, or until the grapes are soft and the sausages are browned. With a slotted spoon, transfer the sausages and grapes to a heated serving platter.

Place the roasting pan on the stovetop over medium-high heat. Add the vinegar, scraping up any browned bits on the bottom of the pan. Reduce the vinegar and juices until they are thick and syrupy. Pour the sauce over the sausages and grapes and serve immediately, accompanied by Al Forno's Mashed Potatoes.

Al Forno's Mashed Potatoes

serves 6

2 pounds small red potatoes,
   quartered

1/2 cup heavy cream

8 tablespoons (1 stick) unsalted
   butter, softened

1 teaspoon salt, or to taste

In a large saucepan, cover the potatoes with 1 inch of water. Bring to a boil, reduce the heat to low, and simmer until the potatoes are soft, about 15 minutes.

Drain and return the potatoes to the saucepan. Over low heat, coarsely mash the potatoes with a potato masher or two large forks, gradually adding the cream and butter. Stir in the salt and serve.

bubba's bunch championship ribs

COOKS

Bubba's Bunch

SOURCE

Weber Grills Barbecue booklet

Not hot and spicy sauced ribs, these are unusual spareribs—bright, clean, tender, and tangy from a lemon juice and vinegar soak. Because they are not sauced, they can be eaten with just about anything, in summer or winter.

Bubba's Bunch, an amateur group of grillers, won first place in the Patio Porkers division of the Memphis in May World Championship Barbecue Cooking Contest with this decidedly different rib recipe, which Weber, the grill company, published in a little booklet.

Aside from the recipe's easy-to-make virtues, we're extremely taken with the way the vinegar soak pulls out every last bit of succulence from the pork, making these ribs mighty tasty. The grilling method adapts easily to an indoor oven, and the marinade works with any kind of pork ribs. It can be used with "back ribs" (meaty ribs cut from high on the rib and generally the most expensive); spareribs (cut from the belly or side, longer and more fatty than back ribs); or "country-style" ribs (made by splitting the blade end of the loin).

If you're flummoxed by the "4 slabs St. Louis–style pork spareribs" called for, not to worry: These are, according to Weber, "a square rib trimmed to remove the flap of meat on the underside of the breast bone, and squared off to more easily fit on the grill." Regular old spareribs sold in a rack will do just fine. The rack can be cut into individual ribs before marinating, and the marinade is sufficient for about 5 pounds.

For the dry rub, Bubba's Bunch uses Willingham's WHAM (available by calling 800-737-WHAM). We use whatever we favor at the moment (see, for example, Memphis Rub on page 119) or one of the innumerable brands now sold in supermarkets and specialty stores. You also might try mixing a mild rub with a very hot one.

serves 4

4 slabs St. Louis–style pork spareribs (see headnote)

1/3 cup fresh lemon juice

1/3 cup apple cider vinegar

2/3 cup water

3 tablespoons lemon-pepper blend

1/4 cup Willingham's WHAM (without salt) Dry Rub or your favorite barbecue rub

If using St. Louis–style pork spareribs, insert a sharp knife between the membrane and the bone on a corner of the back side of the ribs and pull the membrane loose, using your hands. Place the ribs in a single layer in a nonreactive pan.

In a small bowl, combine the lemon juice, vinegar, and water and pour over the ribs, turning them so they are coated and pressing them down into the liquid. Sprinkle the lemon-pepper blend evenly over the ribs. Cover and refrigerate for 4 to 6 hours or overnight. Remove the ribs from the marinade; rub evenly with the dry rub.

To barbecue, place the ribs in the center of the cooking grate, cover, and cook over a slow fire (250 degrees) for 2 to 3 hours, or until the meat pulls away from the bones.

---

serve with

Macaroni Gratin (page 236)

Avocado, Jicama, and Watercress Salad (page 53) or Spicy Coleslaw (page 58)

℘

Double-Chocolate Layer Cake (page 314)

to drink

An Alsatian Pinot Gris or beer

tom valenti's braised lamb shanks
with white bean puree

COOK

Tom Valenti

SOURCE

Kitchen Suppers,
by Alison Becker Hurt

When braised lamb shanks became a fashionable entrée on Manhattan menus, the competition became stiff: Whose were meatier, more succulent, more mouthwateringly irresistible? Again and again, the answer was "those fabulous lamb shanks at Alison on Dominick," a downtown restaurant owned by Alison Becker Hurt. The chef, Tom Valenti, buried the shanks in chopped vegetables, wine, broth, and chopped plum tomatoes and braised them slowly until the meat was tender and toothsome.

Now that the full recipe has been published in Hurt's cookbook, another small secret is revealed: there are anchovy fillets in the sauce —which may be what takes these shanks over the top; you don't taste any anchovy, just beautifully rounded flavor. The White Bean Puree and the sauce with which they are served are as good as the shanks.

Although the original recipe calls for ten lamb shanks to serve six, we have used six shanks without changing the rest of the ingredients. This is purely practical: Six shanks are about the most that can fit in our largest roasting pan.

Use a nonreactive pan, such as a nonstick or enamel-coated pan.

serves 6

6 lamb shanks
   Salt and freshly ground pepper
   to taste
½ cup olive oil
½ bunch celery, cut into medium
   slices
2 carrots, peeled and cut into
   medium slices
1 large onion, diced
5 garlic cloves, crushed
3 cups dry red wine

2 bay leaves
6 anchovy fillets
2 cups veal broth or chicken
   broth
2 32-ounce cans Italian plum
   tomatoes, drained and
   crushed
20 black or green peppercorns

5 cups White Bean Puree
   (page 162)

Preheat the oven to 325 degrees. Place a rack at the lower-middle level.

Season the shanks with salt and pepper. In a large skillet, heat the olive oil over medium-high heat. Brown the shanks in batches on all sides, 15 to 20 minutes. As they brown, transfer the shanks to the largest roasting pan that will fit in your oven and set aside.

Add the celery, carrots, onion, and garlic to the skillet and cook for 30 seconds, being careful not to burn any particles that have stuck to the skillet. Pour 1½ cups of the wine into the skillet and scrape up any browned bits from the bottom. Add the wine mixture and the remaining ingredients and the remaining 1½ cups wine except the White Bean Puree to the roasting pan with the shanks.

Place the roasting pan on the stovetop over medium heat and bring to a simmer. (The shanks should be almost covered with liquid. If necessary, add some water.) Cover the pan with foil, transfer it to the oven, and cook until the meat is very tender, 2½ to 3 hours. Remove the shanks from the liquid and keep warm. Strain the liquid, transfer it to a medium saucepan, bring to a boil, and reduce for 5 to 10 minutes, or until it has the consistency of maple syrup.

Serve the lamb shanks with the sauce on top of the puree.

---

serve with

A sharp winter greens salad

℘

Chocolate Bread Pudding (page 292)

to drink

Cabernet Sauvignon or Merlot

White Bean Puree

This silky puree is a must-serve with the lamb shanks, but it is also an all-around lovely side dish for any entrée with which you might ordinarily serve mashed potatoes. It makes a great dip, too, served warm or at room temperature. Just add raw vegetables or toasted pita bread.

serves 6 to 12

2 pounds dried Great Northern beans

6 cups canned chicken broth, or more as needed (see note)

1 cup white wine

4 garlic cloves: 3 crushed and 1 finely minced

3–4 thyme sprigs or a pinch of dried thyme

2 bay leaves

Salt and freshly ground pepper to taste

1 cup olive oil

1–2 tablespoons butter (optional)

In a large pot, cover the beans with water by 2 inches and soak at room temperature for at least several hours, preferably overnight, changing the water three or four times. Drain.

---

cook's notes

❧ Gourmet stores sell high-quality veal broth. If it's available, by all means use it. Otherwise, a good low-sodium commercial chicken broth is fine.

❧ The bean puree recipe makes loads of beans, about twice as much as you'll need for the lamb shanks. But that's good news: Use the leftovers as a dip or thin them with broth to make a soup.

In a large saucepan, combine the broth, wine, crushed garlic, thyme, bay leaves, and salt and pepper, and bring to a simmer. Cook until the beans are very tender, about 1 hour and 40 minutes. Add a little more chicken broth or water if the liquid is absorbed before the beans are tender.

Puree the beans in a food processor, adding the olive oil slowly and then adding the minced garlic to taste. If the puree seems too thick, fold in a tablespoon or two of butter. (The puree can be made up to 1 day in advance, covered, refrigerated, and gently reheated before serving.) Serve hot.

kashmiri-style leg of lamb

COOK

Cynthia R. Topliss

SOURCE

The Stonyfield Farm Yogurt Cookbook, by Meg Cadoux Hirshberg

This classic Moghul lamb recipe is one you'll make again and again once you try it. The delicate, fragrant seasonings subtly penetrate the lamb, and the yogurt gives it a tender, unctuous quality that's distinctive. All the work—which is so minimal it shouldn't really be called work—is done ahead, so all you have to do is roast the lamb on the day you serve it.

serves 6 to 8

1 5-pound leg of lamb

SPICE MIXTURE

2 tablespoons fresh lemon juice
1 tablespoon grated peeled fresh gingerroot
4 garlic cloves, crushed in a press
1 teaspoon salt
1 teaspoon ground cumin
1 teaspoon ground turmeric
1/2 teaspoon freshly ground pepper
1/2 teaspoon ground cinnamon

1/2 teaspoon ground cardamom
1/2 teaspoon dried ground chile
1/4 teaspoon ground cloves

YOGURT MIXTURE

1 cup plain yogurt
2 tablespoons blanched slivered almonds
2 tablespoons chopped pistachios
1 tablespoon ground turmeric

1 tablespoon honey

Remove any excess fat from the lamb. Using the point of a sharp knife, make deep slits all over the leg. Place the lamb in a large non-reactive dish.

FOR THE SPICE MIXTURE
In a small bowl, combine all the ingredients.

Rub the spice mixture over the lamb, pressing it into the slits.

FOR THE YOGURT MIXTURE

In a food processor or blender, thoroughly blend the yogurt, nuts, and turmeric. Spread over the lamb. Drizzle the honey over the lamb, cover, and marinate for one day in the refrigerator, turning occasionally.

Preheat the oven to 450 degrees.

Transfer the lamb to a roasting pan, cover (aluminum foil is fine), and cook for 30 minutes. Reduce the oven temperature to 350 degrees and cook for $1^3/_4$ hours more, or until meltingly tender. Uncover and serve warm or at room temperature.

---

cook's notes

- You can use a boned leg of lamb, which will make it easier to serve.
- A lovely touch—from a similar recipe in Jennifer Brennan's *One-Dish Meals of Asia*—is to add 10 saffron threads to the yogurt mixture. Soak them for 10 minutes in 2 tablespoons warm water before adding them.
- An easy way to marinate the lamb is in a large zipper-lock plastic bag. Marinating for 2 or even 3 days will deliver an even more flavorful piece of meat. Just be sure to turn it every now and then to redistribute the marinade.

serve with

Rich Red Pepper Soup (page 26)
Saffron rice
Spinach cooked in butter with dried currants

Lemon Sorbet with Apricot-Pistachio Bars (page 310)

to drink

A dry Sémillon Blanc

bodacious porterhouse steaks
with sexy barbecue sauce

First of all, if you're cooking two huge porterhouse steaks on the grill, that's bodacious all by itself. Many aficionados think this is the best steak of all, with the marbled strip of sirloin on one side of the bone and the supple tenderloin on the other. If it's an aged porterhouse, so much the better. And try to get them with their tails, which are usually removed before these steaks hit the supermarket.

COOK

Anonymous

SOURCE

Weber's Art of the Grill,
by Jamie Purviance

Truth be told, this is such a superlative steak that it needs nothing but perhaps a little olive oil and a rub with a cut garlic clove, plus the usual salt and pepper. The truly sexy barbecue sauce is served on the side, so you can choose how much you want to use on the steaks. The sauce is delicious, no question, and it's just as good on chicken or burgers.

serves 4

BARBECUE SAUCE

- ½ cup water
- ½ cup dry red wine
- ½ cup ketchup
- ¼ cup dark molasses
- 2 tablespoons red wine vinegar
- 1 tablespoon Dijon mustard
- 1 tablespoon Worcestershire sauce
- ½ teaspoon chili powder
- ½ teaspoon kosher salt
- ½ teaspoon celery seeds
- ¼ teaspoon curry powder
- ¼ teaspoon ground cumin

STEAKS

- 2 2-pound porterhouse steaks (about 1½ inches thick), at room temperature
- Vegetable oil
- Salt and freshly ground pepper to taste

FOR THE SAUCE

In a medium saucepan, combine all the ingredients and mix well. Bring to a simmer over medium heat and cook, stirring occasionally, until about ²/₃ cup remains, about 30 minutes. Let cool to room temperature.

FOR THE STEAKS

Prepare the grill for direct high heat. Lightly brush both sides of the steaks with the oil and season generously with salt and pepper. Grill the first side of the steaks directly over high heat for 6 minutes. Turn the steaks over and cook the second side for 5 minutes. Continue cooking until the steaks reach the desired doneness.

Remove the steaks from the grill and season again with salt and pepper. Let rest for 3 to 5 minutes, during which time the internal temperature will rise about 5 degrees. You can serve the steaks whole or cut the sirloin strips and tenderloins away from the bones, then cut the meat into ¼-inch-thick slices. Serve warm with the barbecue sauce on the side.

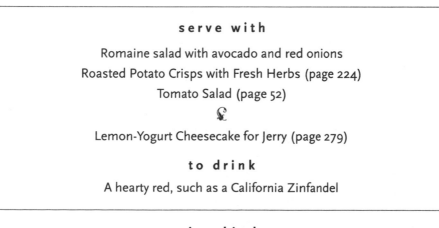

serve with

Romaine salad with avocado and red onions
Roasted Potato Crisps with Fresh Herbs (page 224)
Tomato Salad (page 52)

℘

Lemon-Yogurt Cheesecake for Jerry (page 279)

to drink

A hearty red, such as a California Zinfandel

beer-braised short ribs

When the weather outside is frightful—or even when it's just bleak and you need a little consoling—there's nothing like short ribs to cheer everyone at the table. These especially succulent ribs come from *Snow Country Cooking,* and they're the work of the California cook Diane Rossen Worthington. All the elements are very simple (there's not so

COOK

Diane Rossen Worthington

SOURCE

Snow Country Cooking

much as an herb or a spice here), and we think it's the beer that brings them all together so satisfyingly. Be sure to use a richly flavored beer that's not bitter—Heineken or Sierra Nevada would be a good choice.

For the best taste, make the ribs a day ahead and discard the fat that rises to the top before reheating.

serves 6

5 pounds lean meaty beef short ribs, cut into 3-to-4-inch pieces
  Salt and freshly ground pepper to taste
2–3 tablespoons vegetable oil
3 large onions, cut into thick rings

4 medium carrots, peeled and cut into ½-inch slices
4 garlic cloves, finely chopped
1½ cups beer (see headnote)
1 cup canned crushed tomatoes
1 teaspoon Dijon mustard
  Bottled horseradish cream

In a large bowl or a large zipper-lock plastic bag, season the ribs all over with salt and pepper.

---

cook's note

To brown the ribs using less fat, season them with salt and pepper, then roast on a rack in a preheated 450-degree oven for about 10 minutes, turning once during the cooking.

Preheat the oven to 325 degrees.

In a large, nonstick skillet, heat 2 tablespoons oil over medium-high heat. Brown the ribs on all sides in batches, turning with tongs, 7 to 10 minutes per batch. Remove the ribs with a slotted spoon and drain briefly on paper towels. Place the ribs in a large Dutch oven or heavy flameproof casserole.

In the large skillet, add the remaining 1 tablespoon oil, if needed, to brown the vegetables. Increase the heat to medium-high and sauté the onions for 7 to 10 minutes, or until browned, stirring frequently and watching carefully so that they do not burn.

Add the carrots and sauté for 2 to 3 minutes more, or until softened. Add the garlic and cook for 1 minute more. Add the beer, tomatoes, and mustard. Increase the heat to high and simmer for 1 minute to blend the flavors. Pour the tomato mixture over the short ribs and mix thoroughly.

Bake the ribs, covered, for 2½ to 3 hours, or until the meat is very tender, turning the ribs every 45 minutes. Season with salt and pepper. These are best made a day ahead, refrigerated, degreased, and reheated. Serve with horseradish cream on the side.

---

serve with

Creamy Mashed Potatoes (page 228)
A big green salad

℘

Very Spicy Caramel Pears (page 284)

to drink
The beer you used in the cooking

high-temperature rib roast of beef

This unique way of cooking perfect roast beef has achieved cult status. No elaborate set of instructions, no annotated treatise on the art of roasting, has ever matched this simple formula.

The recipe first appeared over twenty years ago, in an article Craig Claiborne wrote in the *New York Times* about Ann Seranne, a food professional whom he called "an innovative genius in the kitchen."

In that article, Claiborne published five or six recipes of Seranne's. While all of them became beloved standbys, this is the one people remember best. As the original printed recipe became harder and harder to find, we've gotten calls—at least 15 in the past decade alone—asking, "Do you have that recipe for the high-heat roast beef?" By

COOK

Ann Seranne

SOURCE

The Best of Craig Claiborne,
by Craig Claiborne
with Pierre Franey,
edited by Joan Whitman

some miracle of timing, the recipe has been restored to print in this new collection.

The roast will be in the hot oven (make sure your oven is well insulated; see note) for only 25 to 60 minutes, depending on its size. But start at least 5 hours before you want to serve it, which will allow time for the roast to reach room temperature and to finish cooking in the turned-off oven. It will have a crunchy brown exterior and will be perfectly cooked inside to that medium-rare state that most people prefer. Center slices will be rare.

The infallible formula has another bonus: Once out of the oven, the roast can wait at room temperature, and retain its internal heat, for up to four hours before serving. While it is resting comfortably, the oven is freed up for whatever else you

---

cook's notes

≋ Don't attempt this recipe if your oven isn't well insulated—that is, if it is extremely hot to the touch on the outside when it's in use. (Most commercial ovens are not well insulated, which is why restaurant kitchens are so hot.)

≋ The most delicious—and most expensive—roast will be a dry-aged roast, which has to be ordered from a quality butcher well ahead of time.

want to make. We hope one of those things will be Yorkshire Pudding (see page 173).

The crucial instruction is not to open the oven door, not even for a peek, while the roast is in there. Trust us: It is doing beautifully undisturbed.

serves 4 to 8; each rib serves 2

1 2-to-4-rib roast of beef (4½–12 pounds), short ribs removed

All-purpose flour

Salt and freshly ground pepper to taste

½–1 cup beef broth

Remove the roast from the refrigerator 2½ to 4 hours before cooking, the longer time for the largest roast.

Preheat the oven to 500 degrees.

Place the roast in a large, shallow roasting pan, fat side up. Sprinkle with a little flour, rubbing it into the fat lightly. Season with salt and pepper. Put the roast in the oven and bake according to the chart below, timing exactly. When the cooking time is up, turn off the oven. Do not open the door at any time. Leave the roast in the oven

---

Roasting Chart

Weight (without Short Ribs)	Roast at 500 degrees
4½–5 pounds	25–30 minutes
8–9 pounds	40–45 minutes
11–12 pounds	55–60 minutes

This works out to be about 15 minutes per rib, or approximately 5 minutes cooking time per pound of trimmed, ready-to-cook roast.

If you prefer medium-to-well-done beef, add 10 minutes to the maximum cooking time for each size roast.

---

main dishes

until the oven is lukewarm, about 2 hours. If you need to use the oven to cook something else, tent the roast loosely with foil to keep it warm and remove it from the oven.

To make a thin pan gravy, remove the excess fat from the meat drippings, leaving any meat pieces in the pan. Stir in the beef broth. Bring to a boil, scraping the bottom of the pan to loosen the meat pieces. Simmer for 1 minute and season to taste. Serve hot.

---

serve with

Radish and Goat Cheese Wreath (page 3)
Cream of Celery Root with Shrimp Butter (page 46)
Yorkshire Pudding (page 173)
Baked Fennel with Gorgonzola (page 212)
Watercress and endive salad sprinkled with pomegranate seeds

❧

Port Wine Grapes (page 212)
Stilton cheese and crackers with aged port

to drink

Cabernet Sauvignon or a big California Pinot Noir
from the Carneros region

Yorkshire Pudding

serves 8

1 cup all-purpose flour
1 cup milk
⅛ teaspoon freshly grated
    nutmeg

4 large eggs
½ cup beef drippings from the
    roast (see note)

Preheat the oven to 425 degrees.

In a medium bowl, combine the flour, milk, and nutmeg. In a small bowl, beat the eggs until frothy. Add to the milk and stir just until blended.

---

cook's notes

❧ We add salt—about ½ teaspoon—to the flour mixture.

❧ If your beef drippings are less than ½ cup, add bacon grease or melted butter to make up the difference.

Pour the drippings into a flameproof 9-by-12-inch baking dish and place on the stovetop over medium heat or put in the oven. When it is hot and almost smoking, add the batter. Smooth it with a rubber spatula. Place the pudding in the oven and bake for about 15 minutes, or until well puffed and golden brown. For even cooking, turn the baking dish as the cooking proceeds. Serve with the roast beef.

> **tip**
>
> Yorkshire Pudding actually improves if it's left in the refrigerator for several hours (or in the freezer for half an hour), so it's a great idea to make it ahead. Leave the batter a little lumpy and pour it cold into the hot beef drippings in the baking dish for the best puff.

shrimp and corn with basil

COOK
Gourmet magazine staff

SOURCE
Gourmet

In corn season, there are never enough ways to enjoy this toothsome vegetable. Here's an incredibly simple, lively, Americanized version of a Chinese stir-fry that's great for a rainy evening or the day when yet another corn on the cob seems too much. This is a minimalist recipe from *Gourmet* magazine's "Everyday" column, one of those perfectly balanced, satisfying meals you'll make again and again because it's just so good and so simple.

serves 2

2 tablespoons (¼ stick) unsalted butter
Kernels from 2 ears corn
½ pound shelled large shrimp

4 scallions, chopped
¼ cup thinly sliced fresh basil leaves
Salt and freshly ground pepper to taste

In a large nonstick skillet, melt the butter over medium-high heat. Add the corn and shrimp and sauté, stirring, until the shrimp are pink and cooked through, 3 to 5 minutes. Stir in the scallions and basil and season with salt and pepper. Serve immediately.

---

serve with

Tomato Salad (page 52)

℘

Plum and Raspberry Sorbet (page 264)
Zante Currant Cookies (page 300)

to drink

A dry, young Chenin Blanc

---

main dishes

grilled shrimp
or scallops, basque style

COOK

Davis Morgan

SOURCE

*Atlanta
Journal-Constitution*

If the shrimp and scallops are high quality, as they increasingly seem to be, this mix of quickly grilled shellfish tossed in a bath of lemon juice, fresh herbs, and olive oil offers pure, unadulterated flavor. Add pasta or rice or orzo and there, in about 15 minutes, is a sumptuous dinner.

As might be expected, the recipe is from a real person, not a chef. It's the creation of Davis Morgan, an Atlanta resident who was a featured cook in the weekly "Georgia Home Cooks" column in the *Atlanta Journal-Constitution*.

serves 4

½ cup plus 2 tablespoons extra-virgin olive oil

⅓ cup fresh lemon juice (about 2½ lemons), or more to taste

¼–½ teaspoon hot red pepper sauce, or to taste

½ cup coarsely chopped mixed fresh herbs, such as parsley, sage, thyme, basil, marjoram, oregano, and/or chervil

1 tablespoon minced garlic
Salt and freshly ground pepper to taste

1½ pounds sea scallops or large or extra-large shrimp (peeled and deveined, if desired), or a combination of both

---

to drink
Verdicchio or Vernaccia di
San Gimignano

Prepare a medium-hot charcoal fire or preheat a gas grill. Make sure the grill rack is very clean and place it as close to the heat source as possible.

In a large serving bowl, combine the ½ cup olive oil, lemon juice, hot pepper sauce, herbs, garlic, and salt and pepper. Set aside.

In a medium bowl, toss the scallops and/or shrimp with the remaining 2 tablespoons olive oil.

Place the scallops and/or shrimp on the grill as close to the heat as possible. Turn the shrimp after the first side becomes pink, 2 to 3 minutes; turn the scallops when the first side becomes opaque, about 3 minutes. Grill until the second side is pink or opaque; test one piece by cutting into it to make sure it is cooked through.

Add the hot shellfish to the herb mixture. Toss gently and serve immediately.

serve with

Rice or orzo

Savannah Salad with Avocado Dressing (page 50)

℘

Ginger-Mascarpone Icebox Cake (page 286)

main dishes

skillet-roasted mussels

COOK

Reed Hearon

SOURCE

The Rose Pistola Cookbook,
**by Reed Hearon and
Peggy Knickerbocker**

Here is an almost sure bet: Cook mussels this way once, and you will never cook them any other way again. Simply sizzled in a very hot skillet, without any liquid to dilute their flavor, the shells open, releasing their liquid, and the mussels themselves become smoky and intense, almost meaty. They are divine. And at $2 a pound, mussels are still one of the sea's best buys.

Serve with melted butter so that you can pull each mussel out of its shell with a fork and dip it into the butter, and then pop it into your mouth.

The recipe is from a compilation of the dishes served at Rose Pistola, Reed Hearon's acclaimed Italian/Mediterranean restaurant in the old North Beach section of San Francisco. Built around what seems like a city block of wood-burning ovens, the restaurant is long, lean, and stylish. The food is direct and hearty, tweaked up slightly from its mainly Mediterranean origins.

The skillet-roasted mussels at Rose Pistola are cooked over a fire in a *plancha*—a flat cast-iron griddle. These are available in stores where restaurant supplies are sold (or from The Spanish Table, 206-682-2827), but a 10- or 12-inch cast-iron skillet will do just fine.

serves 2

1 pound mussels, scrubbed and
debearded
Salt and freshly cracked pepper
to taste

4 tablespoons (½ stick) unsalted
butter, melted

to drink
A dry Chardonnay, such as
Saint-Véran or Macon

best american recipes 2000

Heat a *plancha* or a large cast-iron skillet over high heat (or over a hot wood fire) until it is extremely hot: When a bead of water dances across the surface and the pan is almost white, it's ready. Spread the mussels in a single layer in the pan: The heat will cause the mussels to open.

The mussel juices will first pool and then burn on the surface of the pan, at which point they are ready to serve. Total cooking time should be 4 to 5 minutes.

Season the mussels generously with salt and pepper and serve from the pan at the table, with the melted butter on the side.

---

serve with

Roasted Black and Green Olives with Whole Garlic (page 8)

Oven-Roasted Canned Tomatoes (page 214)

Creamy Mashed Potatoes (page 228), made with the optional garlic and smoked Spanish paprika

Purslane Salad with Baby Greens and Cabbage (page 54)

℘

Chocolate Mousse with Olive Oil (page 290)

---

slow-roasted salmon

COOK

James O'Shea

SOURCE

Jane Ellis, *House Beautiful*

The idea of slow roasting salmon is a brilliant one. And we know of no more brilliant version than this one from Irish chef James O'Shea, proprietor of the West Street Grill in Litchfield, Connecticut. James got this idea from his Irish mother, who was loath to let the warm oven in her kitchen go to waste once she'd finished her baking, and so put in a bit of salmon to cook in the fading heat.

James embroiders this idea with a rub of olive oil to bring up the flavor and a coat of minced chives, gently pressed into the salmon's flesh. The result, documented in *House Beautiful,* is a sensationally good salmon, delicate and perfectly cooked in just a few minutes — with no fishy aroma in the kitchen.

Once you cook salmon this way, you'll think twice about doing it any other way — it's that good and that easy.

serves 8

8 ¹/₂-pound wild Irish or Atlantic salmon fillets with skin, at room temperature (see tip)
Extra-virgin olive oil
1 cup finely minced fresh chives

Salt and freshly ground white pepper to taste
Sage sprigs, for garnish

---

serve with

New potato salad with fresh dill and sour cream
Tomato Salad (page 52)
Sourdough bread

℘

Rhubarb Soup (page 268)

to drink

Sauvignon Blanc from New Zealand or California

Preheat the oven to 250 degrees.

Lightly brush the flesh side of the salmon fillets with olive oil. Completely cover the fillets with the chives and gently press into the flesh. Season with salt and white pepper.

Place the fillets skin side down on a nonstick or lightly oiled, foil-lined cookie sheet. Roast for exactly 17 minutes. Place the fillets in a serving dish. Serve at room temperature, garnished with sage sprigs.

---

tip

James O'Shea has a clever trick to make farmed salmon taste more like its wild cousins. He wraps it in dried kelp (available in natural food stores) — which is a bit like wrapping it in newspaper — and leaves it overnight in the refrigerator under a small weight, such as a full carton of eggs. The briny flavor of the sea goes right into the fish. Discard the kelp and bring the salmon to room temperature before cooking it.

cook's note

James feels very strongly about his salt. He always uses the best, fleur de sel, if it's available. His source is the Grain and Salt Society: (800) 867-7258.

snapper fillets baked in salt

COOK

Michele Anna Jordan

SOURCE

Salt and Pepper

We've always loved the idea of cooking food in salt —an ancient idea that seals in natural flavors and juices without making the food itself the least bit salty, oddly enough.

Fish—whole or fillets—cooked in salt is in some sense returned to its ocean medium. In this Middle Eastern–flavored dish, the fillets are seasoned with cumin and cayenne and then tucked inside grape leaves, which contribute both flavor and a fuss-free element: you don't have to brush off the excess salt that would otherwise cling to the fish.

These elegant little fillets are fragrant and especially delicious—they're also perfectly cooked, moist, and tender.

serves 6

2 teaspoons crushed black peppercorns	¹/₂ cup water
1 teaspoon ground cumin	2 large egg whites
¹/₂ teaspoon cayenne pepper	12 large brine-packed grape leaves
6 6-ounce red snapper fillets	2 lemons, cut into wedges, for serving
3–4 pounds rock salt or kosher salt	

Preheat the oven to 400 degrees.

> **cook's note**
> You could include some cilantro sprigs inside the grape leaves. You also could substitute seaweed or a bed of herbs for the grape leaves.

In a small bowl, combine the peppercorns, cumin, and cayenne; sprinkle over both sides of each fish fillet. In a large bowl, mix the salt, water, and egg whites into a loose, sticky paste. Spread half of the salt paste on a cookie sheet in a layer about ³/₄ inch thick.

Rinse the grape leaves under running water for 2 minutes and dry thoroughly. Place a layer of 6 leaves down the center of the salt layer and arrange the fillets on top. Cover the fish with the remaining 6 leaves and spread the remaining salt paste over the top, completely burying the fish and grape leaves.

Bake for about 20 minutes, or until the fish is done when an instant-read thermometer registers 130 degrees. Let the fish rest for 5 to 10 minutes. Carefully break apart the salt crust and extract the fish fillets. Serve with the lemon wedges.

---

serve with

Roasted Eggplant Dip
(page 2)

Rice pilaf

Green salad with cilantro
and dill

❦

Melon

Apricot-Pistachio Bars
(page 310)

to drink

A crisp, dry rosé
or Sauvignon Blanc

mediterranean seafood stew

COOK

Jacques Pépin

SOURCE

*Julia and Jacques
Cooking at Home,*
by Julia Child and
Jacques Pépin

Gourmands get into all kinds of fierce arguments about what does and doesn't go into a proper bouillabaisse, the celestial fish soup of the French Mediterranean coast. But the fact is, the frugal French use what's available and looking good at the market. And that's the principle Jacques Pépin has used in creating this extremely simple, endlessly versatile soup that's a meal in itself. Like bouillabaisse, this soup features both saffron and rouille (roo-EE), the exhilarating garlicky mayonnaise that's the color of rust, for which it's named.

Once you have the soup base put together, which can be done ahead of time, the fish cooks very briefly —in fact, it's essential not to overcook it.

As Julia Child points out, the soup base is so good—especially if you let it cook for a long time, about 45 minutes—that you don't even need the fish; potatoes are just as good in this terrific base.

Whatever you do, don't skip the rouille—it's the soul of this dish.

serves 6

1½ pounds fish fillets, such as cod, hake, halibut, red snapper, or sea bass, or a combination of 2 or 3 different fish

1½ pounds small clams, such as littlenecks or cherrystones

½ pound scallops

CROUTONS

24 ¼-inch-thick baguette slices, cut on the diagonal

SOUP BASE

3 tablespoons olive oil

1½ cups chopped onions

5 large scallions (white and green parts), thinly sliced

1 tablespoon chopped garlic

2 cups fresh or canned tomatoes (about 1 pound fresh tomatoes), cored and cut into ½-inch chunks, with skin, juice, and seeds

4 cups fish stock or 2 cups clam
   juice and 2 cups water
1 cup white wine, such as
   Chardonnay
1 teaspoon chopped fresh thyme
½ teaspoon salt, or to taste
½ teaspoon freshly ground
   pepper

¼ cup canned pimiento pieces
¼ cup broth from the soup base
1 large egg yolk
¾–1 cup olive oil
½ teaspoon salt, or to taste
⅛ teaspoon freshly ground
   pepper
⅛ teaspoon cayenne pepper,
   or to taste

ROUILLE

1 slice firm home-style white
   bread, torn into small pieces
6–8 large garlic cloves
⅓ cup cooked potato (1 small
   potato)

1 teaspoon saffron threads,
   or to taste
1½ tablespoons chopped fresh
   tarragon leaves

Skin the fish fillets, if you wish, and cut them into even chunks about 1 inch thick (if you leave the skin on, be sure it has been scaled). Scrub the clams and rinse, if necessary. Rinse the scallops to remove any sand.

---

cook's notes

❧ There are some shortcuts to this recipe: We like to use the clam juice alternative, the excellent diced canned tomatoes made by Muir Glen, and, in a pinch, rouille in a jar from the gourmet store.

❧ We like this soup best made with small shrimp instead of clams. Add them at the last minute and cook just until pink.

FOR THE CROUTONS

Preheat the oven to 400 degrees. Toast the baguette slices on a cookie sheet until they are crisp and starting to color on both sides, about 10 minutes. Set aside.

FOR THE SOUP BASE

In a large saucepan, heat the oil and sauté the onion, scallions, and garlic over medium heat until soft, about 5 minutes.

Add the tomatoes, fish stock or diluted clam juice, wine, thyme, salt, and pepper. Bring to a boil. Taste and adjust the seasonings. Cook at a gentle boil for 10 to 15 minutes, partially covered, while you make the rouille.

FOR THE ROUILLE

Place the bread and garlic in a food processor and process until very finely chopped. Add the potato, pimientos, broth, and egg yolk and process until completely smooth. With the machine running, pour in the olive oil in a slow, steady stream—taking 30 seconds or more—and process until the sauce is completely smooth. Add the salt, pepper, and cayenne and transfer the rouille to a small bowl.

---

serve with

Roasted Eggplant Dip (page 2)
Mixed herb salad
Lemon ice
Tuscan Rosemary and Pine Nut Bars (page 306)

to drink

A stony Provençal rosé

FINISHING THE SOUP AND SERVING

With the soup base at a boil, add the clams and saffron and cook for 2 minutes. Add the fish and scallops, return to a gentle boil, and cook for 2 to 3 minutes, just until the fish pieces are cooked through and opaque and all of the clams have opened (discard any that remain unopened after sitting in the broth for several minutes). Stir in the tarragon, taste, and adjust the seasonings for the final time.

Spoon some rouille onto half of the croutons (2 or 3 per serving). Ladle portions of the seafood and broth into large soup bowls and place several rouille-topped croutons alongside each serving or in the soup itself. Serve hot, with extra croutons and rouille on the side.

on-the-fly noodles with shrimp

We're just as crazy as everyone else about meals-in-a-bowl, which happens to be the subject of Manhattan chef Lynne Aronson's cookbook, written with Elizabeth Simon. Aronson has two restaurants in New York City: Lola and Lola Bowla, where everything comes in a bowl. Her inspiration comes from all over the globe, but we're especially partial to this Asian soup-supper, which is deeply comforting and absolutely delicious.

COOK

Lynne Aronson

SOURCE

BowlFood Cookbook,
**by Lynne Aronson
and Elizabeth Simon**

Don't be put off by the cup of soy sauce here or the list of ingredients: Every one of the elements has an important role to play, so don't leave anything out. And it's especially important not to be intimidated by the pantry ingredients; once you've made this lovely supper, you'll want to make it again, and it's a snap once you have your little Asian arsenal at hand.

serves 6

6 cups water
1 cup soy sauce
1 cup sake
1/2 cup mirin, sweet sherry, or
    sweet vermouth
    Pinch of Shichimi Togarashi
    (page 190)
12 ounces dried soba (buckwheat)
    noodles
1 cup cooked fresh spinach,
    chopped

1 pound boneless skinless
    chicken breasts, thinly sliced
    on the diagonal
6 jumbo shrimp, deveined but
    left in their shells
1 medium onion, thinly sliced
2 scallions (white and green
    parts), cut into 2-inch pieces
3 tablespoons fresh lemon juice
2 tablespoons Asian sesame oil
    Hot chili oil to taste
1/4 cup sesame seeds, toasted
    (see note), for garnish

In a large nonreactive saucepan, combine the water, soy sauce, spirits, and Shichimi Togarashi. Bring to a boil over high heat. Reduce the heat to low and simmer to cook off the alcohol and let the flavors blend, about 30 minutes.

Meanwhile, bring a large saucepan of salted water to a boil over medium-high heat. Add the noodles, return to a boil, and cook until just tender, 2 to 3 minutes. Drain thoroughly in a colander. Divide the noodles and the spinach among six soup bowls.

Add the chicken, shrimp, onion, and scallions to the simmering broth and cook until the shrimp and chicken are tender, about 10 minutes.

Remove from the heat. Add 1 shrimp to each serving of noodles and spinach, then add the chicken and vegetables, dividing them evenly. Ladle the broth into the bowls, then drizzle each serving with lemon juice, sesame oil, and chili oil. Garnish with the sesame seeds and serve.

---

cook's notes

ℒ For most of us, this dish isn't so "on-the-fly." But you can make the broth and chop the spinach ahead, even the day before, and then it's truly speedy to put this one-dish meal together.

ℒ To toast the sesame seeds, spread them in a single layer in a dry skillet. Toast over medium heat, stirring frequently and shaking the skillet so that the seeds don't burn. Watch carefully; they'll turn golden in minutes.

Shichimi Togarashi

If you've never heard of this Japanese seven-spice mix, you owe it to yourself to run out and get some, and not just to make this dish. Shichimi Togarashi is an exhilarating blend of red and brown pepper, mandarin orange peel, white poppy seeds and sesame seeds, nori seaweed, and black hemp seeds. It comes mild, medium, and hot—Aronson votes for hot.

If there's no Japanese market for miles around, you can approximate the flavor with this recipe.

1 tablespoon white sesame seeds

1 tablespoon Szechuan peppercorns

1 small dried hot red chile

½ teaspoon dried orange peel

½ teaspoon crushed dried dark green seaweed, such as hijiki

With a mortar and pestle or in a blender, grind together all the ingredients. Sprinkle this dynamic spice mix on noodles, rice, soup, grilled meat or fish, vegetables—almost anything savory.

---

serve with

Mashed Potato Dip (page 4)

Green salad

℮

Fresh Ginger Cake (page 282)

to drink

Sake, warm or cool, as you like it

spicy codfish cakes with cilantro aïoli

Rhode Island chef Michael Frady lives close to the sea, in an area where codfish cakes are nothing special. But Frady's are unusual: the fish cakes are punched up with jalapeño, ginger, and Thai fish sauce, and they're served in a Thai manner—wrapped in lettuce leaves with mango slices, mint leaves, and a squeeze of lime. Binding it all together is a tropical

COOK
Michael Frady

SOURCE
Out of the Earth, by Kerry Downey Romaniello

take on aïoli, with a big hit of cilantro.

Lighter than crab cakes and more interesting than ordinary fish cakes, these delicious mini–fish burgers in their lettuce wrappers are so good they'll quickly pass out of the exotic category in your repertoire. They can also be served as a particularly gorgeous first course or as finger food with drinks.

serves 4 or 8 as a first course

CILANTRO AÏOLI

- 1 bunch fresh cilantro, stems removed (about 1½ cups leaves)
- 4 garlic cloves, coarsely chopped
  Grated zest and juice of 1 large lemon
- ½ cup mayonnaise, preferably reduced-fat

- 1 head green leaf lettuce, tough stems removed
- 1 large ripe mango or papaya, peeled, pitted or seeded, and cut into thin strips
- ⅓ cup chopped fresh mint leaves
- 1 lime, cut into wedges

SPICY CODFISH CAKES

- 1 pound boneless skinless cod fillets
- 2 scallions (white and some of the green parts), minced
- 1 jalapeño pepper, stemmed, seeded, and minced
- 1 tablespoon minced garlic
- 1 tablespoon minced peeled fresh gingerroot
- 1 tablespoon Thai fish sauce *(nam pla)* or soy sauce
  Grated zest of 1 lemon

  Peanut oil, for frying

main dishes

FOR THE AÏOLI

Coarsely chop the cilantro leaves and place them in a food processor. Add the garlic and lemon zest and process until finely chopped. Add the mayonnaise and process until thoroughly blended. Add the lemon juice and pulse to mix.

Transfer the aïoli to a small serving bowl and set it on a serving platter with the lettuce leaves, mango or papaya, mint leaves, and lime wedges. Cover with plastic wrap and refrigerate.

FOR THE CODFISH CAKES

Cut the fish into 1-inch pieces and finely chop in a food processor, 10 to 20 seconds. In a medium bowl, combine the fish, scallions, jalapeño, garlic, ginger, fish sauce or soy sauce, and lemon zest and stir until blended. Form the fish mixture into patties of about 2 tablespoons each; you should have 16 patties.

serve with

If you're not serving the codfish cakes as an appetizer, you can skip the lettuce wrap and serve with:

Watercress Slaw with Toasted Coconut (page 60)

West Texas Onion Rings (page 202)

℮

Ginger-Mascarpone Icebox Cake (page 286)

In a large skillet, heat about $1/8$ inch peanut oil over medium-high heat until ripples develop in the oil. Carefully slide the patties into the skillet, using a spatula; do not crowd. Cook until golden on the bottom, 2 to 4 minutes. Turn and cook until golden on the other side and opaque in the center. Repeat to cook the remaining patties, adding more oil to the pan as needed.

Place the fish cakes on the serving platter alongside the other ingredients. To eat, put a fish cake, some mango or papaya, and some mint in the center of a lettuce leaf. Sprinkle with a squeeze of lime, then spoon on some of the aïoli. Fold up and eat out of hand.

to drink

A young, crisp Riesling

main dishes

side dishes

Grilled Stuffed Portobello Mushrooms 196

Sugar Snap Peas with Sesame 199

Zucchini and Summer Squash Gratin with Parmesan and Fresh Thyme 200

Warm Leeks with Vinaigrette 202

Green Beans with Parsley-Pecan Pesto 204

Charcoal-Grilled Corn on the Cob with Mayonnaise, Cheese, and Chile 206

Grilled Scallions 208

Broccoli with Cambozola Sauce 210

Baked Fennel with Gorgonzola 212

Oven-Roasted Canned Tomatoes *(Pelati al Forno)* 214

Italian Vegetarian Timbale 216

Northeast Kingdom Maple-Glazed Braised Turnips 219

Creamy Anchos and Onions 220

grilled stuffed portobello mushrooms

COOK

Vincent Scotto

SOURCE

New York

Vegetarian dishes for the grill can be really dreary. Once you get beyond highly seasoned tofu and grilled vegetables, the landscape gets very flat. That's when you need this delectable mushroom "sandwich," which works as well as a side dish to grilled meats or a first course before pasta as it does as a vegetarian main course.

Vincent Scotto, the exuberant chef-owner of Scopa in Manhattan, takes a knife to portobello mushrooms, stuffs them with mozzarella and tomato, and tops them with pesto sauce. A few minutes on the grill and this Italian-accented dish is ready for prime time.

serves 6

6 medium portobello mushroom caps
¼ cup extra-virgin olive oil
6 ¼-inch-thick slices mozzarella cheese

6 ¼-inch-thick slices beefsteak tomato
Salt and freshly ground pepper to taste
½ cup Pesto Sauce (page 198)

Slice each mushroom cap horizontally, making a "sandwich." Brush the caps with oil on both sides and arrange them on a cookie sheet, cut sides up.

---

to serve

For a vegetarian main dish, serve two of these stuffed mushrooms along with a green salad.

to drink

A bright Dolcetto from the Piedmont

Season the mozzarella and tomato slices with salt and pepper. Place a slice of mozzarella on the bottom half of each mushroom, then top with a tomato slice. Finish off with the mushroom top. You can make the stuffed mushrooms up to several hours ahead. If you refrigerate them, let them come to room temperature before grilling.

Start a hot charcoal fire on the grill and place the rack about 6 inches above the fire. Place the mushrooms top down on the rack and grill for 3 to 4 minutes, or until they begin to brown. Turn and grill for 3 to 4 minutes more, or until the mozzarella begins to melt.

Place the grilled mushroom caps on serving plates and drizzle with the pesto sauce. Serve hot.

pesto sauce

You can, of course, use your own pesto sauce or a good commercial brand, but this is Vincent Scotto's favorite blend —and we don't know a better one.

makes about 1½ cups

¼ cup pine nuts

¾ cup plus 1 tablespoon extra-
virgin olive oil

4 cups loosely packed fresh basil
leaves

3 garlic cloves

½ cup freshly grated Parmesan
cheese

Salt to taste

Preheat the oven or a toaster oven to 350 degrees. Spread the pine nuts in a single layer on a cookie sheet and toast for 4 to 5 minutes, or until fragrant and golden brown. Shake the cookie sheet once or twice during the toasting and be careful not to let the nuts burn. Transfer the toasted nuts to a small plate.

In a blender, combine ¼ cup of the oil, 1 cup of the basil, the pine nuts, and garlic. Process until nearly smooth. Add the remaining 3 cups basil and ½ cup of the oil and process until nearly smooth. Add the cheese and pulse to combine. Season with salt.

Cover with the remaining 1 tablespoon olive oil and refrigerate, tightly covered, for up to 4 days, or freeze for up to 2 months.

sugar snap peas with sesame

COOK

Ina Garten

SOURCE

The Barefoot Contessa Cookbook

One day when Ina Garten, author of *The Barefoot Contessa Cookbook,* thought she was getting snow peas delivered to her take-out shop, she got peas all right, but they were sugar snaps, a novelty at that time. On a whim, she tossed them with some dark sesame oil and black sesame seeds to see if her customers would like them. Answer: The next day, she ordered 100 pounds. That was fifteen years ago, and she's still serving this dish, which is one of her best-sellers.

This is one of those divine recipes that's a perfect combination of flavors, tosses together in a few minutes (no cooking), goes anywhere, sits on a buffet table without suffering, and goes with Western dishes as well as Asian ones. Unfortunately, only in California are sugar snap peas available all year long—elsewhere this is an early-summer dish.

serves 6

1 pound sugar snap peas
Asian sesame oil
Black sesame seeds (see note)

Pick through the peas and discard any that aren't perfect. Remove and discard the stem end and string from each pod. In a large serving bowl, toss the peas with sesame oil and sesame seeds to taste. Serve at room temperature.

> **cook's note**
> Black sesame seeds are usually available in Asian markets. If you can't find them, use toasted white ones.

zucchini and summer squash gratin with parmesan and fresh thyme

When summer squashes are overflowing their bins at the farmers' market, this gratin is the right way to use them. Include as many kinds of squash as you can —pattypans, scallops, crooknecks— and the

COOK
Susie Middleton

SOURCE
Fine Cooking

gratin will be even better.

Middleton's mouthwatering, simple combination of fresh vegetables, herbs, and cheese seems to be the essence of summer itself.

serves 6 to 8

ONIONS
2 tablespoons olive oil
2 medium onions, thinly sliced

GRATIN
1¼ pounds small ripe tomatoes, cored and cut into ¼-inch-thick slices
¾ pound zucchini or other green summer squash (about 2 small), cut on the diagonal into ¼-inch-thick slices

¾ pound yellow summer squash or golden zucchini (about 2 small), cut on the diagonal into ¼-inch-thick slices
3 tablespoons olive oil
¼ cup fresh thyme leaves
1 teaspoon coarse salt
1¼ cups freshly grated Parmigiano-Reggiano cheese
Freshly ground pepper to taste

FOR THE ONIONS

In a medium skillet, heat the olive oil over medium heat. Add the onions and sauté, stirring frequently, until limp and golden brown, about 20 minutes. Reduce the heat to medium-low if they're browning too quickly. Spread the onions evenly in the bottom of an oiled 2-quart, shallow gratin dish, preferably an oval one. Let cool.

Preheat the oven to 375 degrees.

Place the tomato slices on a large plate to drain for a few minutes, then discard the collected juices. In a medium bowl, toss the zucchini and yellow squash slices with 1½ tablespoons of the olive oil, 2 tablespoons of the thyme, and ½ teaspoon of the salt. Set aside half of the cheese for the top of the gratin.

Sprinkle 1 tablespoon of the thyme over the onions in the gratin dish. Starting at one end of the baking dish, lay a row of slightly overlapping tomato slices across the width of the dish and sprinkle with a little of the cheese. Next, lay a row of zucchini, overlapping the tomatoes by two-thirds, and sprinkle with cheese. Repeat with a row of squash, and then repeat the rows, sprinkling each with cheese, until the gratin is full.

Season lightly with pepper and the remaining ½ teaspoon salt. Drizzle the remaining 1½ tablespoons olive oil over all. In a small bowl, combine the reserved cheese with the remaining 1 tablespoon thyme and sprinkle over the gratin.

Cook until the gratin is well browned and the juices have bubbled for a while and reduced considerably, 65 to 70 minutes. Let cool for at least 15 minutes before serving.

warm leeks with vinaigrette

COOK

Anonymous

SOURCE

Saveur Cooks Authentic French, **by the editors of** *Saveur*

In spring in France, the big winter leeks that are still around go straight into leeks vinaigrette, a dish we've had many times in French restaurants both at home and abroad. This es-pecially good version of the classic features both peanut oil and nutmeg, a subtle touch that distinguishes it.

Leeks vinaigrette is a classic first course, but we also love it as a side dish.

serves 4

4 large leeks
6 cups chicken broth
2 large shallots, sliced
2 teaspoons Dijon mustard
1 tablespoon red wine vinegar

3 tablespoons peanut oil
   (see note)
Salt and freshly ground pepper
   to taste
Pinch of freshly grated nutmeg
8 flat-leaf parsley sprigs

Remove the roots and outer leaves from the leeks. Cut off all but 2 inches of the green above the white. Slice the leeks in half length-wise, not quite all the way through, so that you can open them like a book. Wash the leeks under cold running water to remove all the sand and dirt and set aside.

In a large skillet, bring the broth to a simmer over medium heat. Place the leeks, all facing in the same direction, in the simmering broth. Reduce the heat to medium-low, cover, and cook until the leeks are soft but not mushy, 10 to 15 minutes. Transfer the leeks to a rack to drain. Add the shallots to the skillet and cook until soft, about 3 minutes, then transfer to a small bowl with a slotted spoon and set aside. Reserve the broth for another use.

In a separate small bowl, whisk together the mustard and vinegar and gradually drizzle in the peanut oil. Season with salt and pepper, then continue whisking until the vinaigrette is smooth and creamy.

Arrange the leeks in circles on a platter or on individual plates and scatter the shallots on top. Drizzle the vinaigrette over the leeks, season with the nutmeg, garnish with the parsley, and serve.

cook's note

The French are mad for peanut oil, though theirs is not usually as aromatic as ours. You can certainly use olive oil here if you'd prefer.

green beans with parsley-pecan pesto

COOK

Barbara Scott-Goodman

SOURCE

Smith & Hawken
The Gardeners'
Community Cookbook,
edited by Victoria Wise

Although we've had—and loved—green beans with pesto before, this version is something special because of the pecans (which have a special affinity for green beans), the parsley, and the lemon juice. All of these elements lighten and sweeten the pesto, bringing out the best in the beans at the same time.

Because this dish is served either slightly warm or at room temperature, it's great for a buffet or a potluck supper. The pesto is also delicious with potatoes, corn, and tomatoes, as well as fish and chicken.

serves 6 to 8

2 pounds young green beans,
   trimmed and left whole
Parsley-Pecan Pesto (recipe
   follows)

Bring a large pot of water to a boil. Add the beans and cook over high heat until barely tender but still firm, 3 to 5 minutes.

Drain the beans in a colander and rinse under cool water. Set aside in the colander to drip-dry, or transfer to a kitchen towel and pat dry.

Place the beans in a large serving bowl, toss with the pesto sauce, and serve.

---

cook's note

Some do and some don't, but we like to salt the green beans in the pot. Once the water is boiling, just add a little salt to taste before dropping in the beans.

Parsley-Pecan Pesto

makes 1 heaped cup

$^3/_4$ cup packed fresh flat-leaf
    parsley leaves
$^3/_4$ cup packed fresh basil leaves
$^1/_2$ cup pecan halves
 2 garlic cloves, sliced

1–2 tablespoons fresh lemon juice
    to taste
$^3/_4$ cup olive oil
$^1/_4$ teaspoon salt
$^1/_4$ teaspoon freshly ground
    pepper

Place the parsley, basil, pecans, garlic, and lemon juice in a food processor or blender and grind as finely as possible.

With the motor running, add the oil in a stream, the salt, and the pepper and continue processing until blended. Use immediately or cover tightly and refrigerate for up to 1 day.

---

tip

The success of this dish depends on having a pesto that really sings. Taste it once it's all together: It may need more lemon, salt, or oil.

charcoal-grilled corn on the cob
with mayonnaise, cheese, and chile

COOK

Rick Bayless

SOURCE

Saveur

Rick Bayless serves authentic Mexican food at his Chicago restaurant, Frontera Grill, and likes to spend his Sundays at Chicago's sprawling Mexican market, New Maxwell Street Market. For *Saveur* magazine, he took readers on a tour of his favorite stalls—which included one that sells a classic street food, corn on the cob. But this smoky, luxurious, spicy corn is another thing altogether from the kind we know.

In Mexico, the corn wouldn't be as sweet as we like it; it would be field corn, which is more savory and substantial. The unhusked ears are first soaked in water, then grilled and husked. Then they're brushed with butter and grilled again, which gives them a smoky flavor. Finally, they're slathered with mayonnaise (or sour cream thinned with a little cream), rolled in grated cheese, and sprinkled with chile. A great trick to know in barbecue season, when the thrill of plain corn on the cob has worn thin.

serves 6

6 ears corn in the husks
3 tablespoons butter, melted
½ cup mayonnaise

⅓ cup finely crumbled queso añejo (see note)
1 tablespoon powdered arbol chile (see note)

---

tip

If you can find field corn—the farmers' market is a good place to start—try it for this recipe. Otherwise, regular sweet corn is fine.

In a large, deep bowl, place the unhusked corn, cover with cold water, and weight with a plate to submerge. Soak for 30 minutes, then drain.

Meanwhile, preheat the grill and adjust the rack to 5 inches above the heat source.

Grill the corn, still unhusked, over a medium-high fire, turning frequently, until the outer leaves are blackened, 15 to 20 minutes. Remove from the grill, and when the corn is cool enough to handle, peel off the husks and remove the silk.

Brush the corn with the butter, return it to the grill, and cook, turning frequently, until browned all over, about 10 minutes. Spread each ear with some of the mayonnaise, roll in the cheese, and sprinkle with the chile. Serve.

cook's notes

🦂 Unless you have a local Mexican market, you probably won't be able to find queso añejo—but you can use Parmesan instead.

🦂 Arbol chile is widely available but it's extremely hot. You can substitute another chile, such as ancho or New Mexican chile, if you like. Either way, don't miss this corn; it's very special.

side dishes

grilled scallions

We've always loved scallions—which are just a toddler version of regular onions, not a whole different vegetable—as a cooked side dish. So we were delighted to see James Peterson recommending them for the grill—or the grill pan: These sweet and punchy little onions work just as well cooked indoors. If you can find

COOK
James Peterson

SOURCE
Essentials of Cooking

baby leeks, they're also excellent treated this way.

A trickle of extra-virgin olive oil finishes off the scallions beautifully just before they come to the table, but in fact we like them best with Peterson's Homemade Porcini Oil.

This recipe is constructed from several notes in *Essentials of Cooking*.

serves 2

1 large bunch scallions
   (about 12)
Extra-virgin olive oil
Salt and freshly ground pepper
   to taste

Homemade Porcini Oil (recipe
   follows), roasted peanut oil,
   or extra-virgin olive oil, for
   serving

Trim the roots and dark green ends from the scallions and brush them with olive oil. Season with salt and pepper.

Grill the scallions on an outdoor grill or in a ridged grill pan on top of the stove over high heat for 10 to 15 minutes, or until tender, turning frequently. Drizzle with oil before serving.

Homemade Porcini Oil

This delicately fragrant, woodsy wild-mushroom oil makes a perfect gift for a fellow cook. Try it over warm asparagus, pasta, or bruschetta. The recipe doubles easily, is child's play to make, and keeps well.

> 3 ounces dried porcini
> mushrooms
> About 1 cup extra-virgin
> olive oil

Check to be sure that the porcini are completely dry; if they feel at all moist or flexible, dry them on a cookie sheet in a low oven before grinding them. Grind the mushrooms to a powder in a blender.

Transfer the powdered mushrooms to a small, heavy saucepan and add enough olive oil to cover generously. Heat gently over low heat, stirring occasionally, for 30 minutes. Keep the temperature at the level of a very hot bath—not so hot that you can't stick your finger in for a second or two. Higher temperatures will destroy the flavor of the mushrooms.

Strain the oil through a fine-mesh sieve into a glass measuring cup and transfer to glass bottles. Seal tightly and keep in a dark place at room temperature for up to 1 month.

broccoli with cambozola sauce

We feel fairly sure George Bush would never have made his famous anti-broccoli proclamation if he'd tasted this sublime dish at Tra Vigne, Michael Chiarello's Napa Valley restaurant. Even if, like Bush, you hate broccoli, we think you'll love it in this soft cloak of buttery cheese touched with thyme and toasted pine nuts. Cooked this way, broccoli is sweet and savory at once. Each bite gives you tender broccoli, the heavenly cheese sauce, and a little buttery toast to carry it all.

This distinctive dish can be a side dish, first course, or the meal itself, with a salad and a simple fruit dessert. You can also leave out the toast and serve the broccoli as a side dish, using a little less sauce and letting it thicken slightly over the heat before tossing it with the broccoli. Don't lose the pine nuts; they make a difference.

COOK

Michael Chiarello

SOURCE

The Tra Vigne Cookbook,
by Michael Chiarello with
Penelope Wisner

serves 4

½ loaf good-quality crusty bread
2 tablespoons (¼ stick) unsalted butter
Salt and freshly ground pepper to taste
½ cup water
2 tablespoons extra-virgin olive oil

1½ pounds broccoli
¼ pound Cambozola cheese (see note)
½ cup heavy cream
1 teaspoon finely chopped fresh thyme
2 tablespoons pine nuts, toasted (see page 306)

Preheat the oven to 375 degrees.

Cut the bread into thick slices about 1½ inches wide and 5 inches long—you will need at least 1 slice per person. In a large ovenproof skillet, melt the butter, add the bread, and toss to coat well. Season with salt and pepper. Toss again and bake until browned and crisp outside but still soft inside, about 15 minutes. Drain on paper towels and keep warm.

In a large skillet, combine the water, olive oil, and salt and pepper, and bring to a boil. Meanwhile, cut the broccoli florets from the stems, leaving about 2 inches of stems attached to the florets. Save the stems for another use.

Add the florets to the skillet, cover, and cook over medium heat for 5 minutes. Uncover and increase the heat to high to boil off any remaining water. Sauté the broccoli in the oil remaining in the pan until cooked through and light brown, about 5 minutes more.

Meanwhile, in a small saucepan, slowly melt the cheese with the cream. Add the thyme and season well with pepper. Place 1 or more slices of bread on each of four warm plates. Arrange the broccoli on the bread and pour the sauce over the top. Sprinkle each serving with pine nuts and serve immediately.

VARIATION

Michael Chiarello suggests making the dish with asparagus instead of broccoli in spring—an equally lovely idea.

---

cook's notes

❦ Trim off the white rind of the cheese before adding it to the cream. Cambozola, which has a rich, mellow, toned-down Gorgonzola flavor, is a supermarket cheese, not one of the great ones according to connoisseurs, but it's just right in this dish.

❦ The broccoli-cooking technique here is perfect—a good chef's trick to add to your repertoire, and simplicity itself. The broccoli comes out sweet, tender, and lightly browned.

baked fennel with gorgonzola

This excellent holiday dish from one of the half-anonymous contributors to Allrecipes.com works for Thanksgiving as well as Christmas—with turkey, ham, beef, almost anything you're serving. The clean taste of the fennel makes a perfect

COOK

Christine L.

SOURCE

Allrecipes.com

balance with the luxuriously rich Gorgonzola. The dish also looks gorgeous, with its golden brown topping and the lacy fennel fronds tucked around the edges. You can make it ahead, even the day before you plan to serve it.

serves 8

4 3-inch-wide fennel bulbs, untrimmed
1³/₄ cups chicken broth
4 ounces Gorgonzola cheese, crumbled (¹/₂ cup)

2 tablespoons fine dry bread crumbs
Salt to taste

Rinse the fennel and trim off the stems, reserving about 1 cup of the tender fronds (if you're making it ahead, wrap the leaves in a towel, seal in a zipper-lock plastic bag, and refrigerate). Trim any bruises or dry looking areas from the fennel. Cut each bulb in half from the stem through the root end.

Preheat the oven to 375 degrees.

Place the fennel bulb pieces in a large skillet and add the chicken broth. Cover and bring to a boil over high heat. Simmer until the fennel is tender when pierced with a fork, 20 to 25 minutes.

Transfer the fennel, cut side up, to a shallow 9-to-10-inch casserole dish.

Boil the broth over high heat until reduced to about $1/2$ cup. Stir in half the fennel fronds. Spoon the broth mixture evenly over the fennel bulb halves.

In a small bowl, mash the cheese with the bread crumbs. Dot the cheese mixture evenly over the fennel.

Bake until the cheese begins to brown and the fennel is heated through, about 20 minutes. Tuck the remaining fennel fronds around the edges of the casserole. Season with salt and serve hot.

oven-roasted canned tomatoes
(pelati al forno)

COOK

Lynne Rossetto Kasper

SOURCE

The Italian Country Table

Amazing things happen to canned tomatoes when you roast them with olive oil, garlic, and herbs; they become almost brazenly meaty and sweet," says Lynne Rossetto Kasper in her new classic, *The Italian Country Table*. Indeed, regardless of the fact that the tomatoes are canned, not fresh, these jammy, scarlet nuggets are irresistible, either by themselves; spread on bread or bruschetta; with salads, beans, polenta, or risotto; or used as a pasta sauce.

The author advises using particular domestic brands of canned tomatoes, which she thinks are richer and better than imported Italian brands. Use tomatoes packed in tomato juice, not puree, and cook them in a nonreactive pan, such as a nonstick baking pan or an enameled cast-iron gratin dish. There are few roasts or chops that wouldn't be just a little bit better with these sweet, meaty tomatoes served alongside.

serves 4 to 6

- 2 28-ounce cans peeled whole tomatoes (preferably Muir Glen, Hunt's, Contadina, or Red Pack), drained, halved, and seeded
- ½–⅔ cup extra-virgin olive oil
- ½ medium red onion, cut into ¼-inch dice
- 5 large garlic cloves, coarsely chopped
- 14 large fresh basil leaves, torn
- 2 4-inch rosemary sprigs
  Salt and freshly ground pepper to taste

Preheat the oven to 300 degrees.

Spread out the tomatoes in a large, shallow pan and sprinkle with the remaining ingredients, turning to coat them with oil. Bake for

$2^{1}/_{4}$ to $2^{1}/_{2}$ hours, basting and turning the tomatoes several times. They're done when their color deepens to dark scarlet and they taste mellow and very rich. Don't let them brown or allow the garlic to brown, or the tomatoes will turn bitter.

Transfer the tomatoes and their oil to a medium nonreactive bowl. Let them mellow at room temperature for up to 6 hours so the flavors can ripen. Refrigerate for up to 4 days or freeze for up to 3 months. Serve at room temperature.

italian vegetarian timbale

COOK

Antonio Carluccio

SOURCE

*Antonio Carluccio's
Italian Feast*

If you haven't seen the ebullient Antonio Carluccio cooking on television or eaten the brilliantly rustic food at his Neal Street Restaurant in London's Covent Garden, you're in for a big treat. Nothing he makes is very complicated, but the flavors are big and memorable. This vegetarian dish is no ex-ception, and it works as a side dish, a first course, or even a vegetarian main dish (just add more vegetables). It's hearty and satisfying, with some of the appeal of lasagna.

For the tomato sauce, you can use a simple pasta sauce or make Carluccio's lovely Neapolitan sauce with basil.

serves 4

4½ ounces broccoli florets (about 1½ cups)

3½ ounces green beans (about 1 scant cup)

¼ cup all-purpose flour
Salt and freshly ground pepper to taste

2 medium zucchini, cut lengthwise into ¼-inch-thick slices

1 large eggplant (about 1 pound), cut lengthwise into ¼-inch-thick slices

4 large eggs, lightly beaten
Olive oil, for frying

2¾ cups Basic Tomato Sauce (recipe follows)

7 ounces fontina or Gruyère cheese, cut into ½-inch dice (⅞ cup)

1 cup freshly grated Parmesan cheese

Preheat the oven to 400 degrees.

In a large pot of boiling salted water, cook the broccoli and green beans until just tender, 6 to 8 minutes. Drain and refresh in cold water. Dry the broccoli on paper towels and slice. Stem the beans and cut them into 3-inch pieces.

Place the flour in a small bowl and season with salt and pepper. Dust the zucchini, eggplant, and broccoli slices with the flour mixture, shaking off any excess. Dip the vegetables in the beaten egg.

In a large skillet, heat 1 inch of oil to 375 degrees, or until a cube of bread quickly browns when tossed in. Fry the vegetables in batches until golden brown on both sides, about 5 minutes. Drain on paper towels.

In a 2-quart baking dish, spread 3 tablespoons of the tomato sauce. Make layers of eggplant, fontina or Gruyère, tomato sauce, Parmesan, green beans, zucchini, and broccoli in the dish. Repeat the layers, ending with a layer of tomato sauce and Parmesan.

Bake for 30 minutes, or until sizzling. Serve hot.

Basic Tomato Sauce

makes about 2³/₄ cups

6 tablespoons extra-virgin
   olive oil
1 medium onion, finely chopped
1 14-ounce can diced tomatoes,
   undrained

6 fresh basil leaves
   Salt and freshly ground pepper
   to taste

In a medium saucepan, heat the oil over medium-high heat. Add
the onion and sauté, stirring, until soft, about 4 minutes. Add the
tomatoes and their juice, reduce the heat to low, and simmer gently
for 10 minutes. Stir in the basil and salt and pepper. The sauce will
keep for up to 1 week in the refrigerator.

northeast kingdom maple-glazed braised turnips

COOK

Brooke Dojny

SOURCE

The New England Cookbook

The upper right-hand corner of Vermont is called the Northeast Kingdom, and it's also turnip country. Vermont maple syrup may seem like an unlikely partner for turnips—and you may not even think you like turnips—but try them this way before you spurn them. This is a delicious side dish, great with turkey or duck. Chances are, most of your guests will ask you what this remarkable vegetable actually *is*.

If you can't find the small young turnips the recipe calls for (they're the sweetest), use larger turnips and cut them up; the dish will still be very good.

serves 6

3 tablespoons butter
1 cup chicken broth
3 tablespoons maple syrup
1½ pounds small white turnips, peeled and halved

1 tablespoon Dijon mustard
Salt and freshly ground pepper to taste
1 tablespoon chopped fresh flat-leaf parsley

In a large skillet with a lid or a Dutch oven, melt the butter. Stir in the broth and maple syrup and bring to a simmer. Add the turnips, bring to a boil, reduce the heat to medium-low, cover, and cook until the turnips are tender, 10 to 20 minutes. Transfer the turnips to a medium bowl with a slotted spoon, leaving the liquid in the skillet or Dutch oven.

Increase the heat to medium-high and boil the cooking liquid until it is reduced by at least half and is beginning to get syrupy, 2 to 5 minutes. Whisk in the mustard. Return the turnips to the sauce, stir to coat, and season with salt and pepper. Reheat gently.

Serve the turnips hot, sprinkled with the parsley.

creamy anchos and onions

Texas Chef Robert Del Grande of Houston's Café Annie took *Food & Wine* magazine south of the border for their Thanksgiving issue and came up with some sizzling recipes. One of our favorites is this spin on traditional creamed onions, made with real cream, not gluey white sauce, and enlivened with sweet, earthy ancho chiles, as well as some fresh tarragon and a touch of lime.

COOK

Robert Del Grande

SOURCE

Food & Wine

These onions are as wonderful with roast pork as they are with turkey, or with any grilled meat or poultry. Best of all, you can make the dish a day ahead and reheat it gently; if the cream has thickened too much, just add a few tablespoons of water.

If you haven't worked with whole dried chiles before, this recipe is a great introduction: it couldn't be simpler.

serves 8

5 medium dried ancho chiles, stemmed and seeded
1 tablespoon unsalted butter
1 pound small white onions, trimmed but with the root end left intact, halved lengthwise
4 garlic cloves, coarsely chopped

1 cup homemade or canned low-sodium turkey broth or chicken broth
2 cups heavy cream
¼ cup fresh tarragon leaves
1 teaspoon salt
1 teaspoon fresh lime juice

In a large cast-iron skillet, toast the anchos over medium heat, pressing down with a spatula, until fragrant and blistered, about 20 seconds per side. Transfer to a small plate and let cool, then cut the anchos into ½-inch pieces.

In a large skillet, melt the butter over medium heat. Add the onions and garlic, cover, and cook, stirring occasionally, until the onions are softened, about 5 minutes. Add the broth and simmer until reduced by half, 6 to 7 minutes. Add the anchos, cream, and tarragon and cook over medium-low heat until the onions and anchos are tender and the cream is thickened, about 10 minutes. Add the salt and lime juice, transfer to a serving bowl, and serve warm.

west texas onion rings

COOK

Lisa Ahier

SOURCE

Food & Wine

Miles from anywhere in the gorgeous Big Bend country near the Mexican border of Texas, chef Lisa Ahier and her husband turned a historic fort into a dream getaway: Cibolo Creek Ranch. There Ahier developed a menu of southwestern-accented meals, including these sensational onion rings—the best by far we've ever tasted. There are a couple of tricks here: the sweet onions, the adobo sauce (we dip into a can of chipotle chiles in adobo), the cornmeal, and the buttermilk. Sweet, sharp, tangy, spicy, crunchy: These are onion rings to die for, best eaten pan to mouth.

serves 6

1½ cups milk or buttermilk
1½ cups all-purpose flour
  2 tablespoons adobo sauce (see note)
  2 large sweet onions (about 1 pound each), cut into ¼-inch-thick slices and separated into rings

Vegetable oil, for frying
1½ cups yellow cornmeal
  1 tablespoon ground cumin
    Salt

In a large bowl, whisk the milk with ½ cup of the flour and the adobo sauce until smooth. Add the onion rings and toss to moisten.

In a large cast-iron skillet, heat the oil to 350 degrees. In a large paper bag, combine the remaining 1 cup flour with the cornmeal, cumin, and 1½ teaspoons salt. Working in batches, dredge the onions in the cornmeal mixture, shaking off the excess. Transfer to a cookie sheet.

Working in batches, fry the onion rings in the hot oil until golden brown, 3 to 4 minutes. Using tongs, transfer to paper towels to drain. Season with salt and serve immediately.

---

cook's notes

- We think these onion rings taste best fried in peanut oil instead of vegetable oil, and we strongly vote for buttermilk in the batter.
- Chipotle chiles in adobo sauce are a great condiment to keep on hand, and they last virtually forever in the refrigerator. They're smoked jalapeño peppers in a spicy sauce. You can find them in Latino markets and some supermarkets.

roasted potato crisps with fresh herbs

These crusty herb-infused potatoes are good alongside summer grilled dishes and wintry roasts. In summer, make them with fresh herbs, if you have them. The winter version is excellent made with dried rosemary and thyme and fresh chives — just cut the amounts in half for the dried herbs.

COOKS

**Sheryl Julian
and Julie Riven**

SOURCE

Boston Globe

This is one of those insouciant recipes in which quantities aren't particularly important, and the seasonings can be changed to suit your whim. The only trick here is to cut the potatoes into the thinnest possible slices. For that, you really need a mandoline or Japanese vegetable slicer — or your own excellent knife skills.

serves 4

Olive oil
1 tablespoon chopped fresh
    chives
2 teaspoons chopped fresh
    rosemary
1 teaspoon chopped fresh
    oregano

4 russet potatoes, peeled and
    placed in a bowl of cold
    water
Salt and freshly ground pepper
    to taste

Preheat the oven to 425 degrees. Sprinkle the bottom of a jellyroll pan or shallow roasting pan with oil and set aside.

In a small bowl, combine the herbs. Slice the potatoes as thinly as possible, using a mandoline or Japanese vegetable slicer.

Arrange the potatoes on the pan in haphazard layers, sprinkling the layers with olive oil, herbs, salt, and pepper.

Roast the potatoes for 20 minutes, then turn them with a spatula. The neat layers will break up, but that's fine.

Roast for 20 to 30 minutes more, turning several more times, until the potatoes are cooked through and crusty.

To remove the potatoes from the pan, lift them with the spatula — they will separate as you do so — and transfer to a serving platter or individual plates. Serve at once.

VARIATION

The potatoes are also delicious scattered with herbes de Provence.

---

tip

If you have no fancy slicing machine and your knife skills are not well honed, you might want to invest in an old-fashioned American tool that's great for making coleslaw, slicing cucumbers, and slicing these potatoes. It's called Feemster's Famous Slicer, and it's in many hardware stores for under $10. It can also be ordered from Sur la Table: (800) 243-0852.

crusty puffed potatoes

A minor miracle, these potatoes look like *pommes soufflés* in a jacket. Little red potatoes are cut in half, rubbed with oil, sprinkled with salt, and then roasted directly on a rack in a hot oven. The high heat makes them simulta-

COOK

Gourmet **magazine staff**

SOURCE

Epicurious.com

neously puff and crisp.

If they are baked cut side down, they become crustier; if they are baked cut side up, they puff high —it's your choice. Do use sea salt, and sprinkle it on generously.

serves 4

8 small red potatoes
2 teaspoons olive oil
2 teaspoons coarse sea salt

Preheat the oven to 475 degrees. Place an oven rack at the middle level.

Rinse the potatoes and dry well with paper towels. Rub the potatoes with oil. Cut each potato in half and sprinkle the cut sides with salt.

Place the potatoes cut side down on a cooling rack and let stand for 10 minutes so the salt can draw some of the water out of them.

---

cook's note

If the potatoes have an egg shape, cut them lengthwise (they will puff higher and get crustier); otherwise, just cut in half crosswise.

Bake the potatoes directly on the oven rack until cooked through, about 20 minutes. Increase the oven temperature to 500 degrees and bake until the potatoes are puffed and golden, about 5 minutes more. Serve hot.

VARIATION

These pop-in-the-mouth potatoes make a fabulous appetizer too—just multiply the recipe depending on the number of people you plan to feed. Serve with a little ramekin of olive oil and a pepper grinder.

---

tips

✢ Oiling the rack will help with cleanup, as will lining the oven floor with foil.

✢ You can make these while a roast is resting; just turn up the oven as soon as the roast is out. They can be prepared in 30 minutes.

---

side dishes

creamy mashed potatoes

Opinions on how to mash potatoes are endless, but we're with *Gourmet* on this one: russet potatoes are the ones to use, a potato ricer or food mill is essential to ensure the right fluffy texture, and real cream (or half-and-half for less hearty eaters), along with plenty of butter, is the secret of truly creamy potatoes. We'd also add sea salt to taste with the butter.

Gourmet listed two wonderful optional ingredients that we think shouldn't be op-

COOK
Gourmet magazine staff

SOURCE
Gourmet

tional at all: garlic cloves cooked along with the potatoes, and this year's favorite "new" ingredient, smoked Spanish paprika. Cooked this way, mashed potatoes are great with everything from barbecue to the Thanksgiving turkey.

Perfect mashed potatoes are made at the last minute, but as *Gourmet* notes, you can always make them a few hours ahead and reheat them in the microwave—they'll still be pretty spectacular.

serves 8

Salt to taste
3 pounds russet potatoes
4 garlic cloves (optional)
6 tablespoons (³/₄ stick) unsalted butter, cut into small pieces and softened

1–1¹/₂ cups heavy cream or half-and-half, heated
Smoked Spanish paprika to taste (see note; optional)

Bring a large pot of salted water to a boil. Meanwhile, peel the potatoes and quarter them. Add the potatoes and garlic, if using, to the pot and return to a boil. Gently boil the potatoes until tender, 15 to 20 minutes. Drain in a colander.

Force the warm potatoes and the garlic, if using, through a ricer or food mill into a large bowl. Add the butter and stir with a wooden spoon, letting the butter melt completely. Add 1 cup of the hot cream or half-and-half and gently stir with a wooden spoon to incorporate, adding more cream or half-and-half to thin to the desired consistency. Stir in the smoked paprika, if desired, and serve.

cook's note

Smoked Spanish paprika comes two ways, hot and sweet — they're both wonderful, depending on what else you're serving. Start with ½ teaspoon if you're unfamiliar with the flavor; you may end up using much more. You'll probably have to mail-order this paprika unless you live near a gourmet superstore. Our favorite brand, Santo Domingo, comes in a little blue can from Formaggio Kitchen: (888)212-3224.

champ

COOK

Margaret M. Johnson

SOURCE

The Irish Heritage Cookbook

It's fitting that the best recipe for champ we've ever tried is from this terrific collection of traditional and new Irish recipes. Along with the goodness of the mashed potato and scallion dish itself, the author contributes some notable champ lore. Sometimes called poundies, champ is served in a mound with a well of melted butter in the center. "Traditionally," she writes, "it's eaten with a spoon, starting from the outside of the mound and dipping each spoonful into the butter. In the old days, the tool used for mashing potatoes was a pestle-shaped wooden implement called a beetle. Thus the old Irish poem:

There was an old woman that lived in a lamp;
She had no room to beetle her champ.
She's up'd with her beetle and broke the lamp,
And now she has room to beetle her champ.

serves 4

2 pounds boiling potatoes, peeled and cut into 2-inch pieces	6 tablespoons (³/₄ stick) butter
¹/₂ cup milk, light cream, or half-and-half	1¹/₃ cups chopped fresh chives or scallions
	Salt and freshly ground pepper to taste

Cook the potatoes in a large pot of boiling salted water until tender, 12 to 15 minutes. Drain and mash.

Meanwhile, in a medium saucepan, combine the milk, cream, or half-and-half and 4 tablespoons of butter. Cook over medium heat until the butter is melted. Add the chives or scallions, reduce the heat to low, and cook until the chives or scallions are soft, 2 to 4 minutes.

Add the potatoes and salt and pepper to the saucepan and stir until blended. Spoon the champ into a deep bowl, make a well in the center, and top with the remaining butter. Serve at once.

cook's note

If there are leftovers, thin them with a little buttermilk to make champ pancakes — just fry them in butter.

to serve

Serve with roast leg of lamb, or a roast chicken.

arroz verde (green rice)

COOK
Jim Peyton

SOURCE
Fine Cooking

If you asked us what we wanted to eat tonight, this emerald green, aromatic rice might well be the answer. Fortunately, it goes so well with so many entrées that there is never a problem fitting it into the menu and, to be honest, it has sometimes been *the* menu—just a bowl of this fabulous rice is enough to make us feel we have dined.

In "Mexico's Surprising Rice Dishes," in *Fine Cooking* magazine, Jim Peyton, a Mexican cookbook author and cooking teacher in San Antonio, writes that he is increasingly amazed by Mexico's world-class rice dishes, many with Spanish antecedents, "which come to light, one after another, like unexpected treasures at a rummage sale."

Peyton introduces this astoundingly good classic (though using milk is an untraditional twist) rather quietly: "Rich and refined, *arroz verde* is one of the most popular dishes I present to cooking classes."

serves 6 to 8

1 cup tightly packed stemmed
    spinach leaves (about
    1 1/2 ounces)
1/2 cup tightly packed cilantro
    sprigs (about 1/2 ounce)
1 1/4 cups homemade or canned
    low-salt chicken broth

1 1/4 cups milk
1 teaspoon salt
3 tablespoons unsalted butter
1 tablespoon olive oil
1 1/2 cups long-grain white rice
1/4 cup minced onion
1 garlic clove, minced

---

cook's note

Although no particular type of long-grain rice is specified in this recipe, both Carolina and Uncle Ben's converted long-grain rice work well.

Place the spinach, cilantro, and broth in a blender and blend until the vegetables are pureed. Add the milk and salt and blend until well combined.

In a medium saucepan, heat the butter and olive oil over medium heat. When the butter is melted, add the rice and sauté, stirring frequently, until it just begins to brown, 3 to 4 minutes. Add the onion and garlic and cook for 1 minute more, stirring constantly. Add the spinach mixture, stir well, increase the heat to high, and bring to a boil. Cover, reduce the heat to low, and cook for 20 minutes. Stir the rice carefully to avoid crushing it, cover, and cook for 5 minutes more.

Remove from the heat and let the rice steam in the covered pot for 10 minutes. Serve hot.

---

tip

Arroz Verde is best served just after it's made, but you can prepare it a day or two in advance if necessary and reheat it in the microwave. To reheat, spread out the cooked rice in a shallow bowl, cover with plastic wrap, vent, and heat on high until the rice is steaming.

Savory Bread Pudding

COOK
Fran Gage

SOURCE
Bradford and Chocolate

We have fallen in love with bread pudding this year—the modest, homey classic turned up everywhere, in both sweet and savory guises. Our favorite to date is this light, airy, herbal bread pudding from celebrated Bay Area baker Fran Gage, who doesn't like to see even a morsel of good bread go to waste.

You can make this very satisfying pudding in minutes from ingredients you usually have on hand: slightly stale bread, eggs, milk, cheese, a scrap of ham, and fresh herbs (even just parsley and scallions are fine). With its crispy top and creamy inte-

rior, this dish works for lunch, brunch, or as a side dish anytime. And you can play with it: add sautéed mushrooms or reconstituted dried porcini, use other cheeses, mix in some cooked vegetables such as bell peppers and zucchini. Just be sure there's an oniony element: scallions or chives.

Gage notes that in San Francisco restaurants, where bread pudding is all the rage, they serve it alongside a variety of meat and poultry dishes, often dressed with the roasting juices.

serves 4

8 ounces slightly stale (not rock-hard) bread, torn into 2-inch pieces

³/₄ cup grated cheese, such as Swiss or cheddar, or a combination of mild cheese and hard grating cheese

¹/₂ cup finely chopped mixed fresh herbs, including scallions or chives

¹/₄ cup chopped smoked ham

3 cups whole milk

5 extra-large eggs

³/₄ teaspoon salt

¹/₄ teaspoon freshly ground pepper

Preheat the oven to 350 degrees. Place a rack at the middle level. Butter a 9-by-12-inch gratin dish.

In a large bowl, toss the bread pieces with the cheese, herbs, and ham, then spread in the gratin dish. In a large bowl, whisk the milk, eggs, salt, and pepper, then pour over the bread.

Bake the bread pudding for 45 minutes, or until golden brown and the custard is set. Serve hot.

macaroni gratin

COOK

Benoit Guichard

SOURCE

Food & Wine

Of the many versions of macaroni and cheese we saw this year, this one conquers them all—and is completely extravagant in every possible way. And if our national pride is slightly hurt by the idea that a French chef has taken one of our few classic dishes and shown us what it could become—well, we'll just eat it.

No American, surely, would ever cook the pasta in milk, though the French are fond of cooking every starch from potatoes to rice to couscous in it. That's three entire quarts of milk, which go right down the drain once the pasta is cooked. There's another little Gallic flourish —the dropping of two trays of ice cubes into the cooked pasta to stop the cooking immediately. And you may wince at the $1/4$ cup of salt. But never fear; this is such a sensationally good version of mac and cheese that we do everything the recipe says, gladly.

serves 8

- 3 quarts whole milk
- 4 garlic cloves, lightly crushed
- 1 tablespoon unsalted butter
- 1 tablespoon all-purpose flour
  Fine sea salt
  Freshly ground white pepper
    to taste
  Freshly grated nutmeg to taste

- $3/4$ cup heavy cream
- $3/4$ pound dried ridged penne
    pasta
- 2 trays ice cubes
- 1 cup grated Gruyère cheese
    (about $31/2$ ounces)
- 2 tablespoons minced fresh
    chives, for garnish

In a large saucepan, heat the milk and garlic over high heat until bubbles appear around the edges. Remove from the heat, cover, and let steep for 10 minutes. Remove and discard the garlic. Measure out 1 cup milk and reserve; set aside the remaining milk until you are ready to cook the pasta.

In a small saucepan, melt the butter over medium heat. Whisk in the flour and cook, stirring constantly without browning, for 1 minute. Remove from the heat and gradually whisk in the reserved 1 cup milk, stirring constantly, until the sauce is completely smooth. Season with a large pinch of salt and generous amounts of white pepper and nutmeg. Return the pan to low heat and cook the sauce, whisking constantly, until thick, about 5 minutes. Remove from the heat, let cool slightly, and stir in the heavy cream. Season with salt.

Preheat the oven to 500 degrees. Butter a 9-by-13-inch gratin dish.

Add ¼ cup salt to the remaining milk and bring to a simmer. Add the pasta and cook, stirring, over medium-high heat, so the milk is just simmering for about 10 minutes, or until al dente. Remove from the heat and add the ice cubes to stop the cooking. When all the ice cubes have melted, drain the pasta in a colander and transfer to a large bowl.

Add the sauce to the pasta and toss to coat. Transfer the pasta mixture to the gratin dish. Sprinkle the cheese over the top and bake for about 10 minutes, or until bubbling around the edges. Turn on the broiler and broil, rotating the dish, until the cheese is golden, 2 to 3 minutes. Let the gratin stand for 5 minutes, then season generously with white pepper, garnish with the chives, and serve.

watermelon salsa

COOK

Sara Gibbs

SOURCE

Butter Beans to Blackberries, by Ronni Lundy

In her completely charming cookbook, Ronni Lundy tells the tale of going to the Ohio Valley Harvest Festival and finding this amazing salsa, the creation of Kentucky chef Sara Gibbs. It was supposed to be a condiment to go on top of something else (which it does superbly), but festivalgoers were demanding cups of salsa to eat on its own, as a salad. Lundy's notes for that day were covered with pink watermelon juice and lots of exclamation points.

You can serve this as either a salsa or a salad. But be prepared: make lots, because people will come right back for more of this refreshing dish. This is sensational barbecue or picnic fare, right with everything from fish to pork. It won't wait, though; this isn't a dish for the buffet table.

serves 4 to 6

4 cups seeded and diced watermelon
⅓ cup minced red onion
⅓ cup minced fresh cilantro
1 tablespoon minced jalapeño pepper
½ teaspoon salt
2 garlic cloves, minced
2 tablespoons fresh lime juice

In a medium nonreactive bowl, toss all the ingredients together. Let stand at room temperature for 30 minutes, then serve immediately.

---

tips

🌿 Using seedless watermelon will save you lots of time spent digging out seeds.

🌿 Don't be tempted to skip the mellowing time of 30 minutes—that's really important for the flavors to blossom.

wine grapes, walnuts, and olives

COOK

Paul Bertolli

SOURCE

Janet Fletcher,
Metropolitan Home

When Berkeley master chef Paul Bertolli of Oliveto goes to the wood-fired oven, out come extraordinary dishes—all of them extremely simple, touched with a little genius and the entrancing flavors this ancient way of cooking produces. Spit-roasted ducks are flavored only with thyme and salt and pepper; wild mushrooms cook in packets in the coals with just lemon juice, olive oil, salt, and pepper.

For those of us who are spitless and have no wood-fired oven, there's Bertolli's terrific side dish/condiment, which is usually cooked on top of a layer of embers and ash but also can be baked in a conventional oven. Because he lives near wine country, Bertolli makes the dish with wine grapes, but plain old Red Flame grapes also will work here. Fall's new crop of walnuts (or plain old walnuts), some French olives, and a few thyme sprigs join the grapes in a bath of olive oil and balsamic vinegar.

This heady dish is a great cool-weather partner for almost anything roasted or broiled: chicken, duck, turkey, or pork. We keep wanting another little spoonful—and so will your guests.

serves 4

2 cups seedless black or white wine grapes or seedless Red Flame or muscat grapes, stemmed

1 cup walnuts, preferably from a new crop

1 cup mixed picholine and oil-cured black olives

2 tablespoons aged balsamic vinegar

2 tablespoons olive oil

3 thyme sprigs

Preheat the oven to 350 degrees.

Combine all the ingredients in a small baking dish. Bake for 45 minutes, stirring occasionally. Serve hot, warm, or at room temperature.

garlicky cranberry chutney

COOK

Madhur Jaffrey

SOURCE

Npr.org

The Indian-born actress Madhur Jaffrey has an extraordinary hand in the kitchen—in fact it's difficult to say which of her talents is more impressive. But if we were compiling a list of the best recipes of our lives, we'd definitely include this sensationally good cranberry chutney, with its equal parts heat, sweet, and tart. No Thanksgiving dinner should be served without it—alongside a more traditional cranberry sauce for those who don't care to be surprised.

makes 2 cups

- 1 1-inch cube fresh gingerroot, peeled
- ½ cup apple cider vinegar
- ¼ cup sugar
- 3 garlic cloves, very finely chopped
- ⅛ teaspoon cayenne pepper, or to taste
- 1 16-ounce can jellied cranberry sauce
- ½ teaspoon salt
  Freshly ground pepper to taste

Cut the ginger into paper-thin slices. Stack the slices together and cut them into very thin slivers.

In a small saucepan, combine the ginger slivers, vinegar, sugar, garlic, and cayenne and bring to a simmer. Simmer over medium heat for about 15 minutes, or until there is ¼ cup liquid left, excluding the solids. Stir in the cranberry sauce, salt, and pepper and bring to a simmer. The sauce will be a bit lumpy, but that's fine.

Simmer over low heat for about 10 minutes, or until it has the right consistency, and let cool in the pan. Store the chutney in a jar in the refrigerator; it will keep for several days.

VARIATION

For an even livelier chutney, mince a jalapeño pepper or two and add to the ginger. Skip the cayenne.

cook's note

This is a great potluck supper item or hostess gift. And it's worth making a double batch, since it keeps well and is so good with leftover turkey or on turkey sandwiches.

cranberry horseradish relish

COOK

Elinor Klivans

SOURCE

Washington Post

Another cranberry relish we love is simplicity itself, and great with poultry, pork, lamb, and even fish.

makes about 1½ cups

2 cups whole cranberries
6 tablespoons sugar
1 tablespoon plus 1 teaspoon
    prepared horseradish

Place the cranberries and sugar in a food processor and pulse until coarsely chopped. Transfer to a small bowl and stir in the horseradish. Cover and refrigerate for up to 4 days.

breads

tuscan flatbread with roasted grapes

At her Los Angeles bakery, Buona Forchetta Handmade Breads, Suzanne Dunaway turns out a cornucopia of remarkable Italian-style breads with chewy crusts and lots of holes in the dough. She discovered the secret of these breads quite by accident one day when she abandoned her dough before kneading it and went off to do something else. Now she makes all her breads this way: stirring the ingredients into a wet dough, letting it rise overnight to develop flavor, and carefully pulling it into place before baking. That's right, no kneading at all. Active work time is just a few min-

COOK

Suzanne Dunaway

SOURCE

No Need to Knead

utes, and the flavor is remarkable. These doughs are virtually foolproof—child's play, really.

This *sciacciatta*, or grape harvest bread, is studded with another serendipitous discovery: roasted grapes. Instead of drying grapes in a very slow oven, Dunaway accidentally roasted them at a much higher temperature—and now she does it all the time. As we do: Once you taste these grapes, you'll never want to be without them.

Roast the grapes a day ahead, make up the batter the night before, and bake the flatbread the day you plan to serve it.

makes 1 large flatbread

1½ cups lukewarm water (85–95 degrees)

1 envelope active dry yeast

¼ cup sugar

1 large egg, lightly beaten (optional)

3¼–4 cups unbleached all-purpose flour

¼ cup olive oil, plus more for oiling bowl

2 teaspoons salt

3 cups Roasted Grapes (page 247)

3–4 tablespoons raw turbinado sugar or white sugar to taste

Place the water in a large bowl and sprinkle the yeast on top. Add the sugar and egg, if using, and beat well. Add the flour, olive oil, and salt and mix well, stirring until the dough is smooth and satiny and pulls away from the sides of the bowl. Place in a large oiled bowl, brush with olive oil, cover, and refrigerate overnight. Remove the dough from the refrigerator and let stand, covered, in a warm place until doubled in volume, about 1 hour.

Grease a 13-by-18-inch cookie sheet with olive oil. Place half the dough on the cookie sheet and stretch it into a very thin circle to the edge of the pan, as you would for pizza (if your fingers stick, rub them with olive oil before handling the dough). Brush the dough with olive oil and spread half of the grapes over the dough.

On a lightly floured surface, roll out the remaining dough to a similar circle and, lifting carefully, place it over the grape layer (you may do this more easily by dusting the circle with a little flour, rolling it up loosely, flour side in, and then unrolling it over the grapes). Press the 2 circles together to push out the air. Dip your fingers in cold water or olive oil and make indentations on the top of the dough. Make holes in the dough by pulling it to the sides of the cookie sheet, about 1 inch at a time. Pulling the holes at random will form small craters all over the dough, with the pan showing through in spots. The dough should be oval and stretched to fit almost the entire cookie sheet. Brush the dough with olive oil and sprinkle the remaining grapes evenly over the dough. Sprinkle with the sugar and let rest for 15 minutes.

Preheat the oven to 500 degrees. Bake for 5 minutes, then reduce the oven temperature to 400 degrees and bake for 20 minutes more, or until golden brown. (Do not let the grapes burn.) Transfer to a rack to cool. Serve warm or at room temperature, cut into strips.

VARIATIONS

❧ As with all the breads in Dunaway's book, you can make smaller loaves in a nonstick or cast-iron skillet rubbed with olive oil and bake them for about 30 minutes. You can even make tiny loaves in a nonstick mini-muffin pan and bake them for 17 to 20 minutes, depending on how much crust you like.

❧ For a bread with a bit more character, try making this with bread flour. You can sprinkle the top with coarse sea salt instead of sugar and add a little chopped fresh rosemary.

To serve

It's mandatory to serve this grape harvest bread with a glass of wine—and a hunk of Gorgonzola also would be welcome. This can be dessert (with a glass of muscat) or a late-afternoon snack. Any leftovers can be toasted for breakfast.

Roasted Grapes

1 teaspoon olive oil
3 pounds seedless Red Flame
   grapes, stemmed

Preheat the oven to 350 degrees. Grease a cookie sheet with the oil.

Spread the grapes evenly on the cookie sheet. Roast for 1 hour, turning once or twice with a large spatula. The grapes should collapse and start to turn brown around the edges. Remove them before they are completely dried like raisins. Set aside while you make the flatbread.

VARIATION

Suzanne Dunaway likes to serve the grapes with broiled quail, tuck them into panettone or plum pudding, or steep them in cognac and serve them over ice cream. They're also delicious stirred into yogurt for breakfast.

beer bread

COOK
Jodi Regan

SOURCE
Allrecipes.com

Here it is: instant bread. In fact, the recipe is a humbling lesson in immediate levitation: Combine self-rising flour and beer, and there will be bread. The yeast in the beer provides not only rising power but also a distinct flavor. Depending on which beer you use, the bread will taste gently or strongly of hops and malt. And the flavor can be adjusted depending on your mood, what you have on hand, and what you plan to serve the bread with. For a bread to serve with cold cuts, such as corned beef and pastrami, try a German beer. For a great bread for grilled cheese sandwiches, an ale is terrific.

This Internet find is from Allrecipes.com, whose Breadrecipes.com is a growing source of both sweet and savory breads, rolls, and muffins.

makes one 9-by-5-inch loaf

3 cups self-rising flour
3 tablespoons sugar
1 12-ounce can or bottle beer

Preheat the oven to 350 degrees. Place a rack at the lower-middle level. Grease a 9-by-5-inch metal loaf pan.

In a large bowl, combine the flour and sugar. Gradually add the beer and stir, first using a wooden spoon, then your hands. The batter will be sticky. Gather it into a rough mound and press it evenly into the loaf pan.

Bake for 50 to 60 minutes, or until a skewer plunged deep into the middle of the bread comes out clean. The top will be crunchy, and the interior soft. Turn the bread out of the loaf pan and let cool briefly on a rack. It can be sliced and eaten immediately or cooled completely and stored in a zipper-lock bag at room temperature for up to 1 week.

swedish knackebrod

COOK

Judith M. Fertig

SOURCE

Prairie Home Cooking

As any fan of Garrison Keillor and *The Prairie Home Companion* knows, the heartland is chockablock with both baking and Swedish food. The two elements come together in this homemade version of rye crisp, which immediately sells out at bake sales in the northern Mid-west. The crackers are shatteringly thin, with a fresh rye taste that the commercial product can't begin to imitate.

You can whip up these crackers in a matter of minutes in the food processor, and they're terrific with cheese spreads, soups, and salads.

makes about 24 crackers

- 1³/₄ cups rye flour
- ³/₄ teaspoon sugar
- ¹/₄ teaspoon salt

- 4 tablespoons (¹/₂ stick) unsalted butter
- ¹/₃ cup plus 1 tablespoon milk

Preheat the oven to 300 degrees. Lightly oil a cookie sheet.

In a mixing bowl or food processor, combine the flour, sugar, and salt. Cut in the butter with a pastry blender or in a food processor. Add the milk a little at a time, stirring with a spoon or pulsing in the food processor until you have a stiff dough.

Roll out the dough as thinly as possible on a floured surface. Cut the dough into 2-by-3-inch strips. Make small holes in the dough with the point of a knife or the tines of a fork.

Bake the strips for 10 minutes, or until golden brown. Remove the knackebrod from the oven and cool on racks. Serve warm or at room temperature. Stored in an airtight container, the crackers will keep for at least 1 week.

VARIATION

Not being Swedish, we can't resist playing with these crackers. We especially like them sprinkled with seeds, such as cumin seeds, as well as coarse sea salt.

greek christmas bread

We're always on the lookout for an interesting new treat for Christmas breakfast—and this gorgeous, delicate, fragrant Greek bread is our choice this year. Aniseeds, raisins, and almonds in a buttery dough are the essential elements here, but the crowning glory is the great cross that tops the bread.

COOK
Good Housekeeping magazine staff

SOURCE
Good Housekeeping Baking

The four ends of the cross are split and curled outward, like a mermaid's tail, and the effect is stunning.

Because the recipe makes two breads, you'll have one to give away or freeze. The bread is especially delicious warm and makes wonderful toast well into the new year.

makes 2 loaves

³/₄ cup warm water (105–115 degrees)
2 envelopes active dry yeast
1 teaspoon plus 1 cup sugar
1¹/₄ cups milk, heated to lukewarm (85–95 degrees)
1 cup (2 sticks) butter, softened
1¹/₂ teaspoons salt

1 teaspoon aniseeds, crushed
3 large eggs
About 7¹/₂ cups all-purpose flour
1¹/₂ cups raisins
2 tablespoons blanched sliced almonds

In a large bowl, combine the water, yeast, and the 1 teaspoon sugar; stir to dissolve. Let stand for 5 minutes, or until foamy. Add the remaining 1 cup sugar, warm milk, butter, salt, aniseeds, 2 of the eggs, and 3 cups of the flour. Beat well with a wooden spoon. Stir in the raisins. Gradually stir in enough of the remaining flour to make a soft dough.

Turn the dough out onto a floured surface and knead for about 10 minutes, or until smooth and elastic, working in about ½ cup of the remaining flour as necessary, just to keep the dough from sticking.

Shape the dough into a ball and place in a large greased bowl, turning the dough to grease the top. Cover and let rise in a warm place until doubled in volume, about 1½ hours.

Grease two large cookie sheets. Punch down the dough. Divide the dough into 2 pieces; cover and refrigerate 1 piece. Turn the other piece out onto a lightly floured surface and reserve ½ cup dough. Shape the larger piece into a smooth ball. Place in the center of one of the cookie sheets and form into an 8-inch round loaf.

Cut the ½ cup reserved dough into 4 equal pieces. Using your hands, roll each piece into a 10-inch-long rope. With a knife, cut a 2-inch-long split in each end. Arrange the ropes on the loaf to form a cross and curl up the ends.

Cover the loaf loosely with greased plastic wrap and let rise in a warm place until doubled in volume, 45 minutes to 1 hour. After 45 minutes, remove the other piece of dough from the refrigerator and make another loaf in the same way.

Preheat the oven to 350 degrees.

In a small cup, beat the remaining egg with a fork. Brush the first loaf all over with the egg wash and sprinkle with 1 tablespoon of the almonds. Bake for 30 minutes, then cover the loaf loosely with foil to prevent overbrowning. Bake for 10 to 15 minutes more, or until the loaf sounds hollow when tapped on the bottom. Transfer the baked loaf to a rack to cool.

Brush the second loaf with the egg wash, sprinkle with the remaining 1 tablespoon almonds, and bake and cool as directed above.

breads

rice bread

COOKS

**Cheryl Alters Jamison
and Bill Jamison
after John Martin Taylor**

SOURCE

American Home Cooking

In 1847, when Sarah Rutledge published *The Carolina Housewife,* rice was the king of Carolina's Low Country cuisine—and the book contained no fewer than thirty recipes for rice bread. Today, rice bread is all but forgotten, gone with the rice plantations. But this truly great bread, with its crunchy exterior and densely textured, chewy crumb, should be an American standard. It's been revived twice in the past decade: first by John Martin Taylor (in *Hoppin' John's Low-* *country Cooking,* 1992, 2000) and this year by Cheryl and Bill Jamison in *American Home Cooking.* The Jamisons used Taylor's method but cut the recipe in half to make a single round loaf—a good idea, since it maximizes the crust.

This is a distinctive bread, not like any other we've tasted—and once you have a taste for it, you'll make it again and again. As Taylor notes, rice bread makes the best imaginable toast.

makes 1 large round loaf, about 12 inches in diameter

1 cup raw long-grain white rice	2 pounds unbleached bread flour
1½ tablespoons kosher salt	(about 7 cups)
1½ quarts water	Vegetable oil
2 envelopes active dry yeast	

In a large saucepan, bring the rice, salt, and water to a boil, then reduce the heat to medium-low. Simmer, uncovered, until the rice is very soft and the water has been absorbed, 20 to 30 minutes. The rice should be moist, not dried out. (Resist any urge to taste what will be a very salty mixture.) Spoon the rice into a large bowl and let cool until lukewarm.

Sprinkle the yeast onto the rice and mix thoroughly. Work in about 5 cups of the flour, 1 cup at a time. When the mixture begins to get stiff and lumpy and you can't believe it's ever going to form bread dough, transfer it to a floured surface for easier working. Knead the dough for 10 to 15 minutes, incorporating some or all of the remaining 2 cups flour if you think the dough can absorb it. When ready, the dough will be transformed into a smooth, elastic mass. Coat the bread lightly with oil and return it to the bowl. Cover the bowl with a clean dish towel and let rise in a warm, draft-free spot until doubled in volume, about 2 hours.

Punch the dough down and knead it lightly for 1 to 2 minutes, forming it into a fat disk while you work. Arrange the dough on a greased cookie sheet. Cover the dough with a dish towel and let rise in a warm, draft-free spot until expanded in size by half, about 1 hour.

Near the end of the rising time, preheat the oven to 450 degrees. If you have a baking stone, which results in a crisper crust, place it in the oven when you start preheating. If using a baking stone, slide the bread off the cookie sheet and onto the stone in the oven. Otherwise, bake the bread on the cookie sheet.

---

tips

❧ For some reason, kneading with a dough hook doesn't work very well with this old-time recipe. The dough seems to want your hands, and the more you concentrate on and enjoy the kneading, the better the bread will be.

❧ Try to mix in at least 6 cups flour. Otherwise, the dough will be too wet and hard to work with.

Bake for 15 minutes, then reduce the oven temperature to 400 degrees and bake for 15 minutes more. If using a cookie sheet, remove it now and return the bread to the oven, placing it directly on the oven rack. If using a baking stone, leave it in place but turn the bread over. Bake for 10 to 15 minutes more, or until the bread is golden brown and sounds hollow when thumped. If it thuds rather dully, it's not ready. If it appears to be getting too dark, reduce the oven temperature to 350 degrees during the last stage of baking.

Cool the loaf to room temperature on a rack. The crusty loaf yields beautiful slices for eating as is or for toasting later.

---

cook's note

In the old days, the bread was baked in a brick oven and the yeast was fresh, not dried. As the culinary historian Karen Hess suggests, you can approximate the brick-oven effect, which makes an especially delicious loaf, by baking the bread under a very large, clean flowerpot. And if you want to use fresh yeast, substitute 1 ounce for the dried yeast, mixing it in the same way.

aunt effie's custard johnnycake

This delectable corn concoction first appeared in a 1931 cookbook, *Cross Creek Cookery*, written by the novelist Marjorie Kinnan Rawlings, author of *The Yearling*, but it's turned up several times since. This year the recipe is back, thanks to the collection of southern recipes *A Gracious Plenty*.

This fork-lifted corn bread has a dense, bready base and a top layer of light custard, unlike any corn bread we've ever eaten. It tastes just fine—some would say better—without the sugar.

COOK

Marjorie Kinnan Rawlings

SOURCE

A Gracious Plenty, by John T. Edge, Ellen Rolfes, and the Center for the Study of Southern Culture

serves 6

- 1 cup cornmeal (see note)
- ½ cup all-purpose flour
- 2 tablespoons sugar
- 1 teaspoon baking soda
- 1 teaspoon salt
- 1 cup buttermilk
- 2 large eggs, well beaten
- 1 cup milk

Preheat the oven to 350 degrees. Grease an 11-by-7-inch baking pan and set aside.

In a large bowl, sift together the dry ingredients. Beat in the buttermilk and stir in the eggs. Quickly blend in the milk. Pour the batter into the pan.

Bake for about 35 minutes, or until golden brown. Serve immediately, cutting the bread into squares at the table.

---

tip

Use stone-ground cornmeal for this recipe. Because it has the germ intact, the corn bread will have more character.

---

desserts

Texas Lemon Bombe 260

Peach Sorbet 263

Plum and Raspberry Sorbet 264

Star Anise Ice Cream 266

Rhubarb Soup 268

Honey-Poached Quinces 270

Port Wine Grapes 272

Danish Berry Pudding (Red Grits with Cream) 274

Caramelized Rice Pudding with Sour Cherry Sauce 276

Lemon-Yogurt Cheesecake for Jerry 279

Original Plum Torte 280

Fresh Ginger Cake 282

Ginger-Mascarpone Icebox Cake 286

Souffléed Lemon Custard 288

Chocolate Mousse with Olive Oil 290

Chocolate Bread Pudding 292

Apple and Armagnac Croustade 295

texts lemon bombe

Certainly the largest dessert in the book, offering generous servings for at least 16, this luscious Texas take on an ice cream bombe is a spectacular showstopper. Jeff Blank, the chef-owner of Hudson's on the Bend outside Austin, Texas, says the meringue-covered ice cream and custard confection was created as "a tribute to Ann Richards with that cotton candy hair." One

COOK

Jeff Blank

SOURCE

Cooking Fearlessly,
by Jeff Blank
and Jay Moore
with Deborah A. Harter

suspects that the glamorous ex-governor of Texas would be flattered to be compared to this huge, snow-white concoction.

Serve it to people who love vanilla ice cream, astoundingly rich lemon custard (lemon curd, really), and meringue as much as we do. But save it for a major birthday, wedding, or other destined-to-be-memorable occasion.

serves 8 texans; 16 non-texans

LEMON CUSTARD
- 2 cups (4 sticks) unsalted butter
- 3 cups sugar
- 24 large egg yolks, plus 8 large egg whites
- Grated zest and juice of 12 lemons (about 2 cups juice)
- 3 tablespoons pure vanilla extract

- 2 quarts rich vanilla ice cream (such as Ben & Jerry's or Häagen-Dazs), softened

MERINGUE
- 16 egg whites
- 3/4 cup confectioners' sugar
- 3 tablespoons 151-proof rum (optional)

FOR THE CUSTARD

In a medium saucepan, melt the butter. Whisk in the sugar and heat until the sugar is dissolved and the mixture is very hot.

In a very large food processor or in two batches in a regular food processor, combine the 24 egg yolks and 8 egg whites with the lemon zest, lemon juice, and vanilla. With the motor running, begin adding the sugar mixture—slowly at first, then faster, until all has been added.

While the mixture is still hot, transfer it to a double boiler. Whisk over simmering water until ribbons of sauce lie on top, like hollandaise sauce. Set aside to cool in an ice bath or the refrigerator.

In the bottom of a bombe mold or a large stainless steel, glass, or plastic bowl, mash half of the softened ice cream, forming a layer about 2 inches thick; refreeze the rest.

Smooth the ice cream layer with a spatula or your hands. Add 2 inches of the cooled lemon custard and immediately put the mold or bowl in the freezer.

Approximately 3 hours later, repeat this layering process. You will have 2 ice cream and 2 lemon custard layers. Cover tightly with plastic wrap and return to the freezer.

FOR THE MERINGUE

In a very large bowl, using an electric mixer, whip the egg whites and confectioners' sugar until stiff but not dry.

Remove the bombe from the freezer and dip the bottom of the mold or bowl briefly in hot water. Place an inverted serving plate over the top of the mold or bowl and flip the mold or bowl and plate over together. Pull off the mold or bowl. Using a pastry bag filled with meringue, give your dessert an "Ann Richards hairdo" (that is, swirl the meringue evenly and completely all over the bombe).

Return the bombe to the freezer for at least 3 hours, or until just before serving.

Remove the bombe from the freezer. It can be served as is, or the meringue can be browned. To do this, use a kitchen blowtorch. Or warm the rum in a small bowl in the microwave or in a small saucepan on the stovetop, pour on top of the bombe, and ignite with the blowtorch, carefully averting your face. Be careful: This is potentially dangerous. Serve immediately.

cook's note

Williams-Sonoma (800-541-2233) offers a miniature blowtorch that's just 5½ inches tall. Called the Kitchen Torch, it sells for about $30.

peach sorbet

COOK

Joanne Chang

SOURCE

Foodline.com

When the fresh, ripe local peaches come in, here's a stunningly good thing to do with an abundance of them. Joanne Chang, who's the pastry chef at Boston's Mistral, devised this gorgeous sorbet, which uses a few drops of almond extract—the same taste that's hiding in the peach's pit—and a jolt of fresh lemon to bring out the best in these most sensual of summer fruits. A pinch of salt rounds out the flavors.

If there are no ripe peaches in sight, you may be able to find the excellent peach puree from France that turns up in specialty stores from time to time.

serves 4

2 cups peach puree (from about 3 pounds very ripe peaches, peeled, pitted, and pureed)

³/₄ cup simple syrup (equal parts sugar and water, simmered together into a syrup), or more if needed

¹/₄ cup water, or more to taste
Juice of ¹/₄ lemon

2 drops almond extract
Pinch of salt

In a large bowl, combine all the ingredients. Taste and adjust the sweetness by adding water to weaken or simple syrup to intensify, if necessary. Freeze in an ice cream maker according to the manufacturer's directions. Or transfer to a 9-inch square baking pan, cover, and freeze until solid. Up to 2 hours before serving, remove from the freezer, let soften slightly, then cut the frozen sorbet into chunks with a blunt table knife. Transfer to a food processor and process until smooth and almost doubled in volume. Serve immediately or transfer to a plastic container, seal tightly, and return to the freezer until serving time.

plum and raspberry sorbet

If nature is taking suggestions for a new fruit, we'd like to recommend a ras-plum, to be made from equal parts of rich, succulent plums and sweet-tart raspberries. This deep burgundy sorbet strikes a perfect balance between the two and, like a great wine made from two grape varietals,

COOK

Stonegate Winery

SOURCE

Recipes from the Vineyards of Northern California: Desserts, by Leslie Mansfield

results in a beautiful blending of flavors. Perhaps not surprisingly, the recipe comes from Stonegate Winery in the Napa Valley, producers of Cabernet Sauvignon, and the contributor of this sublime sorbet to a compilation of desserts from California wine country.

serves 6

1 cup sugar
¹/₂ cup water
¹/₄ cup Cabernet Sauvignon

1¹/₂ pounds red or purple plums, (or a combination), pitted and sliced
2¹/₂ cups raspberries
¹/₄ teaspoon fresh lemon juice

In a small saucepan, combine the sugar, water, and wine. Simmer over low heat until the sugar dissolves. Bring to a boil and cook for 1 minute. Remove from the heat and cool to room temperature.

In a food processor, combine the plums and raspberries; process until smooth. Strain the puree through a sieve into a large bowl. Use the back of a wooden spoon to press on the solids, extracting as much juice as possible. Discard the solids.

Stir in the sugar syrup and lemon juice until well blended.

Chill thoroughly; then pour the mixture into an ice cream maker and freeze according to the manufacturer's directions. Or transfer the mixture to a 9-inch square baking pan, cover, and freeze until solid. Up to 2 hours before serving, remove from the freezer, let soften slightly, and cut into chunks with a blunt table knife. Transfer to a food processor and process until smooth and almost doubled in volume. Serve immediately or transfer to a plastic container, seal tightly, and return to the freezer until serving time.

serve with

Tuscan Rosemary and
Pine Nut Bars (page 306)

to drink

Stonegate Cabernet
Sauvignon

desserts

star anise ice cream

Although everyone knows ice cream is the perfect follow-up to an Asian meal, Asian-flavored ice creams are few and far between. We love this subtle Vietnamese ice cream, perfumed with vanilla and the exotic spice star anise, which is widely used in several Asian cuisines.

Don't be put off the recipe if you don't have any tapioca starch; we made a serious effort to find it, but in the end just made the ice cream without it, and it was delicious. If you can find it, though, the tapioca will add a wonderful texture.

But don't fail to add the little touch of ground star anise when you serve this dessert: It's the perfect punctuation point.

Start the recipe a day ahead so the ice cream will develop flavor.

COOK
Corinne Trang

SOURCE
Authentic Vietnamese Cooking

serves 6

 4 cups half-and-half (plus 2 tablespoons, if using tapioca starch)
 1 vanilla bean or 2 teaspoons pure vanilla extract
 12 whole star anise

 ³/₄ cup sugar, or more to taste
 4 large egg yolks
 1¹/₂ tablespoons tapioca starch (optional)
 1 teaspoon ground star anise

A day before you plan to serve the ice cream, in the top of a double boiler over medium heat, simmer the 4 cups half-and-half with the vanilla bean (if using vanilla extract, add it later) and whole star anise for 30 minutes.

Meanwhile, in a large bowl, whisk the sugar and egg yolks together until thick and pale yellow. Strain the hot half-and-half mixture into a glass measuring cup, discarding the star anise and reserving the vanilla bean for another purpose. Whisk the hot half-and-half into the eggs, 1 cup at a time, so as not to scramble the eggs. If using vanilla extract, add it now.

Return the half-and-half mixture to the top of the double boiler over simmering water until slightly thickened and heated through, 10 to 15 minutes.

In a small bowl, dilute the tapioca starch, if using, with the remaining 2 tablespoons half-and-half and add it to the mixture, whisking well. Continue mixing until you have a custard consistency that coats the back of a wooden spoon, about 2 minutes.

Transfer the custard to a heatproof bowl set over an ice bath and refrigerate overnight or for at least 12 hours.

The next day, freeze the custard in an ice cream maker according to the manufacturer's directions. Pack the finished ice cream into freezer containers, place a layer of plastic wrap directly on the surface, and seal. Freeze until ready to serve.

Lightly dust each portion with ground star anise before serving.

---

cook's note

The flavoring here is very delicate. If you'd like a stronger star anise presence, use 2 cups whole star anise.

---

rhubarb soup

I f you want to understand why the master French dessert chef François Payard keeps winning every award there is to win, just taste this soup, which was his most popular creation on the menu at New York's legendary Restaurant Daniel. The soup itself won an award from *Bartender* magazine—that's because it's so delicious in a champagne cocktail (page 327) as well as with vodka. The secret ingre-

COOK
François Payard

SOURCE
Simply Sensational Desserts

dients are lemongrass and grenadine (which contains pomegranate).

Payard serves the soup with a citrus sorbet and some exotic garnishes, but we find it such a fascinating dessert on its own that we prefer it plain or, as Irish-born chef James O'Shea serves it, with bits of blood oranges. This is one of the most refreshing desserts ever devised.

serves 8

FLAVOR SACHET
Grated zest of 1 lime
Grated zest of 1 orange
1 lemongrass stalk, chopped, or
    grated zest of 1 lemon

SOUP
1 pound rhubarb (about 7
    medium stalks), trimmed
    and chopped
4 cups water

²/₃ cup sugar
¹/₃ cup plus 1 tablespoon
    grenadine

GARNISHES
6 strawberries, hulled
1 mango, peeled
2 passion fruit
8 mint sprigs

FOR THE FLAVOR SACHET

Place all the ingredients in the center of a 4-inch square of cheesecloth. Gather the corners of the square together to form a pouch and tie with kitchen twine.

In a large saucepan, combine the rhubarb, water, and sugar and bring to a boil, stirring occasionally. Remove from the heat, add the flavor sachet, and stir in the grenadine. Cover and let the flavors infuse for 2 hours.

FOR THE GARNISHES

Slice the strawberries lengthwise ¹/₈ inch thick. Stack the slices a few at a time on top of one another and cut the stacks into thin strips. Cut the mango off the pit into ¹/₈-inch-thick slices. Stack the slices and cut into thin strips. Cut the passion fruit in half and scrape the seeds into a small container; save the flesh for another use.

To serve the soup, divide the strawberry strips among 8 dessert bowls. Remove the sachet from the soup and whisk briefly to break up the rhubarb fibers. Ladle the soup over the strawberry strips in each bowl. Arrange the mango slices in a crisscross pattern around the edges of the bowls and scatter passion fruit seeds in between the crisscrosses. Garnish the soup with the mint sprigs. Serve slightly chilled or at room temperature.

---

cook's notes

❧ The early-season spring rhubarb comes from the hothouse, and it's pale and elegant looking. It doesn't have as much flavor as the sturdier field rhubarb that arrives later in the season. If you're using field rhubarb, be sure to cut it into fine dice, or it will be too fibrous.

❧ Payard doesn't advise us about the right temperature to serve the soup. After it's infused for 2 hours, however, it will still be quite warm. It takes about 6 hours to cool down. You can, of course, serve it cold, but we think it has maximum flavor either slightly chilled or at room temperature.

honey-poached quinces

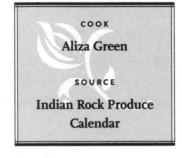

COOK
Aliza Green

SOURCE
**Indian Rock Produce
Calendar**

Quince trees used to abound all over the early American landscape, but now they've become a somewhat exotic fruit, ready to be rediscovered, as they definitely were this year. Legend has it that these deeply lobed yellow fall fruits were Eve's original temptation in the Garden of Eden. That might be so, based on their incredible fragrance. But we don't think Adam took a bite and was seduced forever: A raw quince would've sent civilization in quite a different direction, with its mouth-puckering fierceness.

Quinces need cooking to bring out their seductive flavor, which is somewhere between pear and apple, with another sharp but indefinable taste that seems to come from their wild heritage. But once you have the taste, you're hooked—every fall you'll be looking out for quinces, most reliably found at the farmers' market or an Asian market. A bowl of quinces brings an exotic aroma to the whole house; a lone quince on the shelf will perfume your closet.

The only problem is how to crack these hardest of fruits. We suggest a Chinese cleaver—or don't cut them at all until they're cooked; they'll have more flavor that way.

This heavenly dish of poached quinces from four-star Philadelphia chef Aliza Green accents their natural tartness and fragrance with lemon and spices, including a whole vanilla bean. You'll have leftover poaching liquid; reduce it into a delectable syrup, or even further and you'll have a wonderful quince jelly to serve on crackers with cheese or for breakfast toast.

serves 6

2 cups water, or more if needed
1 cup dry white wine
1/2 cup sugar
1/2 cup honey
1 cinnamon stick

1 vanilla bean, split lengthwise
   and scraped
Grated zest and juice of
   1 lemon
6 large fragrant quinces, such as
   Smyrnas

In a large nonreactive pot, combine everything but the quinces. Stir and bring to a boil.

Peel the skin off the quinces. Slice them in half (preferably with a Chinese cleaver), then in quarters. Cut out the seeds, then cut into 1/2-inch-thick wedges.

Place the quinces in the syrup and return to a boil. Reduce the heat to low and poach gently until the quinces are tender when pierced with a skewer, 15 minutes to nearly 1 hour. You may need to add more water. The quinces will be rosy when they're done. Let cool in the syrup and serve alone or with a cheese course.

---

cook's notes

ℒ To keep quinces for several weeks when they're going out of season, use San Francisco baker Fran Gage's simple trick of poaching them in the oven in a sugar syrup. For 3 pounds of quinces, in a medium flameproof casserole with a lid, mix 1 1/3 cups sugar with 1 1/2 cups water and bring to a boil. Preheat the oven to 325 degrees. Clean the quinces well and cut them in half; dig out the seeds with a sturdy melon baller—or leave them in, as you please. Add the quinces to the syrup and return to a boil. Cover and cook in the oven until the quinces are tender and rosy but still hold their shape, 1 1/2 to 2 hours. Store in the syrup for up to 3 weeks in the refrigerator. Peel (and seed, if you've left them in) before using.

ℒ Simplest of all is to bake the quinces. Rub off their fuzz and place them in a ceramic or enameled cast-iron baking dish. Bake at 325 degrees for 1 hour, or until tender. Peel and remove the seeds and cores before using.

port wine grapes

COOK

Joyce Dodson Piotrowski

SOURCE

Washington Post

As the cheese course returns to American tables, glorious as it is on its own, we find ourselves wondering how to dress it up for special occasions. Joyce Piotrowski, a catering manager in Virginia, has the answer with this minimalist but extremely elegant presentation.

Here the grapes leap out of their serving bowl and into the freezer to become icy little globes, a great match for the chilled port. And in case you still have your champagne saucers in this era of champagne flutes, they're the ideal serving vessel for this frosty dessert. Otherwise, any small glass dish will be fine.

serves 10

6 cups large seedless red grapes
(about 2½ pounds)
2 cups ruby or tawny port, chilled

Stem the grapes and place them on a cookie sheet in the freezer until completely frozen, at least 1 hour or up to 2 days.

---

to serve

Serve a vintage port on the side, possibly with a Stilton cheese and some proper British cheese crackers. Port can be astronomically expensive, but a good domestic brand such as Ficklin won't break anyone's bank.

Place 10 martini glasses or champagne saucers in the freezer to frost.

To serve, divide the grapes evenly among the frosted glasses. Drizzle the grapes with the port and serve immediately.

cook's note

The icy grapes are incredibly refreshing and surprising, but perhaps this dessert is most delicious when the grapes are served about 10 minutes out of the freezer, just as they begin to thaw.

desserts

danish berry pudding
(red grits with cream)

COOK

Anna Pump

SOURCE

Country Weekend Entertaining,
by Anna Pump
and Gen LeRoy

Despite the slightly bizarre original title of this old Danish dessert (it used to include barley meal or buckwheat, hence the "grits"), it is quite delectable. Anna Pump, owner of Loaves and Fishes and the Bridgehampton Inn on Long Island, grew up near the Danish border in Germany, and her mother used to make this pudding to serve after an ample midday meal. Once a humble regional specialty, as Pump notes, it's now served in crystal bowls at elegant dinner parties.

We have our own childhood memories of an American version of this pudding, which came in a packet and was called something like Danish dessert. The secret ingredient was and is red currants, which are available only for a couple of weeks in the summer, usually at farmers' markets. When you see them, grab them and make this dessert. Raspberries and blackberries are also delicious here, but the tart little currants bring another dimension to the pudding.

serves 6

- 2 cups stemmed red currants or raspberries
- 2 cups stemmed black currants or blackberries
- ³/₄ cup sugar
- 1 cup water
- ¹/₄ cup potato starch or cornstarch

- 1 tablespoon fresh lemon juice
- ¹/₂ teaspoon ground cinnamon
- 4 additional cups berries of your choice, such as raspberries or blackberries
- 1 cup half-and-half
- ¹/₂ cup heavy cream

---

cook's note

In the absence of red currants and raspberries, you can make the pudding with a blackberry base, then add blueberries and chopped strawberries during the final mixing.

In a large saucepan, combine the currants or berries, sugar, and ³/₄ cup of the water. Stirring often, bring to a boil and cook for 2 minutes.

In a small bowl, stir together the remaining ¹/₄ cup water and the potato starch or cornstarch. Pour it into the berry mixture while it is still over the heat. Stir until the mixture thickens and becomes clear. Fold in the lemon juice, cinnamon, and additional 4 cups berries. Remove from the heat, transfer to a serving bowl, and chill.

Combine the half-and-half and cream in a serving pitcher. Serve the pudding with the cream mixture on the side.

tip

Currants freeze well: Rinse, stem, and dry them, then spread them in a single layer on a cookie sheet to freeze. Package the frozen currants in heavy plastic bags and keep frozen for up to 3 months.

caramelized rice pudding
with sour cherry sauce

COOK

Joseph Sponzo

SOURCE

The Lake House Cookbook,
**by Trudie Styler
and Joseph Sponzo**

How's this for a fantasy? You marry Sting; you go to live in a sixteenth-century manor house in the glorious English countryside and raise a family; you have a completely organic garden that supplies most of your food. Oh, and you have a brilliant live-in chef, Joseph Sponzo. That's what happened to Trudie Styler, and she's decided to share it all with us in her book, *The Lake House Cookbook.*

So this wickedly rich pudding may be Sting's comfort food, but it's safe to say he's lucky. This is one of those desserts that are unforgettable. It's also a bit of a fuss to make, with its several elements. Fortunately, the cherry sauce is made a day ahead.

serves 8

CHERRY SAUCE

- ½ cup sugar
- ½ cup water
- 1 cup dry white wine
- ½ cup dried sour cherries
- 2 mint sprigs
- ½ vanilla bean, split lengthwise and scraped, both pod and seeds reserved

PUDDING

- 4 cups milk
- 3 cups heavy cream
- 2 2-by-1-inch strips lemon zest
- 2 cinnamon sticks
- 1 vanilla bean, split lengthwise, both pod and seeds reserved
- 1½ cups Arborio rice
- 1 teaspoon unsalted butter, softened
- ½ cup plus ⅓ cup superfine sugar
- 2 tablespoons water
- 2 large eggs plus 1 large egg white

FOR THE CHERRY SAUCE

In a heavy, shallow saucepan, combine the sugar and water and heat gently until the sugar dissolves, stirring frequently. Brush any sugar down from the sides of the pan with a pastry brush. Bring to a boil and boil for 5 minutes, or until just thick.

Add the wine, return to a boil, and boil for 8 to 10 minutes, or until the mixture is syrupy and all the alcohol has evaporated. Add the cherries, mint sprigs, and vanilla pod, scraping the seeds into the syrup. Let cool, then cover and let stand overnight. Remove the vanilla pod and mint.

FOR THE PUDDING

In a large saucepan, combine the milk, cream, lemon zest, cinnamon sticks, and vanilla pod, scraping in the seeds, and bring to a boil over medium-high heat. Remove from the heat and let stand for 30 minutes.

Strain the milk mixture into a large bowl, return to the saucepan, and bring to a boil. Stir in the rice, return to a boil, reduce the heat to low, and simmer, uncovered, stirring frequently, for 25 minutes, or until the rice is tender.

Meanwhile, lightly rub a 6-cup pudding mold or heatproof bowl with the butter.

VARIATIONS

❧ If fresh sour cherries are available, use 1 cup halved and pitted cherries instead of the dried ones.

❧ Sour cherries are wonderful with the pudding, but you can also use dried cranberries, for a holiday version, or blueberries.

To make the caramel, in a small, heavy saucepan, combine the ⅓ cup sugar and water, stirring several times to dissolve the sugar. Bring to a boil, brushing down the sides of the pan with a pastry brush dipped in water. Reduce the heat to low and simmer, without stirring, until the syrup begins to color and turns a deep amber, 3 to 5 minutes. Immediately pour the caramel into the bottom of the prepared mold or bowl.

In a medium bowl, whisk together the remaining ½ cup sugar with the eggs and egg white until well combined. Stir ½ cup of the rice mixture into the egg mixture, then carefully fold in the remaining rice mixture until well combined.

Transfer the pudding to the mold or bowl, smooth the top, cover with a dish towel, and let set for 45 to 60 minutes.

To serve, loosen the edges of the rice pudding with a knife. Cover the mold or bowl with a serving plate, then invert and tap gently to loosen the pudding. If the sides of the unmolded pudding are a little loose, reshape them with a spatula or knife. Serve with the warm or cool cherry sauce.

lemon-yogurt cheesecake for jerry

An Ayurvedic cookbook may seem the least likely place to find an ethereally light but deeply satisfying variation on cheesecake, but that's exactly what this lovely

COOK
Miriam Kasin Hospodar

SOURCE
Heaven's Banquet

recipe is. It's the author's father's favorite recipe in the book, and it's ours too. It goes together in just a few minutes, with no cream cheese to weigh it down.

serves 8

CRUMB CRUST

1¼ cups finely crushed graham crackers or gingersnaps

3½ tablespoons melted ghee (clarified butter, page 135) or melted butter

2 tablespoons raw turbinado sugar or packed light brown sugar

CHEESECAKE

3 cups plain yogurt

3 tablespoons arrowroot or cornstarch

½ cup sugar

1½ teaspoons finely grated lemon zest

Preheat the oven to 350 degrees. Butter a 9-inch pie pan.

FOR THE CRUST

In a medium bowl, mix all the ingredients together. Immediately press evenly into the prepared pie plate—if you wait, the ghee or butter will harden, and the mixture will be difficult to work with. (Once it's hardened, you can never really soften it up again.)

FOR THE CHEESECAKE

Combine all the ingredients in a blender until smooth. Pour the cheesecake into the prepared crust. Bake for 50 to 60 minutes, or until the top is lightly browned in a few places. Chill until firm; the filling will sink slightly. Serve cold.

desserts

original plum torte

COOK

**Marian Burros
after Lois Levine**

SOURCE

Splendidtable.org

Along with everyone else in the New York metropolitan area, we've been making this delectable torte since 1981, when Marian Burros first published it in the *New York Times*. Since then, it's been published every year by popular demand. In August, when the Italian prune plums arrive in the market, all we can think of is "Where's that recipe?"

Here it is, from its latest incarnation on the web. As Burros notes, the reason it's so popular is its lovely, old-fashioned flavor and the lightning speed with which it's made. Summer just wouldn't be complete without enjoying at least one of these tortes.

serves 8

8 tablespoons (1 stick) unsalted butter, softened

³/₄ cup plus 1–2 tablespoons sugar to taste

1 cup unbleached all-purpose flour, sifted

1 teaspoon baking powder

Pinch of salt

2 large eggs

12 Italian prune plums, halved and pitted

1 teaspoon ground cinnamon, or more to taste

Vanilla ice cream, for serving

Preheat the oven to 350 degrees. Place a rack at the lower level.

In a medium bowl, cream the butter with the ³/₄ cup sugar. Add the flour, baking powder, salt, and eggs and beat to mix. Spoon the batter into an ungreased 9- or 10-inch springform pan. Cover the top of the batter with the plums, skin side down. In a small bowl, mix the cinnamon with the remaining 1 to 2 tablespoons sugar and sprinkle over the top.

Bake for 40 to 50 minutes, or until a cake tester inserted in the center comes out clean. Remove from the oven and let cool; refrigerate or freeze, if desired.

To serve, let the torte come to room temperature, then reheat at 300 degrees until warm, if desired. Serve with vanilla ice cream.

cook's note

The little plums have such a short season, and this torte freezes so well and is such a snap to make, that it's a good idea to make several tortes and keep them on hand in the freezer.

fresh ginger cake

COOK
David Lebovitz

SOURCE
Room for Dessert

It seems as though every year there's a cake that captivates us—we can't stop talking about it, we can't stop baking it, and we can't stop eating it. This year, it's this sensational ginger cake, which is a bit like old-fashioned British sticky gingerbread, given an Asian twist with the exhilarating zing of black pepper and fresh ginger. It comes from a superlative cookbook that is for us the dessert book of the year.

David Lebovitz likes to serve his cake in summer with a plum-raspberry compote or sliced sugared peaches or nectarines. In winter, he chooses a dollop of tart lemon curd lightened with a bit of whipped cream. We prefer to add even more spice to the plate with Lebovitz's Very Spicy Caramel Pears (recipe follows), leaving out the cream.

serves 10; makes one 9-inch cake

4 ounces fresh gingerroot
1 cup mild molasses
1 cup sugar
1 cup vegetable oil, preferably peanut
2½ cups all-purpose flour
1 teaspoon ground cinnamon

½ teaspoon ground cloves
½ teaspoon freshly ground pepper
1 cup water
2 teaspoons baking soda
2 large eggs, at room temperature

Preheat the oven to 350 degrees. Place a rack at the middle level. Line a 9-inch cake pan or a 9½-inch springform pan with a circle of parchment paper.

Peel, slice, and chop the ginger or grate it very fine—you should have about ½ cup.

In a large bowl, combine the molasses, sugar, and oil. In a medium bowl, sift together the flour, cinnamon, cloves, and pepper.

In a small saucepan, bring the water to a boil, stir in the baking soda, and add to the molasses mixture. Stir in the ginger.

Gradually whisk the dry ingredients into the liquid ingredients. Add the eggs and mix until thoroughly combined. Pour the batter into the prepared pan and bake for about 1 hour, or until the top of the cake springs back lightly when pressed or a toothpick inserted in the center comes out clean. If the top of the cake browns too quickly before the cake is done, drape a piece of foil over it.

Cool the cake for at least 30 minutes. Run a knife around the edge to loosen it from the pan. Remove from the pan, peel off the parchment paper, and serve.

Very Spicy Caramel Pears

s e r v e s 4

15 whole cloves
 2 whole star anise
 2 cinnamon sticks
½ teaspoon black peppercorns
 4 Bosc, Comice, or Butter pears
 4 tablespoons (½ stick) butter

½ cup packed light or dark brown
  sugar
¼ cup cognac, brandy, or rum
¼ cup heavy cream (see note)
  Vanilla ice cream (optional)

Preheat the oven to 400 degrees.

Coarsely crush the spices with a mortar and pestle or break them up in a plastic bag by smashing them with a rolling pin or hammer.

Peel, quarter, and core the pears, slicing away the fibrous parts in the center. Cut the butter into small pieces and put them in an 8-inch square baking dish with the brown sugar. Put the baking dish in the oven for a few minutes to melt the butter. Arrange the pears in the baking dish, add the spices and liquor, and toss until the pears are evenly coated.

Cover the baking dish with foil and bake for 30 to 45 minutes (Boscs will take longer than the others), or until the pears are cooked through. Remove the dish from the oven two or three times during baking and stir so that the pears will be evenly flavored on all sides. The pears are done when they can be easily pierced with the tip of a knife.

Transfer the pears to a medium bowl with a slotted spoon. Scrape the juices and spices from the baking dish into a medium heavy skillet.

Add the heavy cream to the skillet and cook over medium heat until the mixture turns a deep color, thickens, and caramelizes. Strain the caramel over the pears and serve with scoops of vanilla ice cream, if desired.

VARIATION

You can experiment with the spices here, adding slices of ginger if you like. Lebovitz warns to be careful of the star anise, however, since it can easily become overwhelming. You can also make this dish with sliced apples.

---

tip

If you are serving the pears without the cream, as we do, you can make them ahead and rewarm them to melt the butter before serving.

ginger-mascarpone icebox cake

COOK

Heather Ho

SOURCE

Fine Cooking

This delectable no-bake dessert from the pastry chef at San Francisco's Boulevard restaurant has some of the charm of tiramisu, with the zing of ginger and the voluptuousness of mascarpone. It's a great holiday sweet, for times when oven space is at a premium. Icebox cakes are almost by definition unpretentious, and this one uses plain old gingersnaps as its base.

More virtues: It must be made a day ahead, it travels well (as long as you keep it chilled), and there probably won't be any leftovers to fuss with. It's as good in the summer as it is for the holidays and pairs well with blueberries, mangoes, or peaches.

serves 12

12 ounces gingersnap crumbs (about 2¼ cups; from about 40 Nabisco brand gingersnaps)

5 tablespoons unsalted butter, melted

8 ounces cream cheese, softened

½ cup plain low-fat yogurt

⅔ cup sugar

½ teaspoon pure vanilla extract

½ cup minced crystallized ginger

1 pound mascarpone cheese

⅓ cup heavy cream

Spray a 9-inch springform pan with nonstick cooking spray or butter it lightly. Dust the pan with a little sugar and shake out any excess. In a medium bowl, combine the gingersnap crumbs and butter, rubbing them together with your fingertips to combine thoroughly. Sprinkle half of the crumbs over the bottom of the pan and pat down evenly; reserve the rest.

In a large bowl, with an electric mixer, whip together the cream cheese, yogurt, sugar, vanilla, and ginger until smooth, scraping down the sides. Add the mascarpone and cream and whip until the mixture is thoroughly combined and just holds peaks. Don't over-whip, or the mixture may separate.

Carefully spoon half of the mascarpone mixture over the crust, spreading it evenly to the edges of the pan. Sprinkle half of the re-maining crumbs over the mascarpone mixture in the pan. Top with the remaining mascarpone mixture and finish with the remaining crumbs. Gently tap the pan on the counter to eliminate any air bub-bles. Cover with plastic wrap and refrigerate overnight. Serve cold.

souffléed lemon custard

COOK

Gordon Hamersley

SOURCE

Starchefs.com

This super-lemony souf-flélike dessert has been on the menu at Gordon Hamersley's eponymous Boston restaurant, Hamersley's Bistro, since it opened twelve years ago. All efforts to take it off the menu are greeted with outrage by Hamersley's customers, so he's finally given in and shared the recipe with the rest of us via the Starchefs web site.

Although it seems to have vanished from contemporary cookbooks, versions of this dessert appear in many old American cookbooks. This particular variation is based on a recipe by Craig Claiborne, but it's much richer and has four times as much fresh lemon. What all these desserts have in common is their airy cakelike top and custardy bottom, which turns into a sort of sauce. Hamersley spoons some of the custard onto a plate and garnishes it with fresh mint leaves. Summer berries are an especially nice touch with the custard.

serves 8

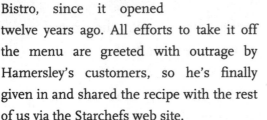

½ cup unsalted butter, softened	2 cups milk
1½ cups sugar	1 cup heavy cream
6 large eggs, separated	½ teaspoon salt
¼ teaspoon grated lemon zest	Fresh mint leaves or berries,
1 cup fresh lemon juice	for garnish
⅔ cup all-purpose flour, sifted	

Preheat the oven to 350 degrees.

In a large bowl, with an electric mixer on medium speed, cream the butter and sugar until fluffy.

Add the egg yolks, one at a time. Add the lemon zest, lemon juice, and flour, stirring until just barely combined. Stir in the milk and cream until smooth.

In a separate large bowl, beat the egg whites until they hold soft-to-medium peaks, adding the salt halfway through. Fold into the custard mixture.

Pour the custard mixture into a 10-inch round cake pan and set into a larger pan filled with 1 inch water. Bake for about 50 minutes, or until the custard is just set. Let cool to room temperature.

Serve on a plate or in glass bowls, garnished with mint leaves or berries.

---

cook's notes

❧ Depending on the eggs, you may have more custard than will fit in the cake pan, especially if it's shallow. In that case, bake the custard in a 2-quart soufflé dish.

❧ You can bake the custard several hours ahead and hold it at room temperature until ready to serve.

chocolate mousse with olive oil

COOK

Teresa Barrenechea

SOURCE

Foodtv.com

Talk about secret ingredients! You might think just a little olive oil has been added here as a novelty, but in fact it's a whopping ³/₄ cup, and it entirely replaces the usual heavy cream—a big bonus for people who can't eat milk products. When Teresa Barrenechea, author of *The Basque Table* and Manhattan restaurateur, made this dessert on the Food Network, the phone board lit up like Times Square. The viewers simply couldn't believe it.

But what's really unbelievable is how absolutely and addictively delicious this mousse is. It has a silky texture, a hauntingly pure chocolate taste, and just a hint of orange. And yes, you *can* taste the olive oil, but it too is delicious. If you're looking to astonish your guests with a minimum of fuss, this is your dessert.

serves 6

6 ounces dark chocolate, chopped
3 large eggs, separated
²/₃ cup confectioners' sugar

¹/₄ cup double-espresso coffee or 1 tablespoon instant espresso powder
2 tablespoons Cointreau
³/₄ cup extra-virgin olive oil

In a small bowl in the microwave or in a small saucepan over very low heat, melt the chocolate. Let cool.

In a medium bowl, with an electric mixer, beat the egg yolks and sugar until smooth. Add the coffee and Cointreau, then stir in the melted chocolate. Whisk until well mixed. Add the olive oil and mix well.

In a separate medium bowl, beat the egg whites until foamy and almost stiff. Gently fold the chocolate mixture into the beaten whites until thoroughly mixed.

Spoon the mousse into a serving bowl, cover, and refrigerate until ready to serve. Serve cold.

VARIATION

At her restaurant, Marichu, Teresa usually serves the mousse with an orange sauce. You can make a quick one by chopping ¼ cup thin-cut marmalade in a food processor, then adding enough water —and a jot of Cointreau—to make a sauce. Heat the sauce gently, then let it cool to room temperature, and serve on the side.

---

cook's note

If you're very unsure about how you'll like the olive oil, use a light olive oil the first time.

---

desserts

chocolate bread pudding

COOK
Martha Stewart

SOURCE
Martha Stewart Living

This supremely delicious but also very homey dessert was one of Martha's Desserts of the Month. And of all the sweet bread puddings we tried this year, it's our favorite. As bread puddings go, it's the gold standard. All the details here — the real vanilla bean, the excellent bread, the high-quality chocolate, the crème fraîche — make a huge difference, so don't expect miracles if you substitute plain old vanilla extract, supermarket bread, and baking chocolate.

You can make the bread pudding ahead of time and reheat it, but it won't be quite as delicious as when it's first made.

serves 8 to 10

- 2 cups heavy cream
- 2 cups milk
- 1 vanilla bean, split lengthwise, both pod and seeds reserved
- 3 cinnamon sticks (optional)
- 1 loaf (about 1 pound) brioche, bakery white bread, or challah
- 12 ounces Valrhona or other high-quality bittersweet chocolate, coarsely chopped
- 8 large egg yolks
- 1/4 cup sugar
- 1 8-ounce container crème fraîche
- 1/2 ounce (1/4 cup) high-quality bittersweet chocolate shavings, for garnish

In a medium saucepan, combine the cream, milk, and vanilla pod, scraping in the seeds, and cinnamon sticks, if using. Bring to a boil, remove from the heat, cover with plastic wrap, and let stand for 30 minutes to infuse the flavors.

Cut the bread into ¼-inch-thick slices. Cut the slices into quarters, setting aside the rounded top pieces. Fill a 9-by-12-inch gratin dish or a deep oval roasting pan with the quartered pieces.

Remove the plastic wrap from the cream mixture and return to a boil. Remove from the heat and discard the vanilla pod and cinnamon sticks. Add the chopped chocolate and whisk until smooth. In a large bowl, combine the egg yolks and sugar and whisk to combine.

Pour the chocolate mixture very slowly into the egg yolk mixture, whisking constantly until fully combined. Slowly pour half the chocolate custard over the bread, making sure all the bread is soaked. Arrange the reserved bread on top in a decorative pattern, pressing firmly so the bottom layer of bread absorbs the custard.

Spoon the remaining custard over the bread until it is completely covered and all the cracks are filled. Place a piece of plastic wrap over the dish; press down to soak the bread thoroughly. Remove the plastic wrap, wipe the edges of the dish with a damp towel, and let stand for 30 minutes.

Preheat the oven to 325 degrees.

Place the gratin dish in a larger pan and add hot water to the outer pan until it is halfway up the sides of the gratin dish. Bake until set, about 35 minutes.

In a small bowl, whisk the crème fraîche until soft peaks form. Serve the pudding warm, garnished with crème fraîche and the chocolate shavings.

---

cook's note

Heat leftover bread pudding in the microwave, about 10 seconds for each serving. Garnish with crème fraîche and chocolate shavings and serve.

apple and armagnac croustade

COOK

Daniel Boulud

SOURCE

*Daniel Boulud's Café
Boulud Cookbook,*
by Daniel Boulud
and Dorie Greenspan

Apple pie, apple tart, tarte tatin, apple croustade —these are among the all-time great desserts, and this one is a knockout. It's also a great recipe for pastry-phobes; if you can't make a good crust to save your life, you can make this croustade and amaze your guests—and yourself.

The croustade is a classic dessert from Gascony, where it used to be made with a pulled dough much like strudel, then brushed with duck or goose fat. Even in Gascony, though, today they use phyllo and butter, as in this recipe. The croustade is built up in sweet buttery layers sprinkled with almonds. The sheets of phyllo are laid down, the Armagnac-warmed apples are laid on the pastry and baked, and then another two layers of caramelized airy phyllo go on top to crown the croustade.

The directions may seem long, but this is actually a simple dessert and requires some attention only during the baking process.

If you have no Armagnac—the wonderful Gascon brandy—you can use cognac or another brandy. But if you do have Armagnac, serve a small glass along with the croustade.

serves 6

APPLES

3 tablespoons unsalted butter
6 Rome apples, peeled, cored, and each cut into 6–8 wedges
2 tablespoons sugar
1 vanilla bean, split lengthwise, both pod and seeds reserved
1/3 cup Armagnac

CROUSTADE

8 sheets phyllo
6 tablespoons unsalted butter, melted
1/2 cup confectioners' sugar, sifted
1/3 cup sliced almonds

Crème fraîche, lightly sweetened whipped cream, or vanilla ice cream, for serving

FOR THE APPLES

In a large skillet, melt the butter over medium heat. When the butter is foamy, add the apples, sugar, and vanilla pod, scraping in the seeds. Cook, stirring constantly, until the apples are lightly caramelized, 7 to 10 minutes. Add the Armagnac and, standing away from the pan, set it aflame. When the flames subside, turn the apples. When the flames have died out and the Armagnac is reduced to a glaze, transfer the apples to a plate and let cool to room temperature. Once cooled, the apples can be covered and refrigerated for up to 12 hours.

FOR THE CROUSTADE

Preheat the oven to 350 degrees. Place a rack at the middle level. Place a 10-inch tart ring or, in a pinch, a 10-inch springform pan minus the bottom on a nonstick cookie sheet. Stack the phyllo on your work surface and cover it with a damp towel.

Remove the top sheet of phyllo (cover the remaining sheets with the towel). Brush the phyllo with butter and dust it with confectioners' sugar. Crumple it and press it into the ring — it should be fairly flat and shouldn't come up the sides of the ring. Sprinkle with about one-fifth of the almonds. Repeat this procedure three more times, until you have 4 buttered, sugared, and almond-sprinkled sheets of phyllo in the ring. Spoon the apple mixture into the center of the croustade, leaving a 1-inch border bare. Working as you did before, butter, sugar, and crumple a sheet of phyllo, fitting it into the ring to cover the apples. Sprinkle this layer with the remaining almonds and cover with another crumpled sheet of buttered and sugared phyllo.

Bake the croustade for about 10 minutes, or until lightly browned, watching carefully to make certain it doesn't brown too much. Remove the croustade from the oven.

Increase the oven temperature to 400 degrees. Butter and sugar another sheet of phyllo, this time crumpling it very loosely so that when you place it on top of the croustade it creates a light, airy crown. Bake the croustade for 7 minutes more, or until lightly browned. Remove the croustade from the oven.

Butter the last sheet of phyllo and once again crumple it to make a crown. Place it on top of the croustade and dust it heavily with the remaining confectioners' sugar. Return the croustade to the oven and bake until the top layer caramelizes evenly, about 5 minutes. Check the progress of the sugar frequently, because it can go from brown to burned in a flash. Pull the croustade from the oven as soon as the top is a golden caramel color and let cool for 5 to 10 minutes.

To serve, lift off the ring and, using two large metal spatulas, transfer the croustade to a serving plate. Serve warm or at room temperature the day it is made, with crème fraîche, whipped cream, or vanilla ice cream.

peanut butter cookies

COOK

Mom-Mom Fritch

SOURCE

Amy Fritch, *Gourmet*

Amy Fritch's grandmother always made these peanut butter cookies, which were her father's favorite—and so good she decided to share them with *Gourmet*'s readers. The editors were amazed: These insanely simple, intense, flourless cookies were the best peanut butter cookies they'd ever tasted.

This is a good recipe to keep in your head: there are just four ingredients, and there's just one of everything—staples almost everyone keeps on hand.

Although you can indeed use either creamy or chunky peanut butter, the recipe works best with the commercial creamy variety. Organic nonhydrogenated peanut butter—just ground peanuts—will work too, and it will taste delicious, but be prepared for some serious crumbling. The hydrogenated commercial product is also sweetened, which may affect the taste of these already quite sweet cookies, so be sure to use the salt tip.

makes about 5 dozen cookies

1 cup creamy or chunky peanut butter

1 cup sugar

1 large egg

1 teaspoon baking soda

Preheat the oven to 350 degrees. Place a rack at the middle level. Grease two cookie sheets or line them with parchment paper.

In a large bowl, with an electric mixer, beat the peanut butter and sugar until well combined. In a small bowl, lightly beat the egg and beat into the peanut butter mixture along with the baking soda until well combined.

Roll level teaspoons of dough into balls and arrange them about 1 inch apart on the cookie sheets. With the tines of a fork, flatten the balls to about 1½ inches in diameter, making a crosshatch pattern. Bake the cookies in batches on the middle rack until puffed and pale golden, about 10 minutes.

Cool the cookies on the cookie sheets for 2 minutes, then transfer with a metal spatula to racks to cool completely. Store in an airtight container at room temperature for up to 5 days.

---

tip

These cookies are especially tasty with an added ½ teaspoon salt. We also like to press a whole roasted salted peanut into the center of each cookie, Chinese almond cookie style.

zante currant cookies

COOK

Anonymous

SOURCE

**Sun-Maid Zante
currant box**

Nothing wrong with good old raisins, but somehow currants strike us as much more interesting and subtle. Possibly it's all those currants in British baking: currant buns, steamed puddings with currants, and, yes, spotted dick.

On the back of the Sun-Maid currant box, you'll find an excellent recipe for these icebox cookies, which are fast to make and fast to disappear. They have a great texture—soft but not crumbly—and they're not terribly sweet. You can keep a roll of them frozen in foil, ready to slice and bake at a moment's notice.

makes about 4 dozen cookies

1 cup (2 sticks) butter, softened	2 teaspoons pure vanilla extract
1 cup confectioners' sugar	2¼ cups all-purpose flour
½ cup sugar	½ teaspoon baking soda
1 large egg	1 cup Zante currants

In a large bowl, combine the butter, sugars, egg, and vanilla. Beat with an electric mixer until light and fluffy. In a medium bowl, combine the flour and baking soda. Stir into the butter mixture, mixing well. Stir in the currants.

Shape the dough into a 12-inch-long roll. Cover and refrigerate until firm.

---

cook's note

We like to add about 1 tablespoon of grated lemon zest to the cookie dough.

Preheat the oven to 350 degrees. Place a rack at the middle level.

Cut the dough crosswise into ¼-inch-thick slices and place on ungreased cookie sheets. Bake for 10 to 12 minutes, or until light brown. Let cool on wire racks.

florentines

COOK

**Catherine Brandel
after Ken Wolfe**

SOURCE

**San Francisco Women
Chefs' benefit dinner
booklet**

A florentine is a good candidate for world's best cookie: delicate, lacy, buttery, shattering delectably at first bite, perfumed with orange and almond, cloaked in the finest chocolate— these are cookies taken to a higher power. And this recipe makes all other florentines seem like Oreos. As a rule, only ace bakers make florentines; they're a little tricky to pry from the baking sheet, and purists insist on making their own candied orange peel as well. But the late Catherine Brandel, longtime chef at Chez Panisse and instructor at the Culinary Institute at Greystone in the Napa Valley, made florentines seem like child's play.

She learned how to make these delectable sweets at the feet of her own cooking guru, Ken Wolfe, and then tinkered with the recipe a bit to make it her own. Now you too can knock everyone's socks off with this legendary recipe.

makes about 3 dozen cookies

½ cup whipping cream

8 tablespoons (1 stick) unsalted butter, melted

½ cup plus 2 tablespoons sugar

4½ tablespoons all-purpose flour

1 rounded cup almonds (6 ounces), coarsely chopped

4 ounces finely chopped candied orange peel (about ½ cup; see Variation, page 320)

⅔ cup chopped bittersweet chocolate (4 ounces)

---

cook's note

If making your own candied orange peel seems out of the question, you can order it from King Arthur Flour: (800) 827-6836.

Preheat the oven to 300 degrees. Oil a cookie sheet (see tip).

In a medium saucepan, combine all the ingredients except the chocolate and bring to a boil. Stir until the mixture is sticky and a little stiff.

Spread the batter on the cookie sheet in circles about 3 inches wide and $1/16$ inch thick. Bake until golden brown, about 20 minutes.

Remove the cookies from the oven and immediately transfer them to a rack. When they are stiff and dry, melt the chocolate in the microwave or a double boiler and dip the cookies in it to coat the bottoms. Place on a rack to dry. Store in an airtight tin, between layers of waxed paper.

tip

If you use parchment paper on the cookie sheet instead of oiling it, you can slide the entire sheet off the pan and onto the rack. That way you won't lose any cookies that harden too quickly and fatally stick to the pan. Use a spatula to scoot them off the paper and onto the rack.

christmas casserole cookies

A jewel of a recipe from the King Arthur Flour web site, this makes unorthodox cookies that are baked and then shaped. They are delicious little sweetmeatlike nuggets—the perfect cookie for adult-and-child teamwork. Even very little kids can roll the baked dough into balls and then in sugar. Because these cookies stay moist for

COOK

Susan Kent

SOURCE

Kingarthurflour.com

up to one week, they are naturals for gift giving. The optional Baker's Special Sanding Sugar and edible glitter called for in the recipe can be ordered from King Arthur: (800) 827-6836. Susan Kent, creator of the recipe, is head of the customer service team there.

makes about 3 dozen 1-inch cookies

2 large eggs
1 cup sugar
¼ teaspoon salt
1½ cups chopped walnuts or
    pecans

1 cup chopped dates
1 cup flaked coconut (sweetened
    or unsweetened, toasted or
    not)
⅛–¼ teaspoon almond extract, or to
    taste
1 teaspoon pure vanilla extract

¼–½ cup granulated sugar, Baker's
    Special Sanding Sugar,
    cinnamon sugar, or the
    sugar of your choice, or
    1 tablespoon edible glitter
    plus 3 tablespoons
    granulated sugar, for rolling

Preheat the oven to 350 degrees. Place a rack at the middle level.

In a medium bowl, beat together the eggs, 1 cup sugar, and salt until pale yellow in color. Add the remaining ingredients, stirring until well combined.

Spread the dough in an ungreased 9-inch square baking pan or casserole dish and bake for 35 to 40 minutes, or until it just barely begins to brown around the edges.

Remove the dough from the oven, transfer to a clean medium bowl, and immediately beat with a wooden spoon, or a metal spoon if your hands are fairly heat resistant. Let the dough cool for about 15 minutes, or until you can handle it, then shape it into 1-inch balls. Roll the balls in the sugar or edible-glitter mixture. (The white edible glitter makes beautiful, sparkly balls.)

Transfer the cookies to racks and let them dry at room temperature for 1 to 2 hours. Store in cookie tins between sheets of waxed paper.

tuscan rosemary and pine nut bars

COOK

Melanie Barnard

SOURCE

Short & Sweet

Melanie Barnard, queen of sweets and author of *Short & Sweet,* assures cookie makers that they too will love the taste of these Italian-inspired bars. Essentially, they are elegant shortbreads and so good that we now automatically double the recipe. Because they keep so well, it's not a bad idea to whip up a batch or two in any off moment (actually moments, and those are few—they take about 10 minutes to assemble). A tin of these in the kitchen will always be good to go.

makes 16 cookies

¹⁄₄ cup pine nuts

8 tablespoons (1 stick) unsalted butter, cut into 10 pieces

¹⁄₂ cup confectioners' sugar

1 tablespoon chopped fresh rosemary or 2 teaspoons dried

1 cup all-purpose flour

Preheat the oven to 350 degrees. Place a rack at the middle level.

Spread the pine nuts on a cookie sheet and place in the oven. Toast, stirring once or twice to prevent burning, until they are a shade darker and fragrant, about 5 minutes. Watch carefully; pine nuts burn easily. Remove from the cookie sheet and set aside.

Meanwhile, in a medium saucepan, melt the butter over medium heat. Remove from the heat and stir in the confectioners' sugar, rosemary, and pine nuts. Then stir in the flour to make a stiff dough.

Spread and pat the dough evenly into an ungreased 8-inch square baking pan. Bake until the bars are golden and firm at the edges, about 20 minutes. Cool the pan on a rack for about 2 minutes, then use a sharp knife to cut into 16 squares. Let the bars cool in the pan for at least 10 minutes before removing them with a small spatula. The bars can be stored, tightly covered, for up to 5 days, or frozen for 1 month.

cook's note

If you'd rather use chopped walnuts instead of pine nuts, do—rosemary and walnuts have a remarkable affinity.

desserts

coconut-walnut bars

COOK

Beth Hensperger

SOURCE

San Jose Mercury News

Let's say you need a *lot* of cookies, and you want them to be special but you don't want to spend hours and hours making them. These bars would be a perfect choice: They're foolproof, everyone raves about them, and they keep well. And be prepared to give out the recipe: At the *San Jose Mercury News,* the editors who first tasted them demanded to have it. Our one caveat is that the bars are extremely sweet; if you don't have a matching sweet tooth, they won't be your favorites.

The bars are baked in two relays: First the buttery cookie crust gets baked, then the coconut-walnut topping goes on. The topping will puff up dramatically in the oven, but don't worry, it goes right down again and makes a chewy top crust.

makes 4 dozen bars

COOKIE CRUST

- 3 cups (6 sticks) unsalted butter, softened
- 1³/₄ cups confectioners' sugar
- 4 cups plus 2 tablespoons all-purpose flour
- 4 teaspoons cornstarch

COCONUT-WALNUT TOPPING

- 7 large eggs
- 3 cups packed light brown sugar
- 1 tablespoon pure vanilla extract
- 1 tablespoon light corn syrup
- 5¹/₂ cups chopped walnuts (19 ounces)
- ⁷/₈ cup flaked sweetened coconut

- 1 large egg, beaten with 1 teaspoon water, for glazing

Preheat the oven to 275 degrees.

FOR THE CRUST

In a large bowl, with an electric mixer, cream the butter and confectioners' sugar until fluffy. Beat in the flour and cornstarch. Press the cookie crust into an ungreased 12-by-17-inch baking pan (a half-sheet pan). Pierce the entire surface with the tines of a fork. Bake until golden brown, 1 to 1½ hours. Let cool in the pan on a rack for 15 minutes.

Meanwhile, increase the oven temperature to 350 degrees.

FOR THE TOPPING

In a large bowl, with an electric mixer, combine the 7 eggs, brown sugar, vanilla, and corn syrup. Stir in the walnuts and coconut.

Brush the cookie crust with the egg glaze to prevent it from getting soggy. Pour in the topping and spread to distribute the nuts evenly over the surface.

TO BAKE

Bake for 25 minutes, or until the topping is set, dry to the touch, and golden brown. Cool completely in the pan on a rack. Cut into 2-inch squares. Keep the bars wrapped in waxed paper and tightly sealed in a cookie tin.

apricot-pistachio bars

COOK
Georgeanne Brennan

SOURCE
Holiday Sweets

These moist, slightly chewy bars simply vanish from the cookie plate. They are sweet but also a bit tart with the profusion of apricots, and the intensely aromatic spices—cardamom and mace—give them a heady Middle Eastern perfume that goes perfectly with the pistachios. And although they're excellent holiday fare, they'd be just as good with early-fall pears or after-dinner liqueurs.

makes about 5 dozen bars

- 1 teaspoon unsalted butter, plus 1 cup (2 sticks), softened
- ½ cup sugar
- ½ cup packed light brown sugar
- 4 large eggs
- 1 tablespoon grated orange zest
- 1 teaspoon apricot brandy (optional)
- ½ teaspoon pure vanilla extract
- 1¼ cups all-purpose flour
- 1 teaspoon baking powder
- ½ teaspoon baking soda

- ½ teaspoon ground cardamom
- ¼ teaspoon ground mace
- 2 cups coarsely chopped dried California apricots
- ½ cup dried currants
- ½ cup coarsely chopped pistachios

ICING
- 1½ cups confectioners' sugar
- 2–3 tablespoons fresh orange juice, or more if needed

Preheat the oven to 350 degrees. Grease a 10-by-15-inch baking pan with the 1 teaspoon butter.

In a large bowl, beat the remaining 1 cup butter and the sugars until light and fluffy. Beat in the eggs, one at a time. Add the orange zest, brandy (if using), and vanilla, beating well to blend.

In a medium bowl, combine the flour, baking powder, baking soda, cardamom, mace, apricots, currants, and pistachios. Stir the flour mixture into the butter mixture and mix well. Spread the batter evenly in the prepared pan and bake for about 20 minutes, or until a toothpick inserted in the center comes out clean. Transfer the pan to a rack and let cool for 15 minutes.

FOR THE ICING

In a small bowl, combine the confectioners' sugar and orange juice, mixing to a medium-firm consistency. Spread on top of the still-warm uncut bars in the pan and let stand until the icing sets. Cut the bars into 1-inch squares.

Store in single layers, separated by sheets of waxed paper, in an airtight container for up to 3 days.

---

cook's notes

🌿 The 10-by-15-inch pan specified here is a slightly unusual size. You can also use a 9-by-12-inch pan, but it will take about 30 minutes instead of 20 and the bars will be slightly thicker, so they should be cut into smaller squares.

🌿 We liked these bars best with just a hint of icing—about half the amount specified in the recipe.

---

sour cream pound cake with strawberries

We have to admit that we're complete suckers for pound cake. We must have tried them all by now, but we still can't pass up an interesting new recipe. So when Molly O'Neill announced that this almond-scented pound cake had rocked her world, we paid attention. And indeed, this is a pound cake quite unlike any other: frankly sweet, with a crackly surface, it makes the perfect raft for terrific strawberries.

COOK

Eva Bone

SOURCE

Molly O'Neill,
New York Times Magazine

It's also an heirloom recipe: Eva Bone passed it on to her granddaughter, Carol Simmons, a strawberry grower in Plant City, Florida—best known as the winter strawberry capital. Yankees may find it hard to give up the classic biscuit shortcake, but southerners will immediately recognize the wisdom of using this fragrant fluffy cake to embrace strawberries and cream.

serves 16

- 1 cup (2 sticks) unsalted butter, plus more for greasing pan
- 3 cups all-purpose flour, plus more for the pan
- 3 cups sugar, plus more for sweetening strawberries
- 6 large eggs, separated
- ¼ teaspoon baking soda
- ¼ teaspoon salt
- 1 cup sour cream
- 1 teaspoon pure vanilla extract
- ½ teaspoon almond extract
- 2 quarts strawberries, hulled and thinly sliced

Sweetened whipped cream, for serving

Preheat the oven to 325 degrees. Butter and flour an angel food cake pan.

In a large bowl, with an electric mixer, cream the 1 cup butter and 2 cups of the sugar. Add the egg yolks, one at a time, beating well after each addition. In a medium bowl, sift together the flour, baking soda, and salt. Sift again. Stir the flour mixture into the sugar mixture in 3 additions, alternating with additions of sour cream. Stir in the vanilla and almond extract.

In a separate medium bowl, beat the egg whites and the remaining 1 cup sugar until the mixture holds stiff peaks. Gently fold the egg whites into the batter. Scrape the batter into the prepared pan. Bake until the cake is golden and a cake tester inserted in the cake comes out clean, 1 to 1½ hours. Cool in the pan for 10 minutes. Run a thin-bladed knife around the edge of the pan and invert the cake onto a rack to cool.

Meanwhile, in a medium bowl, combine the strawberries and sugar to taste and refrigerate for at least 1 hour. When ready to serve, slice the cake and top each serving with strawberries and whipped cream.

double-chocolate layer cake

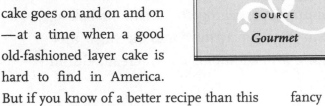

COOK
Ed Kasky

SOURCE
Gourmet

The search for the all-time killer chocolate layer cake goes on and on and on —at a time when a good old-fashioned layer cake is hard to find in America. But if you know of a better recipe than this one, please send it to us—as far as we're concerned, the search is momentarily over. This cake has it all: great chocolate, cocoa, coffee, and buttermilk, for starters. For all chocolate lovers, this is *the* birthday cake.

And you can make it up to three days ahead.

In fact, it's the cake they serve at Engine Co. No. 28, a Los Angeles restaurant. Chef Kasky uses some fancy chocolate in his cake—Callebaut semisweet for the cake and Guittard French vanilla chocolate for the frosting—but we've had great results using less noble brands. Any good semisweet chocolate will deliver the goods.

serves 12

CAKE

- 3 ounces good-quality semisweet chocolate, finely chopped
- 1¹/₂ cups hot brewed coffee
- 3 cups sugar
- 2¹/₂ cups all-purpose flour
- 1¹/₂ cups unsweetened cocoa powder (not Dutch-process)
- 2 teaspoons baking soda
- ³/₄ teaspoon baking powder
- 1¹/₄ teaspoons salt
- 3 large eggs
- ³/₄ cup vegetable oil
- 1¹/₂ cups buttermilk, shaken well
- ³/₄ teaspoon pure vanilla extract

FROSTING

- 1 cup heavy cream
- 2 tablespoons light corn syrup
- 2 tablespoons sugar
- 1 pound good-quality semisweet chocolate, finely chopped
- 4 tablespoons (¹/₂ stick) unsalted butter, cut into small pieces

FOR THE CAKE

Preheat the oven to 300 degrees. Place a rack at the middle level. Grease two 10-inch round cake pans. Line the bottoms with rounds of waxed paper and grease the paper.

In a small bowl, combine the chocolate and coffee and let stand, stirring occasionally, until the chocolate is melted and smooth.

In a large bowl, sift together the sugar, flour, cocoa powder, baking soda, baking powder, and salt. In a separate large bowl, with an electric mixer, beat the eggs until slightly thickened and lemon colored (about 3 minutes with a stand mixer or 5 minutes with a hand-held mixer). Slowly add the oil, buttermilk, vanilla, and melted chocolate mixture to the eggs, beating until well combined. Add the sugar mixture and beat on medium speed until just combined. Divide the batter between the pans and bake until a cake tester inserted in the center comes out clean, 60 to 70 minutes.

Cool the layers completely in their pans on racks. Run a thin knife around the edges of the pans and invert the layers onto racks. Carefully remove the waxed paper and cool the layers completely. The cake layers may be made 1 day ahead and kept at room temperature, wrapped well in plastic wrap.

FOR THE FROSTING

In a medium saucepan, bring the cream, corn syrup, and sugar to a boil over medium-low heat, whisking until the sugar is dissolved. Remove from the heat and add the chocolate, whisking until the chocolate is melted. Add the butter, whisking until smooth.

Transfer the frosting to a medium bowl and let cool, stirring occasionally, until it's spreadable (depending on the chocolate, it may be necessary to chill the frosting to bring it to spreadability).

Spread the frosting between the cake layers and over the top and sides. The cake will keep, covered and refrigerated, for 3 days. Bring it to room temperature before serving.

velvet chocolate cake

COOK

Claire Legas

SOURCE

Scharffen-berger.com

Not just another "sinfully delicious" chocolate cake by a long shot, this is, by some mysterious alchemy of a few simple ingredients, a wonder. It is rich and indeed velvety and—here's the magic —all deep, dark chocolate, but not distractingly sweet.

Scharffen Berger chocolate, a relatively new American-made chocolate, has become a favorite with many professional bakers and pastry chefs. Claire Legas, the pastry chef at Absinthe Restaurant in San Francisco, created this elegant and singular flourless dessert using Scharffen Berger's 70 percent pure dark chocolate, sold in specialty food shops. Truthfully, though, we have used other high-quality bittersweet chocolate in the recipe to equally stunning effect. Part mousse, part cake, this dessert can lead to obsessive desire.

Serve Velvet Chocolate Cake with whipped cream. More good news: If the cake is wrapped tightly in plastic, it will stay moist for up to 4 days at room temperature.

serves 14 to 16

- 1 pound Scharffen Berger 70 percent pure dark chocolate, finely chopped
- 1 cup minus 1 tablespoon heavy cream
- 2 tablespoons plus ½ cup sugar
- 6 large eggs, at room temperature
- ½ cup strong coffee, kept warm but not hot
  Whipped cream, for serving

Preheat the oven to 350 degrees. Butter a 9-inch round cake pan (not springform) or coat it with nonstick cooking spray. Line the bottom with a circle of parchment paper.

In a double boiler, melt the chocolate gently over hot water. Keep warm.

In a medium bowl, with an electric mixer, whip the cream with the 2 tablespoons sugar until the mixture forms soft peaks. Set aside.

In a large bowl, with an electric mixer, beat the eggs on high speed until doubled in volume. Gradually add the remaining 1/2 cup sugar to the eggs, 1 tablespoon at a time. Continue beating until the eggs have fully tripled in volume and are light and fluffy, about 10 minutes.

Pour the coffee into the chocolate and stir until combined. Fold the egg mixture into the chocolate in 3 additions, working quickly to incorporate each addition. Fold in the cream mixture. Pour the batter into the prepared pan. Place the cake pan in a large roasting pan and add enough hot water to the roasting pan so that it reaches halfway up the sides of the cake pan.

Bake the cake for 40 to 50 minutes, or until it still jiggles in the center when gently shaken. Cool completely in the pan on a rack. To unmold, slide a small knife or spatula around the edge of the cake to loosen it from the pan. Cover the top of the cake with a sheet of waxed paper. Place a plate upside down over the paper and invert pan and plate together. Remove the cake pan and parchment liner. Place a serving platter on the bottom of the cake and turn right side up.

Slice the cake and serve with whipped cream.

chocolate-dipped pink grapefruit rind

One of our favorite things about extravagant dinners in Paris is the usual little plate of sweetmeats served with coffee, which inevitably includes candied orange rind. For the frugal French, it's a great way to use something that would otherwise go into the *poubelle*—and that's where citrus peelings

COOKS

**Gale Gand,
Rick Tramonto,
and Julia Moskin**

SOURCE

Butter Sugar Flour Eggs

usually end up in America.

But candied citrus peel is a snap to make, and this version, with pink grapefruit rind, is especially delicious. Dip a long finger of this luscious rind in melted chocolate, and you have a real treat—a refreshing finish to a meal.

makes about 30 pieces

- 1 large pink grapefruit
- 2 cups sugar
- 4 cups water
- 12 ounces semisweet chocolate

Cut a slice off the top and the bottom of the grapefruit to expose the flesh. Cutting from top to bottom and following the contours of the fruit, cut off the rind and white pith in 1-inch-wide strips. Scrape off any grapefruit pulp adhering to the strips, but leave the pith intact.

Cut each strip into smaller strips, about 1/4 inch wide.

Meanwhile, bring a large pot of water to a boil. Pour about 1 quart of the boiling water into a small saucepan, bring back to a boil, add the grapefruit rind, and boil for 30 seconds. Drain in a colander and rinse under cold running water. Repeat the boiling and rinsing process two more times, using fresh boiling water from the pot each time.

In a medium saucepan, combine the sugar and 4 cups water and bring to a boil. Add the blanched rind and reduce the heat to low. Simmer until tender, about 1 hour. Drain in a colander and let cool for 15 minutes, or until cool enough to handle. Using your fingers, arrange the strips on a wire rack so that they do not touch each other. Let cool completely.

In the top of a double boiler set over barely simmering water or in a medium bowl in the microwave, melt the chocolate. Line a cookie sheet with parchment paper or waxed paper. Using your fingers, dip the strips of rind into the chocolate, coating about two-thirds of each strip. Let the excess chocolate drip back into the double boiler. Place the coated strips on the cookie sheet. Let cool at room temperature. Store, refrigerated, in an airtight container for up to 3 days.

VARIATIONS

- To make chocolate-dipped orange rind, use the rind of two large navel oranges and prepare them the same way.
- You can skip the chocolate and just roll the strips in sugar before cooling and drying them.

drinks

uncommonly good hot chocolate

There's good old cocoa and the staggeringly good French hot chocolate, and not much in between. So Richard Donnelly, the owner of Donnelly Fine Chocolates in Santa Cruz, California, set about to make a superlative hot chocolate that is just as easy as cocoa. The secret is using real European bittersweet or semisweet chocolate (Donnelly's favorite is Valrhona Guanaja, a bittersweet)—and milk, not cream. That's the recipe.

COOK
Richard Donnelly

SOURCE
Fine Cooking

But beyond the basics, there's the urgent question of whether you like frothy (our choice) or plain hot chocolate—and whether you'd like it to have some flavorings as well. However you like it, do make this hot chocolate. Very few drinks in the world have its intimate, soul-soothing qualities, and on a bleak day there's nothing quite so welcome. And how about a little cloud of chocolate whipped cream on your cup of hot chocolate?

serves 2

3 cups whole milk
3 ounces bittersweet or
    semisweet chocolate,
    chopped into small pieces

Chocolate Whipped Cream (recipe
follows; optional)

FOR FROTHY HOT CHOCOLATE

In a medium saucepan over medium heat, bring the milk just to a boil. Place the chopped chocolate in a blender and pour in the hot milk. Let sit for 10 to 15 seconds, or until the chocolate starts to melt. Cover with the lid and a folded kitchen towel and blend until completely mixed and frothy, about 30 seconds.

FOR PLAIN HOT CHOCOLATE

In a medium saucepan over medium heat, bring the milk just to a boil. Remove from the heat, add the chocolate, and stir or whisk until well blended.

Top with Chocolate Whipped Cream, if desired.

VARIATIONS

Spicy Hot Chocolate: Add $^3/_4$ teaspoon ground cinnamon and $^1/_2$ teaspoon ground ginger to the milk before heating.

Minty Hot Chocolate: Add 6 to 8 fresh mint leaves to the heated milk and let steep for 10 minutes. Reheat the milk and strain out the mint. Blend with $3^1/_2$ ounces chopped chocolate and garnish each cup with a mint sprig.

Irish Hot Chocolate: Use only 2 cups milk and add $^1/_2$ cup strong coffee. Put 2 tablespoons whiskey in the blender with the chocolate. Top each cup with whipped cream.

Chocolate Whipped Cream

$^1/_4$ cup unsweetened Dutch-
process cocoa powder, such
as Valrhona

3 tablespoons confectioners'
sugar
1 cup heavy cream, chilled
$^1/_2$ teaspoon pure vanilla extract

In a small bowl, combine the cocoa powder and confectioners' sugar. In a chilled medium bowl, combine the cream and vanilla and whip until soft peaks form. With the mixer running or while whisking by hand, gradually pour in the cocoa mixture; whip until well blended.

The whipped cream will keep for several days in the refrigerator.

spring-cleaning tonic

We ran across this recipe in the *Women's Health Letter* and couldn't wait to try it because it reminded us of a superb elixir we once tasted in a Mexican country market. That one was full of pineapple juice, orange juice, a little lemon, and a secret ingredient: fresh alfalfa.

This exhilarating tonic is brimming with vitamins, minerals, and chlorophyll.

COOK

Bonnie Trust Dahan

SOURCE

Women's Health Letter

Greens such as chickweed and purslane are available in the wild, of course, or at the farmers' market. Virtually all variations on the theme are not only delicious but also extremely good for you. We especially like mint and alfalfa sprouts tossed into the mix, along with a little extra lemon juice.

serves 4

2 handfuls mixed fresh herbs, such as parsley, dandelion leaves, mint, chickweed, miner's lettuce, purslane, nettles, and/or plantain

4 cups pineapple juice or fresh orange juice
1 teaspoon fresh lemon juice

Place all the ingredients in a blender and blend on high speed until liquefied. Let stand for a few minutes, then strain and serve.

reverse martini

Lighter, clearer, more refreshing, less potent, and perhaps even more clever than a classic martini, this bottoms-up version was created by Julia Child, who

CREATOR

Julia Child

SOURCE

Gary Regan
and
Mardee Haidin Regan,
Wine Enthusiast Magazine

uses Noilly Prat Dry Vermouth and Gordon's Gin. Julia says, "I can drink two of these." (She did not say in what time frame.) We'll go along with that.

serves 1

Take a large, long-stemmed wineglass, fill it with ice, pour dry vermouth into the glass to within about ½ inch of the rim, and float a little gin on top.

red rooster

COOK

Gigi Linquest

SOURCE

Every Day's a Party,
by Emeril Lagasse

All over Louisiana, this slushy drink accompanies holiday festivities, from tree-trimming parties to impromptu gatherings of old friends. Gigi Linquest told Emeril Lagasse about it, and now he's told all of us.

All you need are some staples you proba-bly have on hand, plus a few hours to freeze the brew. It won't freeze com-pletely because of the vod-ka. The classic sweet-tart combination of cranberry and orange is both festive and refreshing, and the vodka kicks it up considerably.

serves 12 to 16; makes 2 quarts

1½ quarts cranberry juice cocktail
1 6-ounce can frozen orange
    juice concentrate, thawed
2 cups vodka

Combine all the ingredients and freeze in a large plastic container for several hours, or until slushy. (The mixture won't be frozen solid.)

Stir and scoop the mixture into punch cups or wineglasses.

VARIATION

We like this drink even better made with tangerine instead of or-ange juice concentrate.

litchi champagne cocktail

Vietnamese cook Corinne Trang discovered this excellent aperitif in a Vietnamese restaurant in Paris. It's a twist on that old favorite, the kir royale—instead of black currant syrup, the fruit here is the litchi. This exotic drink is instant elegance, and perfect before a light

COOK

Corinne Trang

SOURCE

Food & Wine

Asian meal, especially in summer.

It's simple enough to keep a can of litchis in syrup in the refrigerator, ready to mix with a dry French champagne, which also may be a permanent resident in the fridge.

serves 8

1 11-ounce can litchis in syrup, chilled
1 bottle brut champagne or other dry sparkling wine, chilled

Place a litchi in each of 8 champagne flutes. Add 2 tablespoons of litchi syrup to each flute, then fill with champagne and serve.

VARIATION

Another favorite new champagne drink is one made from Rhubarb Soup (page 268)—just strain the soup, place 2 tablespoons in each flute, and fill with champagne.

credits

Roasted Eggplant Dip by Steve Johnson, Cambridge, MA. Copyright © 1999 by Steve Johnson. Reprinted by permission of Foodline.com.

Radish and Goat Cheese Wreath by Rozanne Gold. From *Entertaining 1-2-3* by Rozanne Gold. Copyright © 1999 by Rozanne Gold (text); 1999 by Tom Eckerle (photographs). By permission of Little, Brown and Company, Inc., and by permission of William Morris Agency, Inc., on behalf of the author.

Mashed Potato Dip by Michel Richard. Reprinted with permission from *Cooking with Patrick Clark*. Copyright © 1999 by the Patrick Clark Family Trust and Charlie Trotter, Ten Speed Press, Berkeley, CA, www.tenspeed.com.

Hungarian Jewish Chopped Liver by Valerie Alia from Allrecipes.com web site, copyright © 1999 by Allrecipes.com. Reprinted by permission of Allrecipes.com.

Roasted Black and Green Olives with Whole Garlic by Marlena de Blasi, in *Regional Foods of Southern Italy*. Published by Viking Press. Copyright © 1999 by Marlena de Blasi.

Apricot Thrones with Cheese and Pecans by Hugh Carpenter. Reprinted with permission from *Fast Appetizers*. Copyright © 1999 by Hugh Carpenter and Teri Sandison, Ten Speed Press, Berkeley, CA, www.tenspeed.com.

Homemade Potato Chips with Crème Fraîche and Caviar by Joachim Splichal from *InStyle* magazine, July 1999 issue. Copyright © 1999 by Joachim Splichal.

Parmigiano-Reggiano Crisps with Goat-Cheese Mousse by Thomas Keller. Excerpted from *The French Laundry Cookbook*. Copyright © 1999 by Thomas Keller. Used by permission of Artisan, a division of Workman Publishing Co., Inc., New York. All rights reserved.

Ceviche Verde by Roberto Santibanez, November 1999. Copyright © 1999 by Roberto Santibanez. Reprinted by permission of Roberto Santibanez.

Florentine Ravioli *(Nudi)* by Giuliano Bugialli from *Food & Wine*, September 1999. Copyright © 1999 by Giuliano Bugialli. Reprinted by permission of Giuliano Bugialli, of Foods of Italy.

Hot Avocado Soup with Poblano by Jeff Vaccaro from California Avocado Commission web site. Copyright © 1999 by Jeff Vaccaro. Reprinted by permission of the California Avocado Commission, www.avocado.org.

Rich Red Pepper Soup by Kathy Born from March/April 1999 *Modern Maturity*. Copyright © 1999 by American Association of Retired Persons. Reprinted with permission from *Modern Maturity* and from Susan Goodman.

Italian Pumpkin Soup by Maria Pia from Palio restaurant press release. Copyright © 1999 Maria Pia. Reprinted by permission of Maria Pia.

Roasted Butternut Squash Soup by Barbara Hom from Russian River Valley Winegrowers press release. Copyright © 1999 by Barbara Hom. Reprinted by permission of Russian River Valley Winegrowers.

The Lentil Soup *(Shurbat al-'Adas)* from *A Mediterranean Feast* by Clifford Wright. Copyright © 1999 by Clifford Wright. Reprinted by permission of HarperCollins Publishers, Inc., William Morrow.

Red Lentil and Apricot Soup by Karena from Allrecipes.com web site. Copyright © 1999 by Allrecipes.com. Reprinted by permission of Allrecipes.com.

Fabio's *Farinata* (Cornmeal and Kale Soup) by Faith Heller Willinger from *The Chefs of Cucina*

credits

Crystallized Ginger Scones by Chuck Williams with Judy Rodgers from Williams-Sonoma catalog (Summer 1999). Copyright © 1999 by Chuck Williams and Judy Rodgers. Reprinted by permission of Chuck Williams and Judy Rodgers.

Kona Inn Banana Muffins from *Learning to Cook with Marion Cunningham* by Marion Cunningham. Copyright © 1999 by Marion Cunningham. Reprinted by permission of Alfred A. Knopf, a division of Random House, Inc.

Mini-Frittatas with Wild Mushrooms by Eileen Weinberg. Reprinted by permission of Eileen Weinberg. Copyright © 1999 by Eileen Weinberg.

Green Chile Cheese Puff from Bear Creek Lodge in Victor, Montana, appearing in *Gourmet*'s staff "Mother's Day Brunch Dishes," May 1999. Courtesy of *Gourmet*. Copyright © 1999 by Condé Nast.

Goat Cheese and Herb Skillet Soufflé by Tamara Holt from *Redbook* magazine, April 1999. Copyright © 1999 by Tamara Holt. Reprinted by permission of *Redbook*.

Caramelized Onion Waffles with Smoked Salmon and Radish Salad by Michael Bauer from the *San Francisco Chronicle*, December 29, 1999. Copyright © 1999 by Michael Bauer. Reprinted by permission of Richard Crocker.

Pasta with Baked Tomato Sauce by Nancy Harmon Jenkins, found at www.cucinaamore.com. From *The Chefs of Cucina Amore: Celebrating the Very Best of Italian Cooking*. Reprinted with permission of West 175 Enterprises.

Spaghetti with Anna's Pesto from *Herbs and Wild Greens from the Sicilian Countryside* by Anna Tasca Lanza. Reprinted by permission of Clarkson Potter/Publishers, a division of Random House, Inc. Copyright © 1999 by Anna Tasca Lanza.

Ziti with Spicy Sausages, Goat Cheese, Tomato, and Parsley by Erica De Mane. Reprinted by permission of Scribner, a division of Simon & Schuster, from *Pasta Improvvisata* by Erica De Mane. Copyright © 1999 by Erica De Mane.

Deep-Dish Pizza and Toppings excerpted from "Deep Dish Pizza" by Anne Yamanaka, with permission from *Cook's Illustrated*, September/October 1999. Copyright © 1999 by *Cook's Illustrated*. For a trial issue of *Cook's Illustrated*, in the U.S. call 800-526-8442. Recipes, cookware ratings, online cooking school, bookstore, and more are available at www.cooksillustrated.com.

Apple and Country Ham Risotto by Frank Browning and Sharon Silva from *An Apple Harvest*, 1999. Copyright © 1999 by Frank Browning and Sharon Silva. Reprinted by permission of Ten Speed Press, Berkeley, CA, www.tenspeed.com.

Egg and Potato Skillet Supper by Sarah Fritschner. Copyright © 1999 by *Courier-Journal* & Louisville Times Co. Reprinted by permission.

Tunisian Chickpea Stew (Lablabi) from *A Mediterranean Feast* by Clifford Wright. Copyright © 1999 by Clifford Wright. Reprinted by permission of HarperCollins Publishers, Inc., William Morrow.

Beer Can Chicken and Memphis Rub excerpted from *The Barbecue! Bible*. Copyright © 1998 by Steven Raichlen. Used by permission of Workman Publishing Co., Inc., New York. All rights reserved.

Garlicky Baked Chicken by Sara Moulton from www.thefoodmaven.com, October 15, 1999. Copyright © 1999 by Sara Moulton. Reprinted by permission.

Indonesian Ginger Chicken from *The Barefoot Contessa Cookbook* by Ina Garten. Copyright © 1999 by Ina Garten. Reprinted by permission of Clarkson Potter/Publishers, a division of Random House, Inc.

Dad's Chinese Chicken Wings from *A Spoonful of Ginger* by Nina Simonds. Copyright © 1999 by Nina Simonds. Reprinted by permission of Alfred A. Knopf, a division of Random House, Inc.

Chinese Lemon Chicken reprinted by permission of Simon & Schuster from *The Wisdom of the Chinese Kitchen* by Grace Young. Copyright © 1999 by Grace Young.

Balsamico Roast Chicken and Potatoes reprinted by permission of Scribner, a division of Simon & Schuster, from *The Italian Country Table* by Lynne Rossetto Kasper. Text copyright © 1999 by Lynne Rossetto Kasper.

Chicken Roasted with Orange, Rosemary, and Bay Leaves from *The Cook and the Gardener* by Amanda Hesser. Copyright © 1999 by Amanda Hesser. Used by permission of W. W. Norton & Company, Inc.

Chicken with Yams, Fennel, and Ginger from *D'Artagnan's Glorious Game Cookbook* by Ariane Daguin. Copyright © 1999 by Ariane Daguin, George Faison, and Joanna Pruess. Reprinted by permission of Little, Brown and Company, Inc., and The Miller Agency.

Chicken Poached in New Beaujolais from *French Chefs Cooking* by Michael Buller. Copyright © 1999 by Michael Buller. All rights reserved. Reproduced here by permission of the publisher, IDG Books Worldwide, Inc.

credits

Grilled Duck in a Jar and Grilled Vegetables in a Jar by Arayah Jenanyan. Excerpted from Smith & Hawken's *The Gardeners' Community Cookbook*, edited by Victoria Wise. Text copyright © 1999 by Smith & Hawken. Used by permission of Workman Publishing Co., Inc., New York. All rights reserved.

Sam Choy's Award-Winning Roast Duck and Dry Duck Marinade from *Sam Choy's Island Flavors* by Sam Choy, 1999, page 207. Copyright © 1999 by Sam Choy. Reprinted by permission from Hyperion and Harvey Klinger Agency.

Awesome Tangerine-Glazed Turkey; Sausage, Apple, and Dried Cranberry Stuffing; and Turkey Giblet Broth by Stacy M. Polcyn from Allrecipes.com. Copyright © 1999 by Allrecipes.com. Reprinted by permission of Allrecipes.com.

Barbecued Turkey Hash by Susan Wyler found on www.thefoodmaven.com 1999. Copyright © 1999 by Susan Wyler. Reprinted by permission.

Twelve-Hour Roast Pork from *Suzanne Somers' Get Skinny on Fabulous Food* by Suzanne Somers. Copyright © 1999 by Suzanne Somers. Reprinted by permission of Crown Publishers, a division of Random House, Inc.

Roasted Sausages and Grapes and Al Forno's Mashed Potatoes from *A Celebration of Women Chefs*, edited by Julie Stillman, and *Cucina Simpatica* by Johanne Killeen and George Germon. Copyright © 1991 by Johanne Killeen and George Germon. Reprinted by permission of HarperCollins Publishers, Inc.

Bubba's Bunch Championship Ribs from Weber Grills Barbecue booklet, 1999.

Tom Valenti's Braised Lamb Shanks with White Bean Puree from *Kitchen Suppers* by Alison Becker Hurt. Copyright © 1999 by Alison Becker Hurt. Used by permission of Doubleday, a division of Random House, Inc.

Kashmiri-Style Leg of Lamb from *The Stonyfield Farm Yogurt Cookbook* by Meg Cadoux Hirshberg. Copyright © 1991, 1999 by Meg Cadoux Hirshberg. Reprinted by permission of Three Rivers Press, a division of Random House, Inc.

Bodacious Porterhouse Steaks with Sexy Barbecue Sauce from *Weber's Art of the Grill*, text by Jamie Purviance. Copyright © 1999. Published by Chronicle Books, San Francisco. Used with permission.

Beer-Braised Short Ribs from *Snow Country Cooking* by Diane Rossen Worthington, 1999. Copyright © 1999 by Diane Rossen Worthington. Courtesy of Weldon Owen Publishing.

High-Temperature Rib Roast of Beef and Yorkshire Pudding from *The Best of Craig Claiborne* by Craig Claiborne with Pierre Franey. Copyright © 1999 by Times Books, a division of Random House, Inc.

Shrimp and Corn with Basil by Gourmet staff, September 1999. Courtesy *Gourmet*. Copyright © 1999 by Condé Nast.

Grilled Shrimp or Scallops, Basque Style by Davis Morgan from the *Atlanta Journal-Constitution*. Copyright © 1999 by Davis Morgan. Reprinted by permission of Davis Morgan.

Skillet-Roasted Mussels from *The Rose Pistola Cookbook* by Reed Hearon and Peggy Knickerbocker. Copyright © 1999 by Reed Hearon and Peggy Knickerbocker. Used by permission of Broadway Books, a division of Random House, Inc.

Slow-Roasted Salmon Article by Jane Ellis from *House Beautiful*, July 1999; recipe by James O'Shea. Copyright © 1999 by James O'Shea. Reprinted by permission of *House Beautiful*.

Snapper Fillets Baked in Salt from *Salt and Pepper* by Michele Anna Jordan. Copyright © 1999 by Michele Anna Jordan. Used by permission of Broadway Books, a division of Random House, Inc.

Mediterranean Seafood Stew from *Julia and Jacques Cooking at Home* by Julia Child and Jacques Pépin. Copyright © 1999 by Julia Child and Jacques Pépin. Reprinted by permission of Alfred A. Knopf, a division of Random House, Inc.

On-the-Fly Noodles with Shrimp and Shichimi Tugarashi excerpted from *Bowlfood Cookbook*. Copyright © 1999 by Lynne Aronson and Elizabeth Simon. Used by permission of Workman Publishing Co., Inc., New York. All rights reserved.

Spicy Codfish Cakes with Cilantro Aïoli from *Out of the Earth* by Kerry Downey Romaniello, recipe by Michael Frady. Copyright © 1999 by Kerry Downey Romaniello. Reprinted courtesy of Spinner Publications, Inc.

Grilled Stuffed Portobello Mushrooms and Pesto Sauce by Vincent Scotto from *New York* magazine, May 24, 1999. Copyright © 1999 by Vincent Scotto. Reprinted by permission of the *Los Angeles Times*.

Sugar Snap Peas with Sesame from *The Barefoot Contessa Cookbook* by Ina Garten. Copyright © 1999 by Ina Garten. Reprinted by permission of Clarkson Potter/Publishers, a division of Random House, Inc.

by Suzanne Dunaway. Reprinted by permission of Hyperion.

Beer Bread by Jodi Regan from Allrecipes.com, 1999. Copyright © 1999 by Allrecipes.com. Reprinted by permission of Allrecipes.com.

Swedish Knackebrod excerpted from *Prairie Home Cooking* by Judith M. Fertig. Copyright © 1999, by permission from The Harvard Common Press.

Greek Christmas Bread by staff from *Good Housekeeping Baking*. Copyright © 1999 by Good Housekeeping. Reprinted by permission of Good Housekeeping.

Rice Bread from *American Home Cooking* by Cheryl Alters Jamison and Bill Jamison. Copyright © 1999 by Cheryl Alters Jamison and Bill Jamison. Used by permission of Broadway Books, a division of Random House, Inc.

Aunt Effie's Custard Johnnycake by Marjorie Kinnan Rawlings from *A Gracious Plenty* by John T. Edge, Ellen Rolfes, and the Center for the Study of Southern Culture. Originally published in *Cross Creek Cookery*.

Texas Lemon Bombe from *Cooking Fearlessly* by Jeff Blank and Jay Moore, Fearless Press, 1999. Copyright © 1999 by Jeff Blank and Jay Moore with Deborah A. Harter. Reprinted by permission of Jeff Blank.

Peach Sorbet by Joanne Chang, August 9, 1999, as found on www.foodline.com. Copyright © 1999 by Joanne Chang. Reprinted by permission of Foodline.com.

Plum and Raspberry Sorbet excerpted from *Recipes from the Vineyards of Northern California: Desserts*. Copyright © 1999 by Leslie Mansfield. Reprinted by permission of Celestial Arts, P.O. Box 7123, Berkeley, CA 94707.

Star Anise Ice Cream reprinted by permission of Simon & Schuster from *Authentic Vietnamese Cooking: Food from a Family Table* by Corinne Trang. Copyright © 1999 by Corinne Trang.

Rhubarb Soup from *Simply Sensational Desserts* by François Payard. Copyright © 1999 by François Payard. Used by permission of Broadway Books, a division of Random House, Inc.

Honey-Poached Quinces by Aliza Green, 1999, reprinted by permission of Indian Rock Produce. Copyright © 1999 by Aliza Green.

Port Wine Grapes by Joyce Dodson Piotrowski from the *Washington Post*, December 22, 1999. Copyright © 1999 by Joyce Dodson Piotrowski. Reprinted by permission of Joyce Dodson Piotrowski.

Danish Berry Pudding (Red Grits with Cream) from *Country Weekend Entertaining* by Anna Pump and Gen LeRoy. Copyright © 1999 by Anna Pump and Gen LeRoy. Used by permission of Doubleday, a division of Random House, Inc.

Caramelized Rice Pudding with Sour Cherry Sauce from *The Lake House Cookbook* by Trudie Styler and Joseph Sponzo. Copyright © 1999 by Trudie Styler. Reprinted by permission of Clarkson Potter/Publishers, a division of Random House, Inc., and by permission of the Wylie Agency, Inc.

Lemon-Yogurt Cheesecake for Jerry by Miriam Kasin Hospodar from *Heaven's Banquet*. Copyright © 1999 by Mariam Kasin Hospodar. Published by E. P. Dutton.

Original Plum Torte by Marian Burros, recipe by Lois Levine reprinted from *The New Elegant but Easy Cookbook*, 1999. Copyright © 1999 by Marian Burros. Reprinted by permission of Simon & Schuster.

Fresh Ginger Cake and **Very Spicy Caramel Pears** from *Room for Dessert* by David Lebovitz. Copyright © 1999 by David Lebovitz. Reprinted by permission of HarperCollins Publishers, Inc.

Ginger-Mascarpone Icebox Cake by Heather Ho from *Fine Cooking* magazine. Copyright © 1999 by Heather Ho. Reprinted by permission of Heather Ho, Pastry Chef, Boulevard, San Francisco, CA.

Souffléed Lemon Custard by Gordon Hamersley/Hamersley's Bistro, Boston, MA. Found on Starchefs.com. Reprinted by permission of Gordon Hamersley.

Chocolate Mousse with Olive Oil by Teresa Barrenechea, found on foodtv.com. Reprinted by permission of Teresa Barrenechea.

Chocolate Bread Pudding by Martha Stewart from *Martha Stewart Living* magazine, October 1999. Copyright © 1999 Martha Stewart Living Omnimedia, Inc. All rights reserved.

Apple and Armagnac Croustade reprinted with the permission of Scribner, a division of Simon & Schuster, from *Daniel Boulud's Café Boulud Cookbook* by Daniel Boulud and Dorie Greenspan. Copyright © 1999 by Daniel Boulud and Dorie Greenspan.

Peanut Butter Cookies by Mom-Mom Fritch from *Gourmet*, submitted by Amy Fritch. Copyright © 1999 by Amy Fritch.

Zante Currant Cookies. Copyright © 1999 by Sun-Maid Growers of California. Recipe is reprinted courtesy of Sun-Maid Growers of California.

Florentines by Catherine Brandel after Ken Wolfe,

credits

index